Co-operatives and Rural Development
in East Africa

CO-OPERATIVES AND RURAL DEVELOPMENT IN EAST AFRICA

EDITED BY

Carl Gösta Widstrand

CONTRIBUTORS:

Raymond Apthorpe, Göran Hydén, Nelson Kasfir,
Patrick McAuslan, S. E. Migot-Adholla,
Dan Nyanjom, Okoro Okereke, Poul W. Westergaard

The Scandinavian Institute of African Studies
Uppsala

Africana Publishing Corporation, New York

The Scandinavian Institute of African Studies has served at Uppsala since 1962 as a Scandinavian documentation and research centre on African affairs.

The views expressed in its publications are entirely those of the authors and do not necessarily reflect those of the Institute or the institutions where they are engaged at present.

Published in the United States of America 1970
by Africana Publishing Corporation
101 Fifth Avenue, New York, N.Y. 10003
Library of Congress Catalog Card No. 78-147089

Printed in Sweden by
Almqvist & Wiksells Boktryckeri Aktiebolag
Uppsala 1970

Contents

Preface

The seminar on "Co-operatives and Rural Development in East Africa" is the sixth seminar that the Scandinavian Institute of African Studies has organized since 1963. As a part of its function as a Scandinavian documentation and research centre on African problems, the Institute has tried to choose topics for these international seminars that would be of interest to academics as well as to planners, administrators and politicians. These topics have included refugee problems, boundary problems and problems of adult education, and scholars from abroad—mainly, of course, from Africa—have been invited to discuss their special topics with Scandinavian specialists and other interested people.

This year's topic was chosen for several reasons. One was the obvious interest in various types of co-operatives as a means of development—economic and egalitarian—that the Governments of Kenya, Tanzania and Uganda have manifested since independence. Another reason was the Scandinavian interest in East Africa in general and especially in the development of co-operatives and co-operative education. A third reason was the question of tradition: whether the knowledge and experience of the functioning of co-operatives that the movements in Scandinavia have amassed during the years of co-operative development would be of any relevance to co-operatives in East Africa, other than in very general terms. Or the similar question of whether East African "traditional" co-operative experience was of any relevance to modern co-operatives in East Africa, other than in very general terms.

These were some of the problems we wanted to discuss and, in discussing them, we experienced the same difficulties as we have had during the other five seminars or that anyone has in discussing a multi-disciplinary topic.

In trying to discuss co-operatives in an East African setting,

7

one is quickly reminded that many of the inherited divisions between academic disciplines do not stand up very well to the hard facts of reality. To divide a discussion of co-operatives into economic, sociological and political sections is hardly possible. The question of efficiency, for example, may be related to or pinpointed by economic calculations; it is related to economic factors and to organisational techniques. But at the same time it is closely related to the social structure in which these co-operatives operate. These social factors express themselves in local political realities. So if one is going to discuss efficiency, the problem is not settled merely by discussing organisational techniques or making economic calculations. One also has to have a discussion on the transformations in the social setting that are necessary in order to realise efficiency. Transformations in the social structure and the culture of a society are obviously political tasks that call for the use of an instrumental ideology and organisation.

I have deliberately made this *caveat* in order to show that we were not indifferent to this type of problem in dividing the seminar into sociological, political, economic and administrative sessions. This is also the way in which the papers have been presented in this volume. In a concluding paper an attempt is made to discuss some co-operative problems "horizontally", that is, in terms of efficiency, democracy, government involvement, power, development prerequisites, etc.

The Institute is very happy to have been able to bring a very distinguished group together for a couple of days in Uppsala. Mr. *Edward Karanja* and Dr. *S. O. Odede,* of the Institute of Development Studies, University of Nairobi, and Mr. *Bismarck Mwansasu* and Mr. *John S. Saul,* of the Department of Political Science, University of Dar-es-Salaam, kindly agreed to introduce the discussions. We were also fortunate in being able to draw upon the combined experience of Dr. *M. Bonow,* President of the International Co-operative Alliance, Mr. *Gabriel Kagaruki,* Director of the Co-operative Education Centre and Principal of the Co-operative College, Moshi, Mr. *M. K. M. Mulinde,* Senior Co-operative Officer, Department of Co-operative Development, Ministry of Marketing and Co-operatives, Kampala, and Mr. *Dan Nyanjom,* Commissioner for Co-operatives, Ministry of Co-operatives and Social Services, Nairobi, who also kindly acted as chairmen of the seminar sessions.

Contributions towards the cost of the seminar from the Swedish Co-operative Centre and the University of Uppsala are gratefully acknowledged.

Carl Gösta Widstrand

Uppsala, May 1970

Carl Gösta Widstrand

Introduction

Co-operation and co-operatives seem to be a very complicated matter to discuss. Co-operation exists as an ideology both in socialist and capitalist countries.[1] Co-operative movements exist all over the world—in Africa as well as in Scandinavia. We talk about primary co-operative societies whether they have 25 or 25,000 members. There was a co-operative rural-development theory in Africa during the colonial period and it is still the same single body of theory that is used. Co-operative primary societies, unions, national unions, international unions and associations all have something in common. Co-operatives are prescribed for rural as well as for urban areas, and are used to handle products for local consumption as well as products for export. Co-operatives transcend different economic activities. And as always when we try to discuss complicated but probably real concepts like justice, love, or co-operation, there is a risk to yield to "aggregism"[2]—the attempt to avoid small-scale field studies by confining analysis and policy to the manipulation of big aggregates—or "single operationalism"—love is a warm puppy, co-operatives are good for you, etc.

Bearing in mind the huge amount of literature on co-operatives that already exists, to which it would seem unnecessary to add as far as general principles and methods are concerned it nevertheless seems, from the very contrast between the success in some circumstances and the failure in others, that their applicability in different stages of rural and peasant society in East Africa is not fully understood. This means that by way of introduction some differences have to be pointed out and some special features of co-operation in East Africa identified.

Most important of all are the basic differences between the various types of co-operatives: *consumers* (although they play a minor part in the East African context), *marketing* and *producer* co-operatives. Important also are the differences within these groups. There is the marketing co-operative which often constitutes a single funnel through which products (tea, coffee, cotton) must pass. The products sometimes never enter the ordinary trade channels until the point of export: they move from primary society to union to marketing board. There is the marketing co-operative, basically organised for the local marketing of, food products, for example. There is the producers co-operative, based on a need to combine against abuses, and there is the *ujamaa* village, an ideologically and politically important new departure. There are obvious reasons for keeping these differences in mind when we discuss co-operatives on a general level, for example, as models for rural development.

As both Göran Hydén and Shem Migot-Adholla have pointed out in their papers membership is compulsory in many marketing co-operatives and their character as voluntary organisations belonging to their members has been lost. This has wide implications for the discussion of the development of voluntary organisations, such as the *ujamaa* villages, and for John Saul's argument that effective marketing co-operatives may eventually only be based on effective production co-operatives, as well as for questions of membership control and participation and members' apathy.[3] There is also a difference in this respect between the countries of East Africa. Voluntary membership is much more widespread in Uganda[4] than in Tanzania.

There are also differences in the way we look at co-operatives, from above or from below, from the government point of view or from the members' point of view, from the activist co-operator's point of view and from the peasant's point of view. A different focus of attention often causes a lot of difficulty in discussion. An additional danger is that those who look at the movement from above very often forget that they have seen the end result of a similar movement somewhere else, they know from experience what ultimate benefits can be reaped, whereas the peasant has a completely different picture of idea of the often new arrangements. European formulas have been exported unaltered (but the demonstration of "truth" does not necessarily entail its acceptance).[5]

Several of these arguments lead back to a more fundamental difference that has to be kept in mind: the various incentives in the starting and the development of co-operatives. Göran Hydén has outlined these differences in his paper as well as the differences between the Scandinavian and the East African experience. Some co-operatives, mainly producer co-operatives, were started because the producers had an urgent need to combine against suspected exploitation. Racial stratification also played a part here. Buyers have many ways of coercing sellers —not merely by false weighing scales but also by keeping the seller waiting expensively in town until he is forced either to accept a lower price or to cart his unsold produce back to the farm.[6] There are also other examples, but many of the organized co-operative undertakings have been instituted from above, by government or government officials. Government also applies considerable measures of control to co-operatives in all the three countries. The differences in the starting of co-operatives, and the question of where the incentives came from are, of course, relevant to the important discussion on membership participation in co-operatives, as Guy Hunter has recently pointed out:

Government sponsored Co-operatives, used to exclude the growth of middle-men or capitalism, are usually not founded by farmers, nor do they always seem to be in the interests of farmers. The whole morale and dynamic of co-operation is thereby lost. Co-operatives are treated as another branch of bureaucracy, the secretaryship is just another job, with opportunity for gains on the side, the Executive Committee is the usual clique of village bosses. This is not a new way of living and working together.[7]

Then there are the differences between the countries, as Lionel Cliffe has pointed out in his paper. Within the countries, the range of variation with which we are confronted makes generalisation very difficult. There are obviously differences, country by country, between the overall social and political and economic settings within which co-operatives work. There are differences between the goals the countries have set themselves: many of the points Lionel Cliffe makes in his paper on Tanzania would obviously be irrelevant to a consideration at the moment of co-operative development in Kenya.

Sometimes the differences between areas within countries are more important. In working towards the goal of *ujamaa* socialism, Tanzania is beginning to become aware of many of these kinds of differences and is beginning to incorporate them in the policy-making process, in trying to adapt the *ujamaa* policy to the realities of the particular areas, John Saul has argued that in the discussion of development in Tanzania —particularly concerning the role of co-operatives in rural development—people have forgotten to take into consideration the different involvement of the people in a particular locality in various new sorts of activity.[8] This has in turn blurred the realities of class formation in contemporary East Africa and the choices between alternative forms or modes of production.

This leads to another type of difference that has all too often been assumed uncritically, the simplified difference between "traditional" and "modern" society that Shem Migot-Adholla discusses in his paper. He and Lionel Cliffe have tried to answer the questions: what aspects, if any, of these pre-colonial social formations survive, and what purposes do these various structures serve? Their answers are much more complicated than the simple dichotomy between "traditional" and "modern". An important question in this context is also: what is the effect of the *ideology of traditionalism,* as represented by the ujamaa ideology (leaving aside the question of how accurate a reflection of reality it is)?[9] I shall return to these and other points in a later chapter on the prerequisite conditions for co-operation, as they are a part of the general discussion on efficiency and the effective contribution of co-operatives to new social development.

Again, by way of introduction, it is necessary to point out that we can not think about these questions in isolation. We can not be only concerned with "traditional" structures and how they contribute to co-operation. We cannot discuss co-operatives, except in relation to the overall strategy for rural development that a country decides on. Any policy that wants to take advantage of "traditional" structures in order to build modern co-operatives will only be able to do so if they are used as part of a general policy designed to maximise other benefits. Let me take, as an example the question of credit. It is often considered a technical question, maybe because of the technicality of the details. But it is not a purely technical question and it is a fundamental question for co-operatives.

It would seem that the rationale for land registration and land consolidation in Kenya is essentially to have a commercial credit scheme for agriculture. There is, of course, the argument that, if a farmer has security of tenure, he will be differently motivated. But land consolidation has been recommended "because then you have a title to land and can borrow on the security of it". Essentially this is one of the two major forms of agricultural credit schemes that are normally introduced into peasant societies,—the other is the marketing co-operative, which precludes the necessity for land registration. Loans can be secured by crops and automatic deductions from crop purchases. This underlines the fact that marketing co-operatives are becoming more and more credit and supply organisations than purely marketing organisations. This again raises a barrage of technical and policy questions. What happens if the creditor does not buy the crop, or if you have to have a transitional period to establish the crop? What if the margin is so small that the co-operative accumulates funds extremely slowly? What if the conditions are less flexible than those of the moneylender? Does the co-operative credit system create an incentive to impose co-operatives from above? Will co-operative marketing monopolies and the scheduling of crops militate against spontaneity and development from below? Will co-operative credit extend the range of temptation for wealthier people to move into co-operatives and manipulate them in their own interest?

But the main point is that the decision as to which kind of credit system to operate—an individual system based on the security of land titles or a co-operative system with other types of security—is one of the *basic decisions about the kind of rural society* that is going to be created. Yet it is regarded as a technical decision.

How various economic systems are related to the total social system is, of course, of major theoretical importance. Although we need studies that go into minute detail on the economic system in order to understand it, we must at the same time try to retain a holistic view, look at the problems of co-operatives against the general background of the much wider question of rural development. Both types of studies were presented at the seminar and, indeed, the rationale for holding the seminar was precisely to compare the two ways of looking at social reality.

S. E. Migot-Adholla

Traditional Society and Co-operatives

The purpose of this paper is fairly limited—to discuss some practical problems and their theoretic implications: specifically, to describe the nature of the indigenous organisational forms in East Africa, and to attempt to show some of their relationships with the modern agricultural co-operatives. The discussion of past practices is very necessary for understanding the present. But the description of the past is undoubtedly useful to those charged with the task of formulating policy only in so far as it serves to indicate possible alternatives. One major interest in the debate on rural development in East Africa centers, among other things, on whether the indigenous communal structures are conducive to development. This and similar questions often seek to answer the problem of ensuring conscious participation by the peasants in the process of agricultural modernisation. It is in this context that co-operatives have recently been most often discussed.

In this ongoing debate two major views predominate: one, a somewhat capitalistic and individualistic outlook; the other, a somewhat romantic-socialist viewpoint. In a study of a co-operative farming scheme in Kisii District in Kenya, Holmquist argues that private land tenure, cash cropping and the expansion of the money economy have "released the individual peasant from a great deal of his traditional dependence on the local community."[1] Co-operation is explained in this study by observing that the individual Gusii peasant is today more dependent on new relationships of trust arising from new cleavages in the community. Holmquist then draws the conclusion that "the most powerful attraction the Scheme has for the individual is profit." This interpretation suggests that participation in the money economy is incompatible with the traditional social structures. In its extreme, this view sees modern agricultural co-operatives as having nothing to do with the indigenous co-operative forms.

But perhaps the most popular view today is that which sees mutual assistance and co-operation as an essential ethic of indigenous African life. Those who hold this view are among the strongest advocates of the promotion of co-operation among peasants. To them, the principle of co-operation is so obviously "natural" to the African peasants that its adoption is thought to be nearly axiomatic. Indeed, the three East African governments have all launched vigorous campaigns for the promotion of co-operatives, arguing that the principles of mutual assistance stem from the traditional past. Co-operatives are thus seen as the necessary vehicles for the realisation of a socialism resembling the traditional African social order.

Although the two views toward co-operation appear contradictory, they both have some approximate validity as explanations of the economic organisations of the pre-capitalist African societies and the modern African peasantries. However, their partiality renders each of them inadequate, for on confronting empirical situations one encounters seemingly "non-traditional" men playing active roles in co-operative societies whose day to day activities may also involve "traditional legitimation". Or, on the other hand, some co-operatives in regions most affected by the money economy are riddled by conflicts and inter-kinship group rivalries almost to paralysis. However, lineage alliances and membership of kinship groups as such are clearly not the most critical factors determining the peasants' participation in agricultural co-operatives. The appeal by the promoters of co-operation in East Africa to traditional ideals of mutual assistance may be expedient for mobilising the peasants and enlisting their participation in the development effort. But, exhortation on the basis of such an ideology has to be complemented by real economic incentives to ensure continued participation.

Some Western scholars, however, have chosen to interpret the "samaritan" appeals characteristic of the current politics of modernisation as an indication of the African's inherent reliance on archaic tradition. Indeed, there appears to be a

persistant professional bias in studies of African social phenomena which exaggerate the natives' respect for the endurance
of ancestral beliefs and practices. Typically the major inadequacy of such studies is their failure to take into consideration the "environmental" contexts in which change is taking
place. Particularily relevant in the explanation of economic
change in Africa is the nature of international economic relations, especially under the colonial situation. Any approach
to economic change in present day Africa which only engages
in abstract discussion of "traditionality" in explaining "re-
ceptivity" or "resistance" to change is clearly mindless to say
the least.

The present essay is an attempt to describe the economic
organisation of the indigenous African society and the structural bases for co-operation. In the second part, the effects
of colonial economic impositions on the indigenous societies
are very briefly reviewed, particularily as they impinged on
the native co-operative ethos. An attempt is made in the last
part of the essay to show the differences between the indigenous modes of co-operation and modern co-operative societies.
Naturally this comparison is pursued only within the limits
of the topic of this paper. The analysis of the implications of
traditional organisational forms on co-operative development
in current times is more exhaustively discussed in later papers.

Organisation of Traditional Economy

It would be difficult to discuss all aspects of the indigenous
society relevant to co-operation. In this brief evaluation, traditional life is discussed fairly broadly omitting idiosyncratic
ethnological references. Naturally there was much variation in
the indigenous societies of East Africa, but they all had certain
common features distinct from those of the money economies
which later affected them. The majority of the people were
engaged in a kind of agriculture, the characteristic feature of
which was consistent with the environmental and technological
constraints: small-scale production. Nor had this to do with
the controversial notion of "limited good" which Western
anthropologists have used to explain the peasants' world view,

insinuating some kind of captive fatalism.[2] Given the hot and humid conditions of tropical climates, bacteriological activity is very rapid. This made storage of grains for long periods very difficult. The low level of technological development and the absence of effective pesticides further made for small-scale agricultural production. In these conditions it was possible to grow crops only sufficient to carry the family comfortably to the next harvesting season. Some individuals, however, managed to produce significant surpluses, but as we shall see later, these were always distributed among the members of the community.

The usual unit of production (and consumption) was, of course, the compound family, comprising several households. Naturally the family did not exist for purposes of production alone; it formed part of a total community with which the individual was identified. A member of the family gave his labour as part of his general social role, and he was rewarded by hospitality while he also shared in the consumption of the product of the joint communal effort. In the indigenous economy land provided the most important resource. However, the relationship between the individual and his family and the land on which he lived and cultivated was more than a purely economic relationship. It was part of his whole social identity. He relied on his land not only for subsistence but also for his recognition as a member of the community.

Under such circumstances land belonged to the community. The most important land holding group was the extended family, comprising the collective group of people derived from a grandfather or any male agnate above the first ascending generation.[3] The concept of the extended family does not refer to readily comparable groups nor to groups similar in composition or having the same degree of solidarity. It refers to groups of wide ranging diversity having disperate functions. Perhaps the use of the term "familistic collectivity" may avoid much of the confusion contained in the concept of the extended family.

No individual *owned* any piece of the land, but its *use* by individuals and families was governed by multiplex imbrications of interlocking rights. Ultimately rights to land use related to notions of good citizenship. But as Brock has observed, the family plots were not operated like a single economic enterprise with a single manager—the family head.[4] The practice was more complicated; among many of the patrilocal peoples, the wife or wives each had household fields assigned for their use. This allocation once made was nearly irrevocable so long as the woman remained a member of the family. Obviously customary rule about who made decisions on the use of the land and who had rights to its proceeds differed greatly amongst different peoples. Such rules, however, were only expressions of the normative practice. Actual practice revealed gradations of deviation from the rule depending, for instance, on the force of personality of different individuals and the nature of relationships between the individuals involved.[5] Given the constrains on production, the range of opportunity for personal advancement under this system was obviously limited. But such limitation had an important consequence on social control.

Some social scientists have sought to explain the apparent contentment of African cultivators by referring to the limited range of their expectations. If the level of expectation and attainment are both low, it is argued, the cultivators must be contented. But what is often not realised is that such a lowering of expectation in the indigenous society was conditioned in part by the structural constraints on expectations exceeding communal norms. The individual maintained a low level expectation not because he lacked ambition but because the cost of high attainment was socially prohibitive. Such limitations did not eliminate gradations in expectations anyway, but their importance concerned the determination of the points at which high or low expectations threatened solidarity. More specifically, the individual remained in the communal group not because he was satisfied materially, but because to step out of this narrow sphere of activity exacted too high costs in terms of societal humiliations and disappointments. Thus, the limitation of expectations became socially an act of communal loyalty. In other words, the limitation was a self-protective measure through which members of the community rationalised costs and avoided social sanctions.[6]

Mechanism of Indigenous Co-operation

The essence of social life in the indigenous society fostered mutual sharing; the distributive system functioned as a method for reconciling the individual's total interests with those of the community. Naturally, it was important that individuals be made to contribute to the general good of the society. Thus, the system had to be coercive in order to make for discretion in the distribution of limited resources. These conditions subsequently formed a mechanism for balancing loyalty and for sharing authority. In other words, the mechanism of indigenous co-operation was ultimately related to other mechanisms of social control within the community. Along with the low level of production of the indigenous society, the nature of gratification to the individual was defined largely in cultural terms. This, however, must be distinguished from romanticised notions of a natural *Gemeinschaft* like that projected by Ferdinand Tönnies. For Tönnies' ideal types meet problems of operational identification in empirical situations. Thus his concept may be adapted in analysis of African rural life only in the narrow sense in which it characterises "the *mechanism* sustaining the social order, rather than the organisation of that order".[7] Since the level of productivity was too low to permit any wide ranging differentiation of remunerative rewards on the basis of achievement, the community tended to reward its less competent members according to needs. But this remained strictly a tendency, for nowhere were the gradations in remunerative rewards completely removed. In addition, rewards in other distributive systems, like the magico-religious system, were often translatable into remunerative rewards. However, the fact that the community was egalitarian in its distribution of remuneration meant precisely that it could not be equally egalitarian in its distribution of authority and social status. The less competent members of the community received roughly the same share of the total material output. But the competent performers who received smaller remunerative rewards than they had earned were given greater relational rewards in the form of social esteem. This arrangement thus compensated the competent performers for the feeling of being deprived the share of remunerative rewards commensurate with their performance. They were rewarded instead by differential distribution of social rewards.

However, the proposal deriving from this argument, that in situations of material equality based on scarcity, differential social rewards go to those most competent, needs to be approached rather warily. For while competent performers were clearly prestigious, the implications of their prestige were muted by cultural factors such as deference to age.

It will be seen, therefore, that co-operation in the indigenous familistic collective was largely related to problems concerned with sharing. The efficacy of the idea of sharing increased with the feeling of dependency, the spirit of sharing being strongest among the less productive. The less competent members of the community, because they benefitted most from redistribution of material rewards, had cause to defend the system more ardently. But material benefit was not the only reason why individuals supported the system. It is clear enough that the nature of support given by the competent members derived from sources other than materialistic. In any case, the distributive system in the indigenous society tended to favour the weak. But without counterveiling forces, the system would have degenerated into one fostering parasitism, and in the long run it would have collapsed. This possibility was offset by the moral value attached to performance and the social opprobium toward the idle consumer. This idea is summarized in the now popular Swahili saying which has replications in many other East African vernaculars: *Mgeni siku mbili; siku ya tatu mpe jembe.* (Be gracious and courteous to the visitor for the first two days; on the third day give him a hoe to help in your garden.)

Sharing in the indigenous system was more concerned with the problem of ensuring subsistence for all rather than servile obedience to some archaic canons. Reciprocity and redistribution in conditions of scarcity made possible the mutual dependence which in turn ensured that while no individual accumulated excessive wealth, no man suffered undue deprivation. It cannot be overemphasised that such an egalitarian distribution of remunerative rewards necessarily implied the coercion of the "collective conscience" upon the individual.

It need hardly be said that the indigenous familistic collectivities were small-scale societies. Concepts such as that of the individuals' right to self-determination or of the community as an aggregate of individuals pursuing their welfare through the coordination of their effort were not easy to understand. The community was "mechanistic" in the Durkheimian sense. Instead of being seen as the link between the individual and the wider world, the community was seen to be the ultimate system. This narrow horizon made the individual totally dependent on the community—economically self-sufficient and geographically identifiable with a particular setting over which it had unalterable rights. In as much, therefore, as the individual and the wider system were not of much consequence to the members of the familistic collectivities, the political struggle between the different kinship groups cannot be called class struggle. It was rather conflict among micro-systems.

Because there were variations in the local micro-sociologies, it should be clear that the maximum unit with which the individual identified was not static. Usually the extended family was the largest most important economic group. Other groups became important for other purposes. For instance, in political matters generally wider units became relevant, the unit expanding in size depending on the issues involved. Thus it can be said with some justification that starting with the family and for purposes of subsistence, the individual's reference unit was characterised by concentric circles representing receding levels of loyalty, the terminal unit being defined in linguistic and cultural terms. In other words, the basis for co-operative organisation was defined by the input demanded by the task at hand, including the persistence of the task. For example, house building, not being a seasonal undertaking, justified the assistance of members of a much wider social unit than, say, cultivation.

Word must be said here about the traditional work groups, so much misunderstood by many Western anthropologists. When the task at hand required little labour, assistance took the form of reciprocal personal arrangement. However, if the task required a sufficiently large labour input to make the mutual exchange of personal assistance inefficient, some organisation of such labour became imperative. For instance, confronted with late cultivation or weeding, precluding the sufficiency of family labour to complete within a given time, need arose for a fairly large labour input. In such cases, large groups, ususally consisting of the young men in some kinship unit performed the task. The work-group, however, was not a permanent institution. Although in some regions it was identified with an age-grade, and task performance represented part of the social role of the age-grade, the group was only incidentally a work group.[8] The group was rewarded by food and drink, but it would be incorrect to conceive of such reward as payment, since it did not represent a measure of earning by individuals in the group nor an aggregate of individual earnings. Performance by the group represented the responsibility of the group toward the welfare of individual members of the community. The work group, thus, was governed by the same "collective conscience" that dictated the performance of other members of the community.

Traditional Co-operation under Change

There is a large body of literature on social change in Africa and it will be unnecessary to add to it, especially with respect to factual description. But the conspicuous omission from many of these descriptions of the colonial situation suggests that their interpretations are deficient. One such striking weakness is that many of them adopt an ideological position that takes the harmony of the predatory nature of capitalist exploitation and Africans' needs for granted. One of the most important effects of colonialism is that it undermined the structural bases of indigenous egalitarianism. For instance, local chiefs were granted more power than those held by the autochthonous leaders, and new rulers were created where no single rulers existed before.

Another effect of colonialism is that it very dramatically started the process of alienation. Thus, it undermined the very roots of communal solidarity and "samaritanism" by forcing a separation of the economic from the social activities: separation of labour from the social essence of man. As Karl Polanyi has very clearly shown, the guiding ideology of capitalism (the motivating force for colonialism) saw land, labour and wealth merely as commodities for sale.[9] And with the introduction of the sale of labour (employment), there was a definite change in the idea of rewards.

Resulting from the introduction of individual responsibility, particularily through wage labour, or the tax system by which it was induced, capitalist ideology propagated the idea of individual earning. The replacement of the idea of sharing by that of earning obviously favoured those performers, who may have had with the new changes, a feeling of being deprived the share of reward commensurate with their input. They were likely to be those people with a kind of competence that did not readily accord them status in the traditional social order. This could be related to their relatively young age; they had not invested much into the community by way of material or social inputs. Nor did they have sufficient skills to obtain any significant entrée into the new alien order which tended to urban based and went along with a certain level of Western education or cosmopoliteness.

Being thus in a situation of "status inconsistency" these people, particularily in the rural areas, had the best advantage of the two juxtaposed social orders. Individualization thus started a kind of polarization that was destined to turn the competent members of the peasant community against the non-competents. This process, however, did not take the form of complete polarization; indeed, it did not proceed at a uniform rate amongst the East African peoples. In any case, one of its most important consequences was the introduction of the idea of ownership, particularily land ownership or individualisation of tenure. Under colonialism, some theories were advanced to justify the vigorous encouragement and sometimes forceful adoption of individual rights and registration of land titles. The argument then was that somehow individual ownership ensured rapid development in that individuals could raise loans for agricultural development against the security of their titles.[10] With the idea of *indivi-*

dual ownership of land went the idea of the sale and purchase of land. The most important implication of these developments to the native social order was, of course, that kinship membership as such would no longer determine an individual's rights to land and his commitments to the lineage group.

We have already seen how an individual's rights to land under the indigenous system defined a whole range of obligations he had to the community. Changes in land holding rules have naturally, therefore, been very crucial factors leading to the erosion of the autochthonous social order, particularily the coercive influence of the "collective conscience". An additional factor in the general erosion of social cohesion has been the ability by the individual to change his residence, that is to move from the lineage-held neighbourhood. The individual who lives on his lineage land among his kinsmen obviously has some obligation toward his familistic community, however minimal. Co-operation in this case is characterised to a significant extent by notions of sharing and differential input depending on competence. Such a mode of co-operation is not based on voluntary association. Nor is it as totally coercive as the autochthonous collective conscience, for the individual can choose to minimize his contribution by choosing to identify more completely only with a much smaller social unit than that relevant under the indigenous system.

The tendency for the individual in this case to maximize output or remunerative rewards does not necessarily imply atomization; rather it implies nuclearization. Even where there are no kinship ties, as in the case of a neighbourhood not occupied by kinship groups, complete atomization has been very difficult to realise. Co-operation in this case, so far as it is based on a *community feeling,* expresses a kind of *Gemeinschaft* that is tied to locality. This form of co-operation may be said to be characteristic of peasants rather than of pre-peasant cultivators. This distinction is very crucial to the discussion of agricultural co-operatives in East Africa today because by participating in a wider market economy, the members of co-operative societies are definitively peasants. By peasants we understand "all those whose ultimate security and subsistence was in their having certain rights in land and in

27

the labour of family members on the land, but who are involved, through rights and obligations, in a wider economic system which includes the participation of non-peasants".[11]

But first let us briefly review some salient features features of agricultural development in this region. The establishment of colonial rule in East Africa and the subsequent setting up of mines and plantations with the necessary adjunct of forced labour—through direct conscription, or indirectly via the imposition of taxes to be paid in cash—affected the natives in a number of ways. They were forced to sell their food surpluses, sell their cattle or seek employment outside their homes to obtain cash. This series of alternatives clearly called for an economic choice, but the consequences were far reaching and had wide ranging social implications. where the production of cash crops was restricted by colonial decrees, as in Kenya, or in ecological regions which could not support profitable cash crops, large sections of the population were "proletarianized" (individuated); their communal anchors were loosened. In such cases, young men left their tribal lands to work in the factories and plantations, and agriculture remained basically of a subsistence kind sustained by women and elderly men.

In other parts of East Africa (and later in parts of Kenya) where the ecological conditions were suitable and no prohibitive restrictions were imposed, the production of cash crops became a very profitable undertaking. Agriculture in these areas, particularily the activities related to the production of cash crops, became the men's task, while the women's duty was to ensure the family's subsistence. In this latter case there arose significant differences among the cultivators oriented to some market and the purely subsistence producers. These, however, were not so much qualitative differences as they were of relative degree. In fact, it may be just convenient, since the cultivators were still very largely (though not entirely) concerned with food production, to see them as peasants. Viewed this way, the internal differences then only distinguish different types of peasants.

Differentiation among peasants in East Africa has been very intimately connected with the process of general agricultural development. In this process, "four variables have been of particular importance in defining the nature of participation in the overall system by primitive agriculturalists through which they acquired, in effect, their peasant characteristics".[12] These variables are (1) the presence of labour-demand centres, (2) the suitability of local ecological environment for cash cropping, including the accessibility of marketing facilities, (3) the presence of white capitalist settlers, and (4) the existence of an indigenous rural "bourgeoisie"—a kind of "kulak" class. To a large extent these variables also influenced the differential rates of the development of modern co-operative societies in East Africa.

Co-operative Development in East Africa

Prior to the end of the Second World War there was little development of co-operative organisations in East Africa. Such co-operatives as existed by 1945 were mainly of European or Asian membership. There were hardly any African organisations in Kenya by that date. Uganda had "few full fledged (African) co-operative societies, though there were many quasi-co-operative marketing societies in operation. Tanganyika by then had the already well-developed Kilimanjaro Native Co-operative Union with its affiliated societies",[13] the Ngoni-Matengo Union and its primaries and the Bugufi Co-operative Society. An important factor which contributed to the slow development of co-operatives, and of agricultural development in general, was a colonial policy that directed attention to the maintenance of law and order rather than to the promotion of social and economic progress for the natives.

Following the war a new approach to colonial policy was put into practice. The new outlook toward agricultural development brought a more positive attitude toward co-operative development. In part, this resulted from internal pressures and representation by certain interests in Britain.[14] Resulting from this change in policy, the already existing co-operative divisions in colonial administration were strengthened and new ones were created where none existed before. A number of factors determined the growth of the earliest co-operatives in East Africa.

Specifically, the first movements were started in those regions where the suitability of environment had favoured production of crops such as coffee, tobacco, and cotton. It is worth noting that the primary motivation in starting these organisations was not the desire to revive some form of a modernist *Gemeinschaft*. Rather, it was more importantly the consideration by the growers of advantages of economies of scale, particularily in reducing the overhead costs, for instance in transportation. The benefit of sharing expensive facilities was clearly obvious to the growers.

It is also important to realise that these early organisations were started in areas of no significant white settlement, and therefore without colonial restrictions, save perhaps regulations which made the sale of crops through co-operatives compulsory. Generally the early co-operative movements were spontaneous, often meeting very little encouragement from the colonial administrators. The subsequent introduction of co-operative regulations in these instances may thus be rightly seen as a form of colonial control of the economic initiatives of the natives. The organisations that sprang up in the postwar years were less spontaneous in that their membership was forced by colonial regulations that sought to ensure proper grading and to preclude the sale of low-quality produce.

Later with the rise of nationalism, co-operative development took a new form: to combat marketing systems and middlemen who exploited the peasant growers. The giant Nyanza Co-operative Union (until recently known as the Victoria Federation of Co-operative Unions), perhaps the largest co-operative venture in Africa, was an outgrowth of political nationalism and general peasant dissatisfaction around 1950–52 with unfair payments, short-weighing of their seed cotton under a zonal monopoly in the hands of Asian agents. The political implications of this movement, as well as others during this period, cannot be overemphasised. Co-operation became the symbol of unity against all forms of colonial exploitation. In many cases the co-operative societies, often sharing their leadership with the local leadership of the incipient political movement, became the natural centres of political opposition. Nor was this a new phenomenon; as early as the twenties, peasants in Tanzania organised in opposition against colonial privilege.[15] This development started an integration between local-level politics and peasant movements which expresses itself in the prominence of co-operative societies in rural politics today.

In the transient situation of East African societies a hard and fast distinction between economic and political matters does not pertain to actual practice. The distinction is one of degree rather than type; moreover, it is one that the peasants themselves hardly make. To assert, therefore, that co-operative development in particular, and rural development in all its overlappings, is essentially rural politics, is only to express a commonplace axiom differently. This becomes particularily true for the post-independence years when co-operation was adopted as part of a policy aimed at the moblization of peasants in the development effort. Apart from its potential efficiency in bulking and marketing, the idea of co-operation has attracted some policy makers as an ideology of life. To this end some themes of traditional communalism have been evoked and propagated through political parties and other organs of communication.[16] This new move raises even more sharply questions about the relevance between autochthonous communal sharing and modern co-operative organizational forms.

Peasant Co-operatives Today

When the boundaries defining the domain of co-operative societies were fixed, they almost invariably tended to coincide with administrative boundaries which were based on lineage units. But such administrative boundaries comprise lineage units much larger than the familistic collective within which the communal co-operative spirit operated. For example, most co-operative unions cover an area corresponding to a District or Area, while societies may cover Locations. These administrative units are also generally identified with tribe or sub-tribe respectively. The new co-operative organisations thus represented an expanded scale of activity; they created a much

31

wider group. But unlike the old order in which an individual was a member by virtue of his birth, the individual was, ideally, invited to become a member in the new and wider organisation. Participation by individuals thus would be, in part, a function of perceived remunerative rewards rather than social obligation. Thus, the act of association in the new organisations is voluntary and recognises the equality of all members.

The new organisations are governed by laws first enacted during the thirties. The regulations retain the same general principles although they have undergone revisions.[17] While these legislations may differ in the fineries of detail, they all embody a common principle. The theory is that an isolated and powerless individual can only by association with others, through mutual support, obtain his own degree of material advantage. Thus, where co-operation was obtained by coercion in the autochthonous order, it is now induced by considerations of individual benefit. Modern co-operatives had been intended as essentially organisations of economic benefit to be secured through trading. In this sense then co-operatives in East Africa today can be seen merely as economic institutions with specialized marketing functions, only tangentially affecting the peasant family's life.

Whereas the indigenous communal spirit of sharing took place as an inseparable part of social life, modern co-operatives confine thenselves to specific functions and are intended to have "rationalistic legitimation". But this development has only been partially accomplished. In actual practice, the canons of the new organisations are not followed flawlessly. The doctrine of equality of the individual members does not exclude the fact that certain aspects of indigenous social relationship, such as the "natural" leadership of elders, persists in some societies. The universalistic tendency in the societies does not preclude the fact that within the neighbourhood the individual's kinship loyalty is efficacious in determining the way he acts. As well as the doctrine of one man one vote, kinship, as indeed other primodial identities, provides an important group around which to organise local-level politics. And being so important institutions in the peasant life, co-operative organisations, and not political party organisations, may perhaps be more central to the rural drama. Control in primary society's committees by micro-systems implies, in the view of many, maximization of benefits by the members of the lineage-neighbourhood group in power. But, of course, the benefit accrues in reality only to a few activists.

In the politics of co-operative societies today two factors play a very important part in patterning the power cleavages. These are socio-economic differentiation and kinship-neighbourhood loyalties, but these variables are not mutually exclusive. Indeed, the relationships between them emphasises important problems in rural development, particularily the problem of effective participation by peasants, and responsible leadership in the co-operatives. The problem we are referring to here also highlights the nature of interrelationships between rural localiteness or *cosmopoliteness* and socio-economic differentiations. The interdependence and interpenetration of class and local lineage alliances, for instance, characterises the politics of the co-operative movement in Maswa District, Tanzania, where for over ten years the movement has been led by a small clique of persons who have had a wide range of commercial and other entrepreneurial experiences. Indeed, it may be generalised that the most ardent promoters of co-operatives have not been cultivators. A number of biographical examinations show these people to have been in a situation of "status inconsistency". Co-operatives thus provided opportunities for their upward mobility.[18]

But in organising support the "activists" relied on local kinship-based followings. In fact, lineage-neighbourhood rivalries became very vital for those engaged in the local-level drama of power struggle. In determining the first leadership of the Maswa organisation, for example, lineage-neighbourhood considerations were most decisive. The architects of the strategy that won elections for the new leaders were all delegates from societies in a single chiefdom.[19] Considerations of lineage or neighbourhood similarly dictate the affairs of primary societies. This practice fosters particularistic tendencies, although it could equally be argued that by ensuring equal participation by lineage-neighbourhood units, it ensures equitable distribution or power, at least in geographical terms. The "double standard" of this suggestion is, of course, not something characteristic only of Africa.[20]

Insufficient participation by peasants, represented by poor attendance at co-operative societies' meetings or non-involvement in activities other than the purely economic, may also be associated with the general level of development in the wider society. Some of the problems encountered by the co-operative movement in East Africa are due to organisational failures of a social and economic nature. Problems of the inefficiency of committeemen, for instance, reflect the transience of society and the low level of a kind of education that ensures informed participation. The social meaning of such inefficiency doubtless deviates from the official notion derived from Western concepts because it involves an attempt to adopt values derived from the autochthonous system in which performance is conditioned by social solidarity. These values deal with multiplex social and economic disruptions caused by the incomplete realisation of a money economy under conditions of great instability.

But despite these inefficiencies, it is clear that co-operative development has met some success in East Africa which has led some people to the hasty conclusion that the most crucial variable must, therefore, be a favourable "traditional" disposition toward co-operation. It is, of course, not so easy to isolate mere association of factors from their causal relatedness. It is clear enough that modern co-operatives are not a direct continuation of the native communal forms, even they may appear to be so. The movement has obviously taken advantage of the given social structures, and its success may be partly attributable to the participants' familiarity with certain ideas of co-operation. Such familiarity, however, can only be a minor factor in explaining the co-operative success in parts of East Africa. The strength of this contention is perhaps best revealed by the examination of deviant cases of co-operative failures or non-existence. The relative absence of co-operative organisations in certain societies where the indigenous organisational forms are still relatively intact only reveals the inadequacy of tradition-based explanations.

34

Naturally, deviant-case analyses will be confounded by the existence of organisations which have been started on government directive. The case of organisations in the resettlement schemes is particularily pertinent. In the case of such organisations, differences in ideological orientations of the national governments come into play. In the former white highlands in Kenya, for instance, commercial farming in the resettlement areas is organised through a series of co-operative societies, membership of which is compulsory. These are reported to be weak, lacking the enthusiasm that comes with voluntary initiative.[21] The compulsory nature of such organisations raises interesting questions about similarity with the coercive nature of the indigenous "collective conscience". The comparison becomes particularily relevant in the case of recently projected measures in Tanzania to make the existing organisations the foci of the new communal villages, *ujamaa* villages.

Analysis of the relevance of indigenous co-operative forms to *ujamaa* villages, however, will have to take account of the heterogeneity of the participants, the "rationalistic legitimation" of the new communities, widened horizons and the increased role of political party and government agencies in effecting changes in patterns of residence and farming practices. There has been a tendency to relocate new settlers in East Africa on schemes that are more or less ethnically homogenous. In more recent bold experiments the Tanzanian government is trying to create ethnically heterogenous settlements, comprising settlers moved from areas of population pressure. The relative freedom of the settlers from customary lineage-group controls may give an added impetus to the change process. But it is a moot point whether the involuntary "mutual self-help" demanded in the new co-operative organisations may not dampen enthusiasm.

The main concern of this discussion has been to determine the relevance of traditional co-operative organisational forms to the present marketing and service co-operatives in East Africa. In attempting to identify any continuities popular notions of "traditional" *Gemeinschaft* and "modern" associational relationships have been approached rather warily. This is prompted by a number of considerations, the most important of which is the gross simplifications inherent in such typologies. There is a primary difficulty in recognising the traditional social forms relevant to co-operation. The transience of social developments in East Africa further makes aspects of "traditionality" and "modernity" inseparably intertwined. The effect is that attempts which rely on clutural explanations for identifying the variables determining the success of co-operatives often miss the real crucial factors.

One major weakness of culture-based explanations is that they tend to have a static view of social life. Thus, many scholars trying to specify what makes the African peasant "tick" tend to treat the existing peasantries as some exotic social type characterised by a basic benevolence and by being relatively undifferentiated. But these assumptions do not obtain in actuality. Socio-economic differentiation and kinship-neighbourhood loyalties emerge into prominence among factors affecting differential participation by individuals in the co-operative organisation. At the same time other variables such as ecology, transportation and availability of market for agricultural goods affect the development of co-operatives. Many of these factors clearly did not pertain under the traditional system. In addition, they represented an expansion of the scale of the activities in which the African peasants are involved today. These factors alone point to the fact that there is no direct continuity between the autochthonous co-operative forms and modern marketing co-operatives.

The rapid development of the co-operative movement in East Africa during the post-war years and after political independence raises a number of problems. One such problem relates to questions of social control, specifically the problem of balancing social justice (democracy) and efficiency. This question, however, ultimately relates to the wider national socio-political environment within which co-operatives are operating. In Tanzania, for example, there is an attempt to ensure the effective participation of the peasants by an ideology that invokes certain features of the African past-adapted to modern conditions. But ideology alone may not ensure such participation. While enthusiasm may be sustained by the nostalgic respect to the past, effective participation will ultimately be kindled by perceived benefits. But these need not be seen purely in economic terms for according to the *Ujamaa* ideology, value encompasses an expression of a relationship as well as a measurement. In propagating the new-look co-operatives, the paradox to which planners must address themselves raises the problem of how to communicate to the peasants the government's long range goals while sustaining their enthusiasm by granting some of their immediate wants.

Lionel Cliffe

Traditional Ujamaa and
Modern Producer Co-operatives in Tanzania

The Origins of Tanzania's Ujamaa Policy

In his paper, Migot-Adholla has ably exposed as a myth the notion that existing co-operatives are a "direct continuation" of the traditional mutual aid common to most African societies in the past. The fact that a few thousand peasant farmers now sell their cash crops to a single *marketing* organisation can scarcely be said to derive from the pattern of life when an extended family worked together to cultivate their homestead, aiding their neighbours at times of harvest and hardship. The additional realisation that the colonial situation with its pressures to replace "sharing by earning" has made this kind of rustic idyll a thing of the past, must also make us vary in seeing to much continuity from the past in marketing co-operatives in rural East Africa.

The recent Tanzania policy of "Socialism and Rural Development" (*Ujamaa Vijijini*) seems, however, to be a somewhat different and novel attempt to mobilise traditional communal values to modern developmental objectives, envisaging the creation of *producer* co-operatives within a village community, in which people will "live and work together for the good of all".[1] This policy is in fact explicity justified in terms of the "traditional *ujamaa* system". It therefore presents an interesting and special test of some of the ideas explored by Migot-Adholla in attempting to show the exact relationships "between indigenous organisational forms and modern agricultural co-operatives".

This paper will focus on this test case and look at the traditional and other factors that have to be taken into account in planning the transformation to "*ujamaa*" in rural Tanzania. This first section will explore the relevance of traditional *ujamaa* at the level of ideas; how this notion in fact influences thinking about rural socialism, and what exactly the policy derived therefrom involves. Subsequent sections will look at the nature of the legacy from the particular traditional forms that existed in Tanzania, the precise nature of the colonial impact, and the problem of dovetailing these features of the inherited socio-economic structure with the possibilities for rational planning of larger scale, modern co-operative production.

First, though, the origin and content of the policy. The appeal of this programme of *Ujamaa Vijijini* is certainly based in part on an appeal to tradition—"the principles upon which the traditional extended family was based must be reactivated (p. 12) . . . we must build on the firm foundations of the three principles of ujamaa living" (p. 4), Nyerere urges in the policy pamphlet. But the relevance of traditional *ujamaa* is more than just as a useful selling device for rural socialism —an attempt to legitimise the policy on the basis of indigenous, and thus hopefully acceptable, values. Traditional forms are seen not only as a convenient myth but as an actual starting point, or at least as a possible operational basis for the creation of *ujamaa* villages:

> We must take our traditional system, correct its short-comings, and adapt to its service the things we can learn from the technologically developed societies (p. 4) . . .

But, President Nyerere adds, "we can *start* with the traditional extended family, but they will not remain family communities" (p. 12); or more flexibly, he suggests that the ultimate group or community "would be the *traditional family,* or any other group of people living according to ujamaa principles, large enough to take account of modern methods . . ." (p. 16) (my italics, in each case). Just how far such "traditional" forms offer an actual operational base for modern *ujamaa* co-operatives we shall examine in the next two sections. Here we must recognise that it it so seen and go on to explore a little further what Nyerere's conception of this "traditional *ujamaa*" is.

The three principles of *ujamaa* living which he sees as being at the roots of all traditional societies, are: mutual respect and obligation (which give rise to the traditions of hospitality and generosity); a common obligation for everyone to work; and the common ownership of the basic goods.[2] In some of his earlier writings he has specifically suggested that these values meant the absence of class or caste divisions, and that even political authorities were subject to certain popular checks and balances. The accuracy of these generalisations will also be discussed in the next section; here it is sufficient to note that the new policy is justified in terms of an ideology of tradition—the myth that African Society were classless and democratic; and that moreover these are the principles which are to be given effect in the new rural society that is to be forged.

If the thinking of the leadership stopped there, Tanzania's *ujamaa* would remain the same kind of rhetoric that "African Socialism" has been reduced to elsewhere, when at most it is used to foster marketing co-operatives and rural self-help within a context of overall capitalist development. In that event *Ujamaa Vijijini* would remain a vision or be restriced to a few utopian experiments. The *ujamaa* village policy amounts to more than that and has to be seen in the context of the Arusha Declaration of commitment to an overall, self-reliant, socialist strategy. What is significant in the new formulations is not just the phrasing of a socialist appeal in terms of indigenous values, but the combination of that with the recognition of the shattering impact on traditional society of the forces of international capitalism, and specifically the urgency of posing an alternative pattern of development which would not so inexorably lead to the formation of distinct classes, even in rural areas.[3] Thus the policy is seen not merely as a blueprint for creating a few co-operative villages, it represents an intention to transform the *whole* of rural society, to "build a nation of such village communities". Indeed, the Second Five Year Plan makes clear that there is to be a "frontal" not a selective approach to *ujamaa* transformation. Thus the villages are not to represent a few rustic islands of communal or co-operative endeavour in a predominantly capitalist economy, as is the case in Israel, or—dare I say it?—Sweden. Moreover, the whole frontal programme of creating co-operative villages is in turn part of a general socialist strategy covering not just the rural areas. Self-reliant, organised and democratic rural communities would play their part by promoting a much broader–based, labour–intensive development of the agricultural sector with important consequences for the growth of the internal market and the diminution of international dependence. The existence of such rural communities would also make possible effective mass mobilisation behind the policy which will alone ensure in the long run a socialist society in which the "interests of the peasants and workers" are in fact paramount.

That the *Ujamaa Vijijini* policy has to be set in this wider context, as an alternative to rural class formation and thus one of the foundations for socialist development of the *whole* society, is often overlooked by commentators and even by those who are responsible for implementing rural development policies. There is a tendency to focus on the micro aspects of *ujamaa* villages and see them as merely another set to be added to the existing list of rural capital projects. An earlier draft of the new Development Plan had in fact to be reworked by the planners as the political leadership felt that those sections dealing with the rural sector did not give sufficient weight to the frontal approach to *ujamaa*. This narrow interpretation is also evident in the fact that in practice, almost all of of the several hundred communities now designated as "*ujamaa* villages" are in fact *new* settlements in that they have only recently been initiated; people have been brought to "live together" but are only slowly and as a second stage being encouraged to "work together" on a co-operative basis. Few attempts have as yet been made to tackle the far more taxing problem of transforming *existing* patterns of cultivation. However, there is now emerging a different emphasis away from the starting of new, *ujamaa* settlements. This frontal approach will concentrate on seizing the opportunities to be derived from larger-scale, co-operative production, especially of those cash crops whose promotion is receiving economic priority, and on the working out of regional, macro strategies to effect this kind of transformation. There is. in Migot-Adholla's terms, a shift of focus from the "coercive, collective conscience" resulting from "membership" in a new settlement, to a "rationalistic legitimation" in terms of the benefits of increased mutual aid and labour co-operation within existing communities.

Indigenous Modes of Production and Productive Relations

As the next section will make clear the possibility of direct continuity from forms of production that are no longer traditional may be an unrealistic hope, but in working out strategies for transformation to modern producer co-operatives it is useful to discover to what extent particular societies did correspond to the *ujamaa* ideal and how far this legacy persists. For whatever the accuracy of Nyerere's generalisations and whatever the nature of any particular traditional society, it will have *some* operational relevance for the creation of modern forms of co-operation—even if only in a negative sense. Some form of mutual aid was almost certainly a feature of all pre-colonial communities. Whether, and to what extent it persists is of some interest. But many of the other communal values which Nyerere and others posit applied, if at all, only within the family so other features of the structure of the larger society into which the *ujamaa* family had to fit, must also be isolated for they may have impeding or facilitating consequences if there is an aim to expand the *scale* of effective co-operative organisation. Moreover, the relevance of pre-existing socio-economic structures has to be admitted even if they have been profoundly reshaped for the new forms have been derived from, and owe their particular shape to, the earlier configurations.

Three factors, which embrace Nyerere's three principles, would seem to be vital in determining the point of departure for modern *ujamaa*:

(1) *Stratification & Differentiation*—what quantitative and qualitative socio-economic differences were to be found within a community?

(2) *Land tenure*—What rights in land were held by which individuals and groups?

(3) *Mechanisms of co-operation*—what activities were carried out on a communal basis and what was the nature of the co-operating group.

Of course, ultimately, these questions should be phrased in the present tense. Yet, a brief analysis of what was will assist us not to get a picture of the present situation, but to see it in a dynamic framework; for it is not so much the depth of, say, class cleavages which is now of concern but the inevitability and rapidity of their emergence. Any attempt to answer these three questions must refer to the pre-existing modes of production, which would have had some determining effect on all three of these elements.

An interesting recent paper[4] in fact provides a basis for the examination of pre-colonial societies. In this, Goody suggests that the typical African farming system precluded the emergence of a feudal landed class. Agriculture was conducted by a fairly sparse population in a situation where land was plentiful but soils were relatively infertile, and conducted without the use of animal power, only with the hoe and other hand tools. Consequently, there was a tendency to shifting cultivation, holdings were not so fixed, not so productive, nor land values as high as in most parts of Eurasia where feudalism developed; thus, Goody argues, "there were no landlords, (although) there were of course lords of the land". In addition, the technological character of production meant that it was essentially small-scale, and economic specialisation (except perhaps in iron and tool making) was almost unknown. While much of Tanzania would correspond to this pattern, two kinds of area would constitute important exceptions.

First, the highland, banana-staple areas—in the mountains of the north-west, in the south western highlands, and west of Lake Victoria—were supporting fairly dense, settled populations and yielding sufficient surplus to support more complex, hierarchial societies. But only in the north-western, "interlacustrine kingdoms" did anything of a "feudal" economic system, with a landed class or caste, actually emerge. In one such area, Bukoba District, despite two pieces of post-independence legislation, it is proving quite difficult to get rid of the remnants of the "feudal" *nyarubanja* land tenure system there. Elsewhere, a certain element (local-chiefs in Rungwe near Lake Malawi[5] specific clans in Pare[6]) had some powers of allocation of land, and with the introduction of cash crops and severe land shortage these groups have often been able to obtain a privileged economic position and to retain considerable political influence. The intensive nature of cultivation, the differentiation that has resulted from the uneven access to cash crop opportunities, and the continued influence of those who in the past controlled access to land, together present great obstacles to the creation of *ujamaa* co-operatives in these areas. So far the only efforts to start *ujamaa* activities have been through resettling people from these overcrowded areas in *new ujamaa* villages in bordering areas or in other districts; and, more recently, to reframe government programmes for the development of peasant tea and dairying in a more co-operative framework.

At the other extreme, the large areas of dry, tsetse-infested bush represent a second exception to the shifting cultivation pattern. The limited population that lived in these vast areas was often pastoral (like the Masai) or semi-pastoral (like the Gogo) or even in some very remote pockets still reliant on hunting and gathering (the Hadza and Sandawe of north-central Tanzania, for instance). Understandably these groups were highly segmented and the people can still be aggressively egalitarian and independent. While they had been militarily dominant in recent times the cattle herders had not established their fiefdom over a whole society as was the case in Rwanda. Livestock were owned by an individual family head, although sometimes they were herded together with those of other families or loaned out. Grazing rights were communal in that everyone (at least within the community that habitually "occupied" a locality) had access, which meant that in the economic sense grazing land was a "free" good. There could still be great differences in "wealth"; individual herds ranging from a handful to a thousand cattle or more.

These pastoral areas have been the least touched by the colonial impact. A lack of concern for, and of understanding of, the indigenous system by which this harsh environment

44

was exploited has meant that few rational plans for development have been formulated.[7] Efforts are, however, now being made to give more priority to livestock development and co-operative ranching associations are being introduced as the basis for improved range management.

Two problems are immediately posed in connection with these new ranching programmes by the pre-existing social and economic practices. The combination of individual ownership of animals with communal and/or "free" grazing rights, makes it difficult to institute control to ensure more rational pasture-use, now necessitated by a denser population and overgrazing. No *individual* has an incentive to reduce or limit his stock, as he will then only be worse off *vis-a-vis* his neighbours, and differentation and consequent differences of interest make agreed collective solutions difficult to obtain. Equally the ranching associations which are being created seem to lend themselves to manipulation (of such thing as membership and dipping fees—levied in some associations on a per capita basis and not according to number of animals) by the larger cattle owners.[8]

In most of the other inhabited parts of the country, occupied by the great majority of the population, a kind of agricultural system that corresponds in varying degrees to the general pattern described by Goody had emerged, that is one based on some form of shifting cultivation. The fallow need not be so long and thus the degree of permanence was greater in the less arid areas—near the coast, or the great lakes—or where new forms of socio-political organisation,[9] or improved implements (iron hoes, etc.) were available. In these areas a fairly settled population lived in large, and usually scattered, extended family homesteads (*kaaya*), each wife or sub-family often cultivating its own plots, and (where tsetse allowed) family herds of livestock were grazed on the surrounding, unused lands. In much of the south of the country, livestock had been almost unknown, at least for the last hundred years (because of tsetse), and in these and other drier and more marginal areas, there was a system of more widespread shifting, in which small islands of thicket or woodland would be cut and burnt, cropped for a year or two and then left to go back to bush. Rights in land were seldom as well defined as in the highland areas, and in the more marginal districts especially, there was something approaching free access to land.

Patterns of kinship and inheritance in some instances (e.g. among the Sukuma) encouraged the out-migration of younger sons or other family members. Especially in the drier areas, there was only limited economic specialisation and differentiation, although in livestock areas larger cattle owners would live off their herds by exchanging grain surpluses produced by poorer neighbours. Again, depending on how marginal the area, there was a tendency for these societies to be segmented.[10] In some of them, however, chiefly elements were emerging in the 18th and 19th centuries, drawing tribute, but also being considered responsible through rain-making and other powers, for the general prosperity. These elements, some of whom were in fact strengthened and yet made less responsive by colonial rule, were later well-placed to get access to education, cash crops and other resources. However, apart from the introduction of cotton in Sukumaland, in the East Lake and in parts of the Eastern-Coast area, and more recently islands of tobacco in the *miombo* woodlands of the west of the country, many of these areas are even now only involved in the cash economy to a very limited extent—except in so far as some of the areas of this type are *indirectly* involved in the capitalist sector. The dry, central areas like Singida Region, or Kigoma Region in the extreme west, and the more remote parts of the South-West for instance, have become source areas for labour migrating to work on the sisal and other estates.

We can now sum up this very brief and oversimplified survey of the pre-colonial economic patterns in Tanzania. Production was constrained by the simple technology, and over much of the country by an inhospitable environment; it was on a very small-scale; it was organised on the basis of the family; and as the Migot-Adholla paper reminds us, this usually meant that the family was divided up between wives and sons, and seldom farmed as a single unit. Likewise, labour was organised on an individual household basis,[11] members of the wider family, other kin, neighbours or age mates being drawn in when tasks or circumstances warranted. The actual form of co-operation shows interesting variations; sometimes being confined to the family, with conflict as the basic feature of inter-family relations (e.g. in the Singida example mentioned in footnote 10), or between other kin. It is clearly relevant to the planning of *ujamaa* transformation to know whether there are these kinds of precedents for mutual aid on anything but a family basis. Age group organisations, like the *basumba batale* in Sukumaland may thus have some contemporary relevance; in other areas, Lushoto District for instance, a small group of age-mates on occasions formed informal but permanent labour exchange teams undertaking a wider range of farming operations together than was the general case; and in some villages this pattern can still be found. Abrahams[12] describes the oft-ignored neighbourhood groups (*bazengwa bichane*) as the basis for a co-operative team in parts of Nyamwezi, which cultivated and threshed their millet on a joint basis and which were at the root of the more recent spread of grassroots nationalist political organisation in the area.

Apart from the persistence of such legacies, significant regional differences in the extent of differentiation and in land tenure had already grown up in the pre-colonial period, and the general effect of the colonial impact has been to emphasize and compound the differences, as we shall see in the next section.

The Colonial Impact

The general pattern of social change stemming from the colonial presence is well-known, and amply summarised by Migot-Adholla, even though one still sees discussions of pre-colonial Africa in terms of the "anthropological present" tense! Yet, there have been relatively few attempts, particularly in recent years, to chart precisely the economic forces for change at work on a given society and their social consequences.[13] We can, however, indicate that there were marked variations in this impact in Tanzania, it being most dramatic in the highland (and high-potential) areas which often were exposed to settler encroaching ment as well as to the introduction of permanent, relatively highpriced, cash crops, notably coffee. By no means all the more marginal shifting agricultural areas were deemed suitable for cash crops, and thus many of them are not as yet completely given over to a more individualistic, cash-oriented system—although some areas near Tanga and around Morogoro saw the development of the sisal plantations, while other areas adjusted to an agricultural system requiring limited labour inputs from the males of the family as so many were seeking work on these estates.

Where the impact was heaviest, there have been marked tendencies towards economic *stratification,* and a "class" of larger farmers, sometimes combining trading, transporting and other business activities is in evidence. On many occasions it was the already slightly privileged elements, those with traditional political power, control over land, or just those who had a little more land or who got in first with cash crops or schooling, who enhanced their relative socio-economic status in this way. The further differentiation of the already privileged from the rest of the population was not always the pattern. In Lushoto, for instance (as in several other places) some educated commoner elements successfully challenged the political and later economic position of a traditional ruling clan.

The process of differentiation was often linked with decisive changes in land tenure. The extra acreages for cash crops and increased population, the resulting monetary values attaching to land and the fact of permanent, tree crops tended to lead to the occupation of all land, to *de facto* individual partition and eventually freedom to dispose of, and a market in land. Again, the process seems to be well under-way in the highland areas, and to a more limited extent in a few of the other areas where cash crops have been grown for some time.

Some forms of *co-operation* still persist, but the employment of casual (or even permanent) labour has tended to replace it in areas most exposed to capitalist development. Even within a given district for instance Lushoto, analysis showed that in those villages most taken up with production for the market (areas growing coffee, tea, vegetables) mutual aid on some-

48

thing like the traditional basis had virtually died out, while it was an accepted practice in villages more remore from the international market place.

The present situation which has to be faced in thinking of moves towards socialist forms is one that varies from one part of the country to another. In the more "developed" highlands, every pocket of land is occupied, people are used to production for the market and if they need any extra help they hire it. One can find both poor peasants and maybe even landless prepared to offer their labour, together with a growing set of local notables depending on such labour and with a vested interest in maintaining an individual pattern of farming. If these better-off "kulaks" are also politically influential at the grass roots level, the prospects for implementing *ujamaa* farming through the local institutions (at least without some minor, local "cultural revolution") are somewhat remote. There are, at the other extreme, areas where cash crops are only now being introduced, where people are ready to seize at such chances and can be made to see the logic of introducing methods and activities or opening up new land on a co-operative basis, and where indeed traditions of labour exchange between recognised groups are not dead. But, whatever the kind of structural position that has arisen, the scope for introducing co-operative forms of working and residence cannot be fully appreciated without reference also to the potential of the area and, specifically, the possibilities for effective and economic co-operative production.

The Rationale for Co-operative Production

The trends, then, in Tanzania are away from those forms of traditional co-operation that existed and towards a more individualistic pattern and "the beginnings of a class system in the rural areas".[14] But in one sense this process has not gone far enough; exploitation neither was sufficiently marked in the inherited system nor has it become pronounced enough to create profound discontents and conflicts in the countryside. In the absence of the kind of "revolutionary situation" which has made possible agrarian socialism in such diverse circumstances as those of U.S.S.R., China, and Cuba, consciousness and the necessary incentives for change must be provided by other means. There has to be some "rationalistic legitimation" for *ujamaa* co-operatives—especially as any form of forced collectivisation has not only been expressly ruled out on ideological grounds, but is probably beyond the present capacity of enforcement agencies. Yet if the transformation to *ujamaa* agriculture is to be through persuasion not force, there has to be an "argument" with which to persuade.

One possible set of benefits which could provide the incentive to bring people together are to be derived from the "villagisation" aspect of the new policy. In all but a few societies people have resided on their own scattered plots, and even in densely populated highlands, there are in most instances no single clusters deserving the label "villages". The Tanzania leadership has for several years[15] extolled the advantages of people moving physically together—people can then be more easily and cheaply be provided with social services and other amenities and with extension and other advice, and generally could be more efficiently mobilised. But the new, *ujamaa* policy implies more than this and indeed to much stress on its "living together" aspects rather than the "working together" may not only obscure the co-operative theme but be even dysfunctional for achieving the overall objectives.

This is firstly because local government or party personnel may attract people into new villages with the provision of schools and water supplies, but may then find it difficult to proceed with co-operativisation of production, or even ignore this second stage altogether. Or, even if such efforts towards co-operation are made, they will not necessarily have been conceived in such a manner and on such a scale that there is in fact the possibility of increased productivity. Yet a frontal approach affecting a large part of the population will only be within the limits of Tanzania resources if it does lead to significant increases in production. The appropriateness of some of the newly settled *ujamaa* villages planned on the basis of economic provision of services is partly a matter of scale. In Rufiji District, where one village has some 3,000 families resettled from flooded areas, and in the sparsely populated Handeni District where several villages of up to 250 families have been formed, there just may not be enough cultivable land within reasonable distance to support such a concentration. Added to which, the advantages of larger-scale efficient labour organisation which, in the absence of heavy mechanisation, is the main advantage of co-operative production, are only likely to accrue when the working groups are fairly small at least until people are more used to this system of work, and until the organisational capability of village leadership is higher.[16a]

The fact that the whole experience in forming *ujamaa* villages has been one of sponsoring new settlements around a government-built core of services, is seemingly having two further unfortunate effects. It is doing anything but foster an attitude of self-reliance among the villages that are formed. Also, this emphasis has created a general impression, among the public and officials alike, that identifies the policy of *Ujamaa Vijijini* only with the process of moving people to unoccupied areas of land. People may, understandably, resist this version of *ujamaa*; in areas where there is little spare land, the whole *ujamaa* idea seems as a result to have little relevance; and finally the relevance of co-operation to *existing* areas of cultivation and the whole "frontal approach" are thus neglected.

These considerations all suggest a conclusion that the incentives which in the long run are going to determine the success of this frontal attempt at *ujamaa* transformation have to be sought in the potential benefits of co-operative production. Economies may result from the greater ease of providing what the economists call "indivisibilites" for a larger organised collectivity—especially mechanised equipment. But the lack of success of large-scale mechanisation as well as the overall economic strategy of self-reliance, suggest that this will not be the answer for most of the rural areas, at least in the first stage. We are thus left with seeking opportunities for more effective labour use through co-operation. There are several circumstances where such incentives may arise from increased production through co-operation. Obviously, there are possibilities of economies of larger scale through better organisation of labour, and through the familiar advantages of specialisation.[17] A slightly different opportunity is presented in many of the agricultural systems in Tanzania, which have under-utilised labour for long periods of the year—for the introduction of additional activities, which may not be possible except with co-operation. These might include new crops—which may only be possible by overcoming seasonal labour bottlenecks through a division of labour (for instance, more cash crops can be planted once the food is ensured by another team)—new non-agricultural activities (cottage industries etc.), and capital investment through labour-creation of irrigation works, storeage facilities and the like.

A further incentive can be derived from *ujamaa* patterns of production, as compared with the present individual pattern, but this one is not simply a matter of greater overall productivity. The facts of economic indivisibilities and differentiation mean that there are many improvements which are not available to some, or most, of the individual peasants in an area; others which are only available through hiring labour additional to that of the family. A good example is a tractor which is only economic if there is a certain minimum number of acres. Or dairy cattle offer another: where they are being introduced in many highland areas they require spare land for grass leys and fodder crops—as well as cash outlays. Surveys carried out in Lushoto District of 151 peasant farms,[17] showed that 52% of that sample had 5 acres of land or less. In this case, depending on the size of the family and its minimum subsistence needs, anything up to half of the population would not have sufficient land to be able to benefit from this dairying development as long as it was introduced on an individual basis. More generally, then, one of the incentives for co-operative production is that opportunities might be thereby made available to a wider group of people. Of course, one could even go further, and, as a tactic, introduce all innovations in a co-operative form, and thus sweeten the pill.

Such benefits can, in theory, be derived from *ujamaa* farming. For this to actually happen, careful planning and good organisation is necessary. Specifically, a thorough study is demanded into the kind of crops and other productive activities that exist in a particular farming system, and into the new ones which could be usefully introduced given existing market and labour potential, and finally to determine at what precise point economies of scale are to be obtained in these activities. Ideally, therefore, it should be possible to identify for a given area what activities should have priority as a focus for co-operative production, and what size of group or area of land would be most appropriate. These findings could then be matched with what is known about the inherited patterns of labour and other features of the social structure to define the most likely social unit for co-operation. Land tenure and differentiation patterns as well as local leadership characteristics also have to be brought into the equation as they may well present obstacles to the actual implementation of *ujamaa* activities. What this kind of local planning for *ujamaa* might entail can perhaps be illustrated by a case-study based on research that has been carried out in Lushoto District.[18]

Prospects for Ujamaa Transformation: A Case study

Lushoto District consists of a *massif* formed by the western Usambara mountains and an area of surrounding plains stretching to the Kenya border. It is situated some 100 miles inland from the northern port of Tanga, from where there are road and rail connections to the foot of the mountains. The Usambaras form a plateau, which is deeply dissected, with very steep slopes surrounding small valley bottoms and one or two larger basirs. Rainfall and soil types are extremely varied. The cultivation of maize and bananas in what was, for the most part, a fertile area, led to much of these uplands heavily settled by the 19th century. By that time a strong centralised kingdom had been established over the Usambaras and much of the area around under the rule of the Kilindi dynasty.[19]

The kingdom had already started to break up under the impact of the coastal trade before the arrival of the Germans, but Kilindi overrule through the paramount chief and local chiefs, was rather precariously preserved as a colonial instrument until the early 1950's. Much of the agricultural development in this area during the colonial period was in the form of European settlers on coffee and, later tea estates and smaller mixed farms, but the same crops were also introduced on peasant shambas to a limited extent. This precipitated a problem of land shortage, already noted as early as 1906. Chiefs were used in the early days to recruit (often forcibly) farm labour, and later to enforce terracing and other highly unpopular anti-erosion measures, propounded as a check to the ever-decreasing soil fertility. It was their identification with these measures which as much as anything led to the successful opposition to Kilindi dominance.[20] Some members of the traditional ruling group retain a degree of influence; they occupy key positions in the local Lutheran Church and the co-operative, and have been known to win elections as district councillor etc. But beyond that they may be feared and respected by the local population often because of their traditional rain-making powers.

The Shambala people, untypically for Tanzania, resided together in village clusters of upwards of 20–30 families. The villages were social units usually consisting of a single, or two or three related, lineages. Some were "royal" villages. The lineage, particularly the dominant lineage in a village, held claim to the land and seems to have exercised allocative rights. The Kilindi chiefs had access to land, and to the labour of slaves as well as the surplus of their subjects in the past, but seemingly enjoyed the produce of the land by virtue of their political position rather than retaining land rights as a landlorded caste. Land was cultivated by individual families, and the growing population pressure thus enforced permanence of cultivation, and the effect of production for the market has lead to a situation characterised by virtual individual ownership, a market in land (with some residual extended family control over sales) and great fragmentation.

The patterns of land tenure and social and economic differentiation which have emerged from this past, affect the possibilities for a move towards *ujamaa* in several ways. The density of settlement precludes much possibility of starting

54

new settlements, except for a few on the plains below—but these are hot, unhealthy and unpopular—and the existence of clustered village obviates much of the necessity. However, there are some areas of settler farms, forest and mission land —and even some neglected shambas belonging to Shambala with large holdings—which might yield elbowroom. But the highly fragmented nature of the holdings,[21] and the tenacity with which they are held, provide a logic for, but present obstacles to, rational, larger-scale co-operative land use. In addition, the differentiation in land-holding poses problems for the encouragment of labour exchange. There is a small proportion of large land-owners, in addition to the estates —one we interviewed had some 80 different plots—who would probably have to be left out of the initial efforts to develop co-operative activities, except in so far as they occupy un-used land. A further problem found within every village is the wide range of distribution of land-holding. Farmers' estimates of their own acreages are not always reliable, but a quarter of our farmers said they had less than 2 acres; a third 6 acres or more; another survey in central parts of the District found that one third of the farmers owned two-thirds of the land.[22] Such variance while not enormous could well lead to a lack of mutuality in exchange, or to it benefitting the larger land holders, unless land "ownership" was not the sole basis for distribution of product. (If not, those with little land could in fact be contributing labour to the larger owners for no return.) These problems are compounded by the character of local leadership; traditional elements and newer political actors who have grown up to challenge them have little legitimacy, and are often (as was traditionally the case) caught up with using their status to allocate land and other resources in their own interest.

On the more favourable side of the balance sheet, some forms of co-operative activity still persist, although the extent seems to vary very greatly. Of course, traditional authorities were able to command labour for various purposes, and today in many areas a whole village is frequently called out to help with road building, and various "public works", the necessity and general benefit of which are generally understood, we found. In addition, there was a tradition of co-operation in the carrying out of certain agricultural tasks. Usually, relatives and other villagers would be provided food in exchange for help with weeding and clearing; the harvesting of maize in its many stages seems to have been traditionally a joint endeavour, large groups bringing in the *risha* (strings of cobs) of maize for each family in turn. Beyond this, it was the case, and still is on occasions that a handful of age mates (usually younger farmers) would come together on a more permanent team basis and regularly carry out tasks together on each shamba in turn. This practice seems to have been associated with the important ritual of blood-brother-hood (*mbuya or amini*). The persistence of these customs and their variability can be gauged from a comparison of responses of farmers from 6 of the eight villages in our sample. In two of our less developed villages som 80% of our respondents regularly participated in some co-operative work, all of it agricultural; in another couple of "middle" villages, one in a newly-opened forest area, which have limited cash crop production, the proportion is almost half; while in two villages, in Mlalo and in Soni Divisions—both so heavily populated and given over to cash cropping that they are almost peri-urban, only one person out of a combined sample of 40 had recently done any communal work; indeed in Mlalo we were told "such activities are no longer practiced since 1963!"

We can thus see that there is a tradition of village solidarity and a legacy of agricultural co-operation in some parts of the district, yet the presence of interests likely to be resistant to a more co-operative and egalitarian system, and the people's attachment to their scarce, fragmented plots imply the need for marked incentives and careful political preparation to support a possible transformation. It remains therefore to see how a strategy towards *ujamaa* can in fact be posed which will in fact appeal because it is phrased in terms that will help to solve the particular problems facing the area. In fact, the district as a whole faces a near crisis situation compounded of a number of problems. As we have seen there is growing population pressure, deteriorating fertility, little improvement in traditional methods, and limited production for the market which, in one view, may well "result in one of the most impoverished smallholder economies to be found in East Africa".[23]

The answer to the population pressure can only in small part be solved by movement of population; the surrounding plains are scarcely likely to be made inhabitable enough to meet a large increment. The peasants are conscious of a competition for land within the mountains and are in many villages pressing for the allocation to them of either forest or estates. The possibilities of making additional land available are virtually limited to the extent encroachment on forest reserves and settler farms as thought ecologically, and politically desirable. Where such land is released it would usually be more profitable to continue to exploit it as a single unit on a large scale—which implies the need to make it available to a village co-operative, rather than has been the case up to now, of dividing it into individual plots, a process which has tended anyway to result in political notables and larger farmers getting much of the extra land. In addition, village-owned forest areas, perhaps linked with some small-scale co-operative timber saw-milling, would produce an acceptable incentive for the necessary retention of forest cover.

Two further problems of land use—erosion and fragmentation—could well be tackled on a co-operative basis, and indeed may necessitate such an approach. The reclamation of badly eroded slopes and the planting of grasses and trees as a protective measure are only likely if the owner of the affected land can be compensated or can work other plots—such exchanges of land and labour would be much more easy within a village co-operative. Equally there is some anti-erosion, reclamation and irrigation work that necessitate a joint approach—a whole valley or slope may have to be tackled simultanously to reap the benefits, and the work would anyway be beyond the scope of one man. The fragmented nature of plots makes not only the possibility of this kind of local public works remote but makes even rational cultivation of many crops difficult. A process of pooling land and labour could probably be the only way to achieve larger scale production while still giving gainful employment to a large population—or, at least, the only way which would avoid the concentration of land in a few hands and the emergence of a labouring class, and of landless unemployed.

In fact, the economies of production of several of the crops which are given priority in the district—notably tea, vegetables and dairy products—each in different ways show advantages of larger-scale co-operative activity. Experience in introducing tea on a smallholder basis has shown that "blocks" of tea would be more economical of supervision and of the daily transportation to the factory than scattered tiny plots. The dissected topography and the problems of organising the labour-intensive nature of the work indicate that such tea co-operatives should be relatively small in size—equivalent perhaps to a small team within the village. A co-operative of such co-operative teams might then be responsible for running the factories.

Vegetables which represent enormous potential, could be further propagated with co-operative irrigation in order to make use of hill-sides instead of merely the valley bottoms as at present. Their expansion also depends on improving the very inefficient still private and ad hoc, marketing arrangements. The advantages from phasing production and deliveries, from organising guaranteed markets suggest the need for collective action, but the necessity for quick handling of perishables suggests in turn the need to match co-operative production with co-operative marketing at the local level, as opposed to building up something equivalent to the large co-operative primary societies which now exist for the marketing on non-perishables. The advantage of joint, dairying ventures stems more from the possibility of thus allowing more than the better-off section of the community to benefit. The economies of scale, especially in an area like Lushoto, are not likely to be marked, except that research has indicated that two or three improved cattle on common pasture proves more economic than just one.[24] But a handful of neighbours, or even a TANU cell might be able to pool resources—one man planting pasture, while others guarantee him a share from their food plots, and yet others planting fodder crops or collecting grasses for stall feeding from the area around. Again, a larger co-operative for marketing and provision of credit, insemination and other services would be useful, and is in fact being planned by government.

These considerations of the actual modes of production of some of the crops which might be further developed in the area has not only indicated the possible advantages of co-operation but told us something of the particular scale and form of co-operation that might be appropriate. If we try and tie these tentative conclusions in with the sociological variables, we begin to arrive at some idea of what might be possible as well as appropriate.

In general, a strategy of socialist development in Lushoto might have the following elements: first, it would centre on the existing villages rather than the existing marketing societies or other larger units; the village as a unit would be the basis for organising co-operative labour activities on irrigation, anti-erosion, provision of forest, orchard or grass cover and other public works and social services, and might have areas of forest or estate attached to it; the production of other crops, especially the more profitable cash crops, could be made more rational and benefit every one if small teams, perhaps based on such traditional vestiges as the maize harvesting or other labour exchange groups, or the young men's blood brother groups, or the TANU ten-house cell were formed in order to promote pooling of land to overcome fragmentation, and pooling of labour to overcome labour bottlenecks, and thus achieve some specialisation, a division of labour and larger-scale production. The specifics of the programme would have to be worked out in relation to the existing situation and potential within any particular village.[25]

Such a plan, however, neglects the all-important question of implementation.[26] The need to explain potential benefits, the vacuum in the local leadership position, and suspicion of government-sponsored plans for agricultural improvement in the colonial period, all contribute to the difficulty. Beyond this, stratification has developed sufficiently in some areas to throw up rich peasants, often politically influential, likely to resist these kinds of moves.

We saw in the first part of this paper that the policy of rural socialism in Tanzania uses the myth of traditional co-operation as the basis of its appeal. In addition, although the differentiating, individualistic effects of the colonial economic impact are recognised, there is some feeling that traditional forms can also provide an operational basis for *ujamaa* transformation. Part of the general argument of this paper has been a concern that a voluntary, "frontal" approach to *ujamaa* must have in addition a clear rationale, offering some visible betterment to the life of the peasants. The Lushoto case study has tried to show how an outline for possible *ujamaa* producer co-operatives might be worked out on the basis of economies of production in a given physical and social environment, and that any remnants of pre-existing patterns of mutual labour exchange (particularly if they were on a non-kinship footing) might be one useful element in such a plan.

However, the problem of implementation, posed in the Lushoto case by the existence of more economically privileged and politically influential elements, deriving their status from both traditional and/or modern, capitalist roots, remains severe. The general question of the responsiveness of elite-controlled local institutions to socialist goals raises a basic issue of ideology and praxis in Tanzania's attempts to create rural *ujamaa*. One wonders how far a call to build socialism limited to an appeal to "tradition", or even to the economic benefits of larger-scale co-operative production (which have been one of the concerns of the paper) might not have to be tempered with attempts to develop a consciousness of the emerging class differences, and the resulting exploitation, amongst the peasantry. The most effective mix of tactics between emphasising the unity and consensus of traditional, egalitarian *ujamaa* as opposed to the promotion of awareness of conflict and differentiation through a class-oriented approach—is a difficult one to find. But in trying to establish the point of balance, the people and leaders of Tanzania can only benefit from more local empirical studies, not of "traditional" but of *existing* rural societies and the trajectory of development they are following.

Göran Hydén

Co-operatives and their
Socio-Political Environment

On paper, the three East African Governments are all committed to the use of co-operative institutions for the purpose of rural development. Kenya's *Sessional Paper* No. 10 of 1965 puts emphasis on the need for "mutual social responsibility" in the process of development. It is also implied that co-operatives are particularly well suited for participation in rural development, because they have "direct roots in African tradition".[1] A Tanzanian Government Paper states: "There is no other type of organization which is so suited (as co-operatives) to the problems and concept of rural development."[2] The recent *Common Man's Charter* in Uganda makes its contribution. It further states that Uganda must embark upon a "massive education" to re-orient "the attitudes of the people towards co-operation in the management of economic institutions, and away from individual and private inrichment".[3]

While the first post-independence development plans in Tanzania and Uganda are remarkably reticent about what the two Governments expect the co-operatives to achieve, the 1966–70 Kenya Development Plan contains a specific programme of co-operative development, boosted by the phrase that "there is only one course of action open to the nation, and that is to strengthen the co-operatives to play their role adequately".[4] In contrast, the Second Kenya Plan (1970–74) is more cautious than the First Plan in assessing the role of co-operatives, while the Second Tanzanian Plan (1969–74) puts renewed emphasis on co-operatives, by linking them to the system of *ujamaa* villages. As part of Uganda's "Move to the Left" co-operatives have been given complete or almost complete control over the processing of coffee and cotton.[5] In another policy statement co-operatives in Uganda have been promised greater participation also in other economic activities than agricultural marketing and processing.[6]

Thus in 1970 the policy aspirations of the three Governments remain high, though they have chosen different routes of co-operative development. In Kenya, the effort is to consolidate already existing marketing co-operatives and turn them into multi-purpose institutions, offering a wider range of services to the members. In Tanzania the main emphasis lies on building up co-operative institutions around the new collective producer villages. In Uganda expansion of the role of co-operatives is envisaged in non-agricultural activities.

In this paper the discussion will be focussed on marketing co-operatives, the economically most significant in all three countries. This does not mean, however, that the points raised here are irrelevant for the understanding of other types of co-operatives. At least to a certain degree, all co-operatives in Africa face similar problems, because of the general state of underdevelopment of the continent.

The Analysis of Co-operatives

The question thus arises, to what extent do the problems of co-operatives in East Africa fall within the realm of the theories of underdevelopment or within that or organizational theories? How much can be explained with reference to the general character of the social environment and how much with reference to the administrative and managerial arrangements of co-operatives? How effective can co-operatives be in terms of transforming their socio-economic environment? Which institutional changes will increase the effectiveness of co-operatives as agents of change in the rural areas? In discussing these questions, this chapter will be focussed more specifically on the interaction between rural marketing co-operatives and their environment. The character of the environment is used to explain management problems in the co-operatives.

The view taken here is that co-operatives are organizations which compete with other organizations to secure sufficient resources in order to achieve their objectives. Crucial to any analysis of co-operatives, therefore, is the *amount of support,* financial, material and human, that they can obtain. An organization, however, cannot function adequately without a *consciousness of its objectives* and a *will to realize them* on the part of its members. Organizations are also dependent upon their *ability to store information,* so as to avoid policy inconsistencies. Yet another aspect of organizational performance that is important relates to the *ability* of an institution *to recombine its parts* in order to more successfully achieve its objectives under changing conditions.

I shall here be concerned with two particular aspects of the environment: the general socio-economic character of East African societies; and the government attempts to overcome socio-economic obstacles to co-operative development.

Co-operatives and their
Socio-economic Environment

The character of the environment becomes particularly important in the case of co-operatives, as their democratic management structure legitimizes a high degree of openness to the environment. Elected members of the management committee are expected to bring to bear on the operation of their societies or unions outside opinions and demands. Unless all committee members share the same objectives, the process of managing co-operatives becomes very difficult. In order to more easily understand this point, it may be justified to draw a comparison with the situation in Europe at the time co-operative institutions were in formation there.

The growth of co-operative institutions in northern Europe, among consumers as well as producers, was based on the ideological commitment of their members to the notion that they had something to gain from co-operating. A number of factors at that time contributed to the emergence of this consciousness. First of all, the increasing dependence on middlemen, who were not members of the rural community. The scale of economic activities had increased to such an extent that the rural community could no longer serve as a self-sufficient unit. The co-operatives were a reaction against this; an attempt to defend the economic interests of the ordinary peasant against increasingly more powerful outside interests. There was not only a social but also an economic reason for co-operation.

This new spontaneous form of co-operation was further made possible by the absence of strong social ties based on kinship. The nuclear family system had already been sufficiently established to make the peasants realize that their strongest allies were not their relatives but the other peasants who shared the same economic fate. Another factor of importance was the general decline in society at that time of the belief that human beings were unable to control their environment. The free religious movements in Scandinavia of the late 19th century, which drew their membership from the same category of people as the co-operatives, emphasized that through a new moral consciousness men could achieve what they wanted. This input of religious self-confidence was not unimportant in the growth of co-operatives in Scandinavia. In short, what I am saying here is that the de-structuration of the old rural communities under the influence of new economic (capitalist) forces had increased to such an extent that it caused a genuine counterreaction among the free peasants.[7]

In some parts of East Africa, co-operatives have been formed spontaneously in reaction to the "Asian middlemen". We should be aware, however, that the forces in operation in East Africa have not been the same as in Europe. Those who took the initiative in challenging the Asian merchants were not the ordinary peasants, but the African "entrepreneurs" in the countryside, who found the Asians standing in their way. These entrepreneurs, by appealing to the peasants and telling them that they were "their men", as opposed to the Asians, who were "outsiders", managed to use the co-operatives to strengthen not only their own economic position but also their political control over the countryside. Racial stratification thus helped the formation of co-operatives in East Africa. The story of the growth of the co-operative movement in the Bukoba and Mwanza areas of Tanzania illustrates this.[8]

Though the story in Kenya is slightly different, the same

element is important. When the Office of the Registrar of Co-operatives was first established in Kenya in 1945, its duty was to promote both co-operatives and trade among Africans. On the one hand, the Registrar was expected to assist the middlemen, on the other, he was expected to create institutions opposing them. He was deliberately placed in this impossible position by the colonial Government, which did not like the idea of co-operatives among Africans. The Registrar in his first annual report also complains that the Africans he met were only interested in knowing how to establish their private business and to outdo the Asians.[9] Thus, in so far as the commercially more active members of the rural areas entered into the co-operatives, they used these institutions to undermine the monopoly of the Asians.

As co-operatives have more recently come to face more competition from private African traders, however, this ideological impetus has declined in importance. Other criteria, notably economic performance, have become more important in determining the attitudes of peasants towards their co-operative institutions. Today, co-operative societies and unions in East Africa are still under the influence of people with a wider view and experience of the world outside the local rural community. To this category belong teachers, priests, traders, administrators and politicians. They often get into leading positions, because the ordinary peasants believe them to be more able to defend the interests of the local community than they are themselves. The peasants give them full support in return for the favours or rewards that they can secure from the "outside world". Co-operatives in East Africa are thus very often ruled on the basis of already existing informal "patron-client" relationships.

The importance of this "vertical" relationship is reinforced by the fact that social ties based on kinship and other local institutions are still more important than the mutual loyalty between peasants in different village communities. The "horizontal" ties of economic interest have not yet replaced the "vertical" ties of social obligation based on such units as the clan, village, etc. While the former were most important in the formation of co-operatives in East Africa.

Contrary, therefore, to what is sometimes maintained, that co-operatives are particularly suitable to Africa because of the traditionally communal orientation of its rural inhabitants, special difficulties arise out of the problem of combining traditional and modern forms of co-operation. The former were by and large based on social obligations rather than economic interest; though equality existed between kinship units, within these units, relations were inegalitarian;[10] traditional forms of communalism were based on production (often in an emergency situation); in so far as it was a separate function, marketing was usually a family matter.

What has been said above about the socio-economic conditions in East Africa has definite implications for the management of co-operative institutions. The committee members in a co-operative society or union are usually elected on the basis of local constituencies—a village, location or division, etc. Unlike the situation in Europe, where elected committee members shared an interest in fighting a common enemy, the contradictions in East Africa are still regarded as those between different local communities: village against village, division against division, etc. A committee member is there to fight for his own interest or that of his constituents.

This renders the process or managing co-operatives extremely difficult. Each committee member is pulling in his own direction or seeking coalitions based on non-economic principles. There is no real consciousness of the common objectives, certainly no strong will to realize these objectives. Favouritism and corruption are often the result of planting democratically managed co-operatives in this kind of environment. Committee members who deliberately use their position for other purposes than that of promoting the economic welfare of all members can easily be re-elected as long as they are socially acceptable to a majority of the electorate.

It must be noted, however, that the situation in East Africa varies from area to area. At least two different patterns can be distinguished. There are first, the economically more advanced areas of East Africa (the Central Province and parts of the Eastern Province in Kenya; the Kilimanjaro, Bukoba and Mwanza Districts in Tanzania; Buganda in Uganda).

Here, because investment in land and agricultural development is profitable, people who are primarily businessmen also
qualify as farmers and thereby as members of co-operatives.
The tendency in these areas is towards the concentration of
the ownership of profitable land in the hands of those who
are also the economically most active members of the rural
communities; those who already, by virtue of their resources,
can grasp new opportunities to get richer. The extent to which
this has taken place in the areas mentioned above may vary.
By and large, however, the trend is the same in all of them.

For the co-operatives this means that businessmen are often
found in positions of leadership inside the co-operatives. They
contribute to the management of these institutions their business experience. The general efficiency or productivity of co-
operatives in these areas, both because of the economic base
and the business experience of many of their leaders, is generally higher than in other areas. At the same time, however,
there is often a price to be paid for this. The businessman
cum co-operative leader is usually able to divert some of the
money of the co-operative institution for purposes connected
with his own private activities. It may be for further improving
agricultural production on his land or it may be for building
up political support in the area. The latter is not uncommon.
It must be remembered that very few, if any, businessmen
become co-operative leaders because it is commercially profitable. They belong to co-operatives because these institutions
in the rural areas offer a convenient platform for political
campaigning and the maintenance of social control over the
population in the area. While the businessman acts in order
to build up his economic position while in his business, he
acts in order to boost his social and political position while
in the co-operatives. This is one of the important aspects of
current socio-political change. Co-operatives assist in institu-
tionalizing the power of the already economically privileged.

In the economically less developed parts of rural East Africa
the incentive on the part of those, who have originated from
these areas and who have made themselves positions elsewhere
in the country to re-invest in land and agriculture is much
weaker. Co-operatives in these areas are never or rarely in-

fluenced by this category. Though the elite fulfils their obligations to relatives, they never develop any serious interest in the co-operatives. The problem co-operatives face here is a different one—the general lack of management and business experience on the part of the committee members. Besides ordinary peasants, teachers, local-government, officers or politicians usually constitute the membership of the committees. As in the first category, management is by and large a political process, characterized by rivalry between relatively self-contained social units, represented on the co-operative management committee. The weak economic base of co-operative institutions and the general lack of economic entrepreneurship of their leaders limit the effect of co-operatives on the process of social change in these areas.

Both categories of co-operatives described above have one thing in common—they often become more of a liability than an asset to the ordinary peasant. In the case of the first type, the co-operative becomes an instrument to perpetuate and deepen the exploitation of the peasant. In the second case, co-operatives become highly unimaginative and lacking in initiative to change the environment. Overhead costs grow and the individual peasant member of the co-operative has to pay for the maintenance of these unprofitable institutions.

I am aware that it is easy to lose the time perspective in this kind of analysis. What has been described above may only be phases in the development of co-operative institutions that will soon be replaced by a more constructive sequence. In the economically more advanced areas, where a certain degree of exploitation already takes place, the peasants may soon realize their economic position and unite against the already privileged members of the community. The growing contradiction of social forces in these parts of East Africa may strengthen the basis for a co-operative *movement* against exploitation. At least in parts of Kenya (Machakos and Meru), there have been cases of ordinary peasants voting teachers and traders out of office in co-operative societies. This takes place in the absence of any socialist leadership at the national level.

It is true that the great mass of the people in the East African countries is still, in Marx's own frank words, formed by "simply addition of homologous magnitudes, much as potatoes in a sack form a sack of potatoes".[11] The peasants live in similar conditions but do not enter into a mutual productive intercourse. Production on a small piece of land does not admit of any division of labour, any application of scientific methods, any variety of talent and social relationships. Each individual peasant remains almost self-sufficient. Being unaware of their common social interest, they do not form a class. In this respect the situation in East Africa differs from that in, e.g., China. There peasants had long lived under severe social oppression. Their common fate was further strengthened by such factors as the common field of production created by the vast irrigation systems. The war against the Japanese and the civil war that led to the victory of the Communists finally incorporated the Chinese peasants into the mainstream of development in that country.

All these factors are absent in East Africa and the traditions there are different. Nevertheless, a new social consciousness among peasants may develop much faster in East Africa than it ever did among peasants in other parts of the world. The examples from Kenya, quoted above, indicate this. The reasons for believing that this new phase of development in the rural areas of East Africa may come soon are as follows: the absence of an established feudal system, as in Latin America, that holds back the resolution of contradictions; the urban-rural continuum—the interaction between village and town in Africa being much more intensive than in other parts of the world during the initial, dramatic phase of urbanization; the more extensive exposure to mass media and the more rapid development of a consciousness about the outside world.

It may be argued, therefore, that governments should not interfere in the process of socio-political change in the rural areas until "antagonistic contradictions" have developed in the communities. Government interference will not resolve contradictions as long as they are based not on economic factors but rather on social ones (e.g., clan, village or tribal origin). Under these circumstances it will also be difficult to create among the peasants by means of political education a subjective consciousness of the importance of economic inequalities and their elimination. Intervention by government in this situation may well be the same as abortion—killing the offspring before it has had a chance to show what it is capable of. Government intervention certainly is not, as I shall argue further below, an automatic solution of the problems of co-operative development.

There are at least two immediate dangers in having bureaucratic government or party institutions directing co-operative development from above. The first is that overhead costs will increase and the charge for development on the peasants will become even heavier. Control over co-operative institutions by governments instead of by individual businessmen will not help the peasants. Under present conditions they would probably prefer a situation where the latter were in control, if for no other reason than that the businessmen can much more easily deal with the peasants on a personal basis than a bureaucratic government institution ever can.

The other danger lies in the ambiguous role government must play. It must, on the one hand, act on behalf of the peasants, as their representative and, on the other, as their master. In the general stage of underdevelopment the role of master easily becomes the more important. Certainly, the East African experience does not contradict this statement. Marx's lamentation about the general incapacity of traditional rural communities in dissolution to play a significant role in the great evolution towards socialism is still to a large degree valid. "The isolation of the village communities, the lack of links between their lives, this locally bounded microcosm ... permits the emergence of central despotism above the communities."[12]

The danger of despotic rule over peasants seems particularly imminent in the economically little advanced parts of East Africa, where co-operative institutions are weak. In the absence of other strong institutions, the government or party official can easily become a local despot, very much in the same way as the traditional chief before independence.

To sum up under the prevailing socio-economic conditions, co-operative institutions in East Africa easily turn into "battlefields" for local political interests. The character of the rural communities does not lend itself to the principle of modern co-operative management, as developed in Europe. Nor have co-operatives in East Africa made a significant contribution to the emergence of a more egalitarian society. John Saul has summarized the problems of co-operatives in the following phrase: "Socialism is necessary for co-operatives and not vice versa."[13] Co-operatives cannot become effective agents of socio-political change in the direction of more egalitarianism unless the "right" conditions exist. The question is, to what extent can these conditions be created by political, administrative and educational measures?

The Government and the Co-operatives

The belief in government circles in East Africa has been that the "consciousness" and the "will" of co-operative organizations can be strengthened by applying a mixture of regulatory and educational measures. The environmental obstacles can be overcome through legislative control and extensive education. Here I shall be concerned with some aspects of the experience gained in these efforts. In order to fully understand how government actions affect co-operatives in different parts of East Africa, it is necessary to distinguish between three ways in which co-operatives were started: in opposition to Asian dominance in business, for local political reasons, e.g., a person wanting to show others that he is doing something useful for his community, and through central government initiative.

The first category belongs primarily to the period before independence, the second to the period just around independence, and the third to the time after independence. Though there are exceptions,[14] the most successful in terms of survival and business expansion have been co-operatives belonging to the first category. Several factors have contributed to this: (a) they were started for economic and not political reasons, (b) they were able to lay a solid economic foundation for their activities, thanks to the favourable prices on the world market in the 1950s, and (c) many were able to benefit from proper economic advice from Europeans who had no political interest in these organizations as political platforms.

The vast majority of co-operatives belonging to the second category, at least in Kenya, have failed or are now dormant, because the economic feasibility of these societies was never seriously considered. Much the same applies to the third category, though a slightly higher proportion of those started by governments have remained in existence. In some cases, this is due to adequate preparation. In others, however, co-operatives have been allowed to operate despite financial losses, because governments have been reluctant to acknowledge their failures or for other reasons have allowed them to continue to function.

Though there are important differences between co-operative societies and unions within each of the three countries, government control measures have usually been applied universally.[15] This means that no distinction has been made between the, economically speaking, relatively successful unions and their opposites or between those which had previously developed an autonomous status vis-à-vis the government and those which were partly or totally dependent on government support for their survival. The explicit reason for increasing central control over co-operatives has been financial mismanagement and the feeling that the government can save the poor peasants from exploitation by economically more active members of the rural communities. Implicit in the measures, however, has also been the desire to reduce the autonomous power of some of the larger co-operative unions.

The control measures applied have been most extensive in Tanzania, the most drastic action being the government "takeover" of 16 co-operative unions in the country in 1968 on the grounds of mismanagement and embezzlement. All the elected management committees were replaced by government-appointed caretaker committees. Also in Kenya the powers given to the Commissioner for Co-operative Development (the principal government employee concerned directly with co-operatives) are significant. The 1966 Co-operative Societies Act gives him the right to insist that all cheques written by a society be countersigned by a Co-operative Officer. He can also insist that small mono-crop or single-purpose societies be amalgamated into sufficiently large viable multi-purpose units. He has the right to dissolve society committees that are not performing their duties satisfactorily (though this particular right has not been applied as frequently as in Tanzania). Co-operative societies also have to submit monthly trial balances for approval by the Department for Co-operative Development.

Though there has been a decline in cases of deliberate mismanagement and embezzlement, this has been obtained at what seems a high cost. The new regulatory measures have considerably reduced the organizational autonomy of the co-operatives and made them "handmaidens" of the governments. The character of co-operatives as voluntary associations, belonging to their members, has been lost.

This has become particularly serious in the case of those co-operatives that were founded long before independence and had developed a sense of autonomy, financially and otherwise. The tendencies toward centralized control have not been received favourably by co-operative institutions like the Kilimanjaro Co-operative Unions, the Bukoba Co-operative Union and the Victoria Federation of Co-operative Unions—now the Nyanza Federation of Co-operative Unions—in Tanzania or by the Meru and Nyeri District Co-operative Unions in Kenya. Though these control measures have had the effect of eliminating the most serious financial irregularities, they have in other respects had negative implications. At least in Kenya, staff in co-operative unions report that administrative overhead costs have increased as a result of the new control measures from above. Much more time is now spent on filling in forms or writing reports to satisfy the Co-operative Department. Much of the incentive to act as co-operative leaders has disappeared. The co-operative societies and unions are no longer theirs. External goal-setting has further reduced the capacity of these organizations to compete successfully with other institutions in the rural areas. They are unable to capture the attention and interest of the peasants.

It is no coincidence that self-help groups in Kenya are much more successful in mobilizing support for their activities than co-operatives are. Particularly remarkable in this connection are the *mabati* groups. These consist exclusively of women, who jointly collect money to employ a local artisan to build a roof on somebody's house. (In the old days, women used to do this themselves, but nowadays the process is so complicated that a *fundi* must be employed.)

Co-operatives started by politicians at the time of independence or by the government thereafter are often kept alive artificially by the Co-operative Department. This may be done by various means, bank overdrafts being the most common in Kenya. The notion is that they can overcome their crisis and eventually become economically viable. The prospects are very often bad and the experience gained so far in Kenya not particularly encouraging. The ordinary member has to pay a much higher price than if he sold to a private trader. Thus, it is not surprising that, where the opportunity exists, peasants prefer to sell to the trader rather than to their society or smuggle their produce across the border to a neighbouring country where the price is more attractive. The social and political costs of maintaining economically unviable units are also high. Opportunities for committee members and staff to learn management techniques are limited, as most important matters are decided by representatives of the Co-operative Department. The learning capacity of the co-operative societies under these conditions is limited; they act on "transfusion" from another institution. They never get opportunities to develop structural arrangements on their own. They become cripples with little ability to adjust to changing demands and supports.

Another aspect of the paternalistic or tutelary relationship to the Government under which co-operatives are expected to flourish in East Africa is the danger of administrative overload in the latter. Policies devised by the Co-operative Department are often such that they do not consider the administrative and managerial capacity of co-operative unions and societies. Very often these policies cannot be implemented, because there is not the qualified staff to execute them. This has been a serious problem in Kenya and may well be one reason why the Government strategy now is to consolidate and

74

improve the quality of already existing co-operatives. Over-ambitious targets have already created serious disappointments and reactions against the government. Moreover, as usual, it is the peasant who has suffered.

The danger of giving the co-operatives more than they can swallow results either from a strong ideological commitment on the part of the government to the promotion of co-operatives or from an institutional struggle between individual ministeries or departments to boost their position *vis-à-vis* one another. In the first case, which applies to Tanzania, it is the general acceptability of co-operative values and the security of these organizations that cause administrative overload. In the second case, of which Kenya is an illustration, it is the marginal position of co-operative values and the insecurity of these organizations that create this problem.

The regulatory measures mentioned above have had a limited impact on the socio-political environment of co-operatives. The fundamental obstacles discussed earlier in this chapter still remain. Though the control measures have relieved the co-operative management from some difficulties, they have created new ones, the more important of which have been outlined above.

It would be wrong, however, to discuss government attempts to promote the growth of co-operatives without mentioning the supporting activities. Of these, co-operative education is the most important in all three countries. Educating staff in financial management and organizational techniques, as well as training committee members in committee procedures and other aspects of management have so far been the main educational activities. In all three countries a large number of co-operative leaders have been able to acquire new skills in running their organizations. At the same time, however, it must be noted that, with the exception of Tanzania, where extensive correspondence education is available to ordinary members, co-operative education has been confined to elected leaders and appointed staff only. Another limitation of co-operative education so far has been its exclusive emphasis on the transmission of knowledge, while little attention has been paid to strengthening the motivation to work for a co-operative purpose. There is also evidence that the newly acquired knowledge of several committee members and employees has not always been used for the common good of their organization.

Though there are visible results of government efforts to promote the growth of co-operatives, less embezzlement and greater familiarity with financial administration being the most significant, neither the regulatory nor the supporting activities of the Co-operative Departments in the three countries have eliminated the fundamental obstacles to a strong co-operative *movement*. Factionalism in the committees remains prominent. So does the tendency for already privileged people to become leaders of the co-operative societies and unions, thereby preventing the latter from developing into a front of poor peasants against wealthier groups, both inside and outside the rural communities. There is also evidence that the government control measures have the effect of reducing the commitment of members and leaders alike to their organization. Goal-setting by government institutions instead of by the co-operative leadership itself adversely affects the "consciousness" and the "will" of the co-operative institutions. The heavy load of duties imposed upon co-operatives by governments in East Africa also reduces the capacity to store and use information adequately and limits the ability to recombine their parts in changing conditions of operation. Routine activities take precedence over creative thinking. The co-operatives become bureaucratic and inflexible—organizational cripples.

The Future

The previous account has been relatively pessimistic. As agents of change, co-operatives have so far played a limited role. A number of co-operative societies and unions have no doubt been able to increase their productivity and grow economically stronger, but in most cases at the price of widening inequalities in the local communities which these institutions serve. The principle of "promotion of the economic welfare of the members" has rarely been strictly followed.

About half the co-operatives registered in East Africa are now defunct. Overhead costs are often much higher than is economically justified. Loan repayment has been fairly satisfactory. Participation in the affairs of the co-operative society by ordinary members has been generally limited to the collection of money. On all these criteria, therefore, the performance of co-operatives in East Africa can at best be called moderately successful.

It is easy to become too pessimistic in an account like this. Our time perspective is very narrow and the standards applied in judging these co-operatives are identical with those we would use, let us say, in Scandinavia. Moreover, I am quite aware that several people who have worked in the co-operatives in East Africa have experienced genuine progress in their institutions. While this must be acknowledged, there is, as indicated above, room for improvement. The question thus arises: What are the implications for the future of the experience, gained so far?

If socialism is necessary for co-operatives, it must be concluded that in East Africa the proper conditions for the growth of co-operatives do not exist. Nor have co-operatives yet been able to contribute to socialism in any significant sense. This at least is true of marketing co-operatives in all three countries.

Can the right conditions, then, be created through political, organizational and educational means? The answer is not an outright affirmative. For example, nationalization of the more important means of production in the country will, not automatically turn people into co-operators. The conditions in the East African countryside are such that the necessary change in attitude that must accompany structural changes in a socialist direction is extremely difficult to achieve. The *ujamaa* villages in Tanzania, the performance of which it may be too early to assess now, will doubtless throw some light on the question to what extent major structural changes in the rural areas also produce a corresponding change in attitude and motivation among the people affected by them.

In the meantime it should be pointed out that deliberate intervention in the growth of an organization usually incurs costs and may well have unintended negative consequences. Every organization has its own life cycle. A period of stagnation is often an integral part of the growth of an institution —a springboard towards a more constructive period. Like human beings, organizations learn from their mistakes. In view of this, a policy implying extensive intervention in the various activities of co-operatives may backfire.

It may even be argued that a quicker way to socialism than deliberate politico-bureaucratic intervention in peasant society and its institutions is to allow a further de-structuration of the rural communities. As indicated above, ordinary peasants develop a new consciousness about their role in society as a result of feeling exploited by the more wealthy members of their respective communities. This spontaneous process of change is, at least in Kenya, of great importance for the emergence of new conditions in the rural areas. If it is aborted too early through deliberate government intervention, socialist conditions may be more difficult to achieve in the countryside.

I am not arguing that the governments should completely refrain from influencing the process of social change. The alternative discussed here is not based on a belief in a complete laissez-faire approach. What I am arguing is simply that government intervention will resolve contradictions in favour of socialism only if these contradictions are based on the question, who owns the means of production? In most parts of rural East Africa contradictions or conflicts between groups are of a different nature. Government attempts to resolve them will not lead to more socialism, except under very specific conditions.

I am also convinced that the governments in East Africa could do a lot in order to reduce the importance of conflicts based on social factions inside the co-operatives. Ones such step would be to re-orient co-operative education more towards the ordinary members. Only if the latter are able to challenge the leadership of their co-operative society or union on the basis of economic performance will they be able to exercise their democratic control constructively. Improved education in financial matters among ordinary members would make it possible to shift from a particularistic type of conflict to a universalistic one. Instead of arguing in the general meetings about *who* has mismanaged the affairs of the society, the argument could be on the basis of more objective criteria of performance. If members could be made to understand the balance sheets and shown that in comparison with the neighbouring society theirs has done better or worse, new criteria for electing members to the management committee would most likely develop.[16]

It can also be argued that an important part of the Government's policy of creating better conditions for the development of co-operative institutions is to improve the productivity of these institutions. So far, co-operative societies and unions have fallen short of private companies or public corporations in terms of economic efficiency. Overhead costs in the former have been considerably higher. Transmission of knowledge to the co-operative leadership has not proved sufficient as a means of increasing efficiency. What may in the long run turn out to be more effective in making people more efficiency-conscious is to create a system of bonus payment, related to the output of the employee. The more he does, the higher the payment he receives. This principle, which was a basic tenet of the "scientific management school", requires the setting up of fair standards that can be used to assess the performance of each employee. This is no easy task, but it should not prove impossible.

In my view, measures of this kind are likely to have a more positive impact on the development of co-operative institutions in East Africa than the indiscriminate expansion of these organizations which was the main strategy during 1960s in all three countries. Improving the efficiency of co-operatives is also a precondition if policies aimed at a co-operative monopoly in marketing certain agricultural products are to benefit the peasants.

The purpose of this paper has been to discuss the limitations imposed on the development of co-operative institutions in East Africa. Particular emphasis has been placed on the problems of making co-operatives into something more than just marketing institutions. The politico-bureaucratic control measures applied in all three countries have not fundamentally changed the conditions under which marketing co-operatives operate. Moreover, these measures have to a certain extent reduced the capacity of these institutions to function satisfactorily. In many cases, the co-operatives have been turned into organizational cripples.

The next step must be to encourage a process of improvement in management from inside the co-operatives. This cannot be done only by the transmission of knowledge of the financial aspects of management. It is equally important to encourage a new motivation among leaders and rank-and-file members alike which will honour the principles of equality and fairness to all members. Finally, peasants must be encouraged to pay more attention to their co-operative societies and participate more actively in the society affairs. This can only be achieved if the co-operatives can prove that they are economically more productive than private companies or public corporations.

J. P. W. B. McAuslan

Co-operatives and the Law in East Africa

The three East African countries of Kenya, Tanzania and Uganda with which this paper deals have all stated at some time since independence the importance they attach to co-operatives and their role in the process of development. Any discussion of this role in practice must touch on the law relating to co-operatives for the law is one of the chief mechanisms both for translating policy about co-operatives into action, and for preventing such policies being put into action. By this I mean that the law is not a neutral spectator of the development process but is a set of rules and principles which are created and set to work by sets of individuals and these individuals may very well misunderstand or disagree with each other or approach the rules with different pre-conceptions about what is right and desirable in their operation so that the rules and their application in practice may be far removed from the pronouncements of policy which preceded them. There is a limit to the extent to which alterations of the law can remedy this state of affairs but at the very least a case can be made out for discussing the law on co-operatives, and attempting to pin-point some of its gaps, defects and problems and this is what this paper sets out to do.

The subject matter of this paper will be discussed in the following order: production co-operatives and land tenure; powers of and controls over service co-operatives; co-operative credit; conclusions. These topics do not add up to an exhaustive survey of co-operatives and the law but they do cover those matters which are important in any discussion of co-operatives and development and on which a lawyer might be expected to have something useful to say.

Production Co-operatives and Land Tenure

It is clearly impossible to survey the land tenure laws of East Africa, yet since production co-operatives are so intimately connected with the ownership and use of the land, some discussion of tenure and how it affects these co-operatives is necessary, the more so since an insistent argument for these co-operatives is that they are in keeping with traditional notions of land ownership and use. What then is the position? First, the general law must be discussed.

There is a fundamental division to be made here between the received or imposed English law, and the indigenous customary law, though as we will see, the former has influenced the development of the latter a great deal. English land law rests on two fundamental principles—the sanctity or rightness of individual ownership, and the existence of divided rights of ownership. The former principle needs little explanation; the latter does. A feudal heritage and the demands of a modern capitalist economy have combined to create and stamp upon English law the principle that it is not land but estates or interests or rights in the land which are the subject of ownership and these estates, being an abstract entity, a product of the mind, can be and are frequently divided up amongst several different people and on different planes of time in respect of the same piece of land. Thus a person who wishes to borrow money from a bank in order to improve his farm will have to provide some security for the loan. He will create a mortgage over his farm; the effect of this is that he, the mortgagor will have given some of the rights in the land to the bank, the mortgagee, for instance, the right to sell the land and pass a good title on to the purchaser, if the mortgagor does not repay the loan, and use the purchase price to repay the loan, or the right to appoint some-one to receive the income from the farm which will be used to repay the loan. But the mortgagor will retain some of the rights in the land; the right to live on the land and cultivate it, the right to leave it to his heir in his will, the right to sell it or lease it, subject to the mortgage, to a third person. If ownership is thought of as embracing the right to receive an income from land, the right to alienate the land (sell, lease, leave by will) and the right to use the land, it seems that in this example both the bank and the farmer "own the land"; English law however says that neither own the land, (though the farmer is in physical possession of the land and can obtain legal remedies to prevent others e.g. squatters from trying to obtain physical possession of the land) instead both own interests in the land which they can use in certain carefully defined circumstances. Again English law recognises and gives effect to the fact that a right to the future possession of land is economically valuable and commercially marketable; thus a person may be given a "future interest" in a piece of land (to A for life, *and then to B*) which he may deal with and protect, just as the law will facilitate dealings with physical things such as coffee and ginning machines.

The first principle has affected the second in two important ways; generally, the person in actual physical possession of the land or with the right to actual physical possession is vested with the rights of management over the land i.e. powers of cultivation, and alienation; (the right to receive an income from the land is a right which is frequently separated from other rights of ownership e.g. the absentee landlord) and secondly there has always been a marked reluctance to accept that the state has or should have any kind of overriding powers of control on the ownership and use of the land.

To generalise on customary land law in the same way as I have on English land law is foolish yet must be attempted if only in a negative way. There is still I think a widespread belief amongst many politicians and other policy-makers in East Africa that customary land tenure was communal co-operative land tenure. It is doubtful whether this was ever universally the case; certainly since anthropological investigation has taken place, such a view cannot any longer be entertained. There are varieties of communal tenure, some with a high individualistic content as Mugerwa[1] has shown, and much communal tenure was anything but an idyllic co-operative society as Potekhin[2] has pointed out. During the British colonial period individual land tenure either emerged through economic pressures—land hunger, the growing of cash crops

—or via direct legislative intervention e.g. the Buganda Agreement of 1900 and the consolidation and registration of holdings amongst the Kikuyu in the 1950's[3] so that today, at any rate for the cultivators of East Africa—as opposed to the pastoralists—and these are the vast majority, it would be a fair generalisation to say that their customary law now recognises some individual rights in the land which range from full ownership, that is the right to use, receive an income from, and alienate subject only to the state's control but not traditional tribal control, to use for life only—what in English law would be called a life interest in the land—with restrictions both on alienation and types of use permitted. Where customary communal control exists, it may be exercised by a clan or family head or a traditional political head though increasingly these functions have been taken over by modern local equivalents such as village development committees, local land boards or local authorities.

Many customary land laws, both because of the persistence of traditional notions and under the impact of modern economic developments permit dealings with the land which imply the existence of the notion of divided rights of ownership e.g. the landlord/tenant relationship where the tenant must pay rent and the landlord has certain rights of re-entry, and the conditional sale where the vendor and his heirs have the right to get "his" land back from the purchaser and his heirs in certain circumstances. However to say that dealings recognised by customary law imply divided rights of ownership is not to say that the average peasant farmer in East Africa thinks in terms of "owning an estate in the land"; I would be prepared to state categorically that he does not: rather, as has been observed of peasants generally, he thinks in terms of owning the land, the actual soil, grass, etc. and is in no way concerned with abstract notions however convenient lawyers and economists find them in discussing and creating rights in the land. I will return to this point and its importance later.

To turn now to the land laws of the East African states only Kenya has adopted a legal framework for the co-existence of the two systems of land law, the transfer of land and the

84

rights therein from one system to the other, including the transfer of communal rights with which we are particularly concerned here. Where land is governed by customary law, it is called Trust land, and is vested in the local county council by the Constitution. The council is required to:

hold the Trust land vested in it for the benefit of the persons ordinarily resident on that land and shall give effect to such rights, interests or other benefits in respect of the land as may under the African customary law for the time being in force and applicable thereto, be vested in any tribe, group, family, or individual.[4]

Thus the council owns the land as a trustee under a duty to give effect to the customary rights of the residents on the land, who are in the nature of beneficiaries under the trust, whether those rights are communal or individual. The county council, after consultation with the persons affected, may however request the government that the title to the land vested in it be registered, and this sets in motion the process of consolidation of land and adjudication of rights in the land carried through by committees of local people which ultimately results in a title to the land being registered under the Registered Land Act; from thenceforth the land and dealings with it are governed by a statutory system modelled on the English Law of Property Act, and Registered Land Act of 1925; the system therefore is founded on the English system of divided rights of ownership.

The Kenyan Registered Land Act came into effect, under another name, in 1959 and does permit groups of people up to a maximum of five jointly to own rights in a piece of land, either as joint proprietors or as proprietors in common. The distinction is important. Where land is owned jointly "no proprietor is entitled to any separate share in the land and consequently ... on the death of a joint proprietor his interest shall vest in the surviving proprietor or the surviving proprietors jointly";[5] this would provide the legal framework for a small collective farm. On the other hand, where land is owned in common, "each proprietor shall be entitled to an undivided share in the whole and on the death of a proprietor his share shall be administered as part of his estate"[6]

85

(estate here means all the property a person leaves at his or her death); this would provide the legal framework for a small co-operative farm. These provisions were not however put into the Act with production co-operatives in mind, but in order to provide for the situation where a father dies leaving sons who wish to work the land together because that is the custom. The limit of five was fixed in order to prevent excessive refragmentation of the land, as was the limit to the size of a plot of land which could come into being as a result of partition,—the demarcation and division on the ground of the individual shares—and provisions exist both in the Act and in the general (English) land law for the five registered proprietors to hold the land on behalf of themselves and others who cannot be registered as joint proprietors and/or for those who are deprived of land through the operation of the rules on partition to receive compensation from those who retain land, which may take effect as a right to receive an income from another's land.

These provisions have been set out in some detail to show their inadequacies in two respects. First, though they may be couched in fairly straightforward legal prose they involve complicated legal ideas and principles and so assume a high degree of sophistication amongst those who will be making use of them. This complexity of concepts and the stress laid on shares in the land, whether divided or undivided, is a characteristic of the English law on co-ownership and the complexity may be an unavoidable necessity in any law of co-ownership but it detracts from the usefulness of the law when it is to be applied to peasant farmers, for it conflicts with their fundamental belief in the importance of owning and physically possessing a piece of land. To a lawyer trained in English law, a right to an income from a piece of land, or a right to use land which is in the ownership of someone who has a duty to look after your interests as well as his own in the land, is as good as owning the land itself, but this is not so to the Kenyan peasant farmer and this is one reason why these provisions are something of a failure in practice; they are incompatible with the "gut reaction" of the peasant to his land.

Secondly, these provisions are inadequate in that they do not make provision for two types of production co-operative which do in fact exist in Kenya, the first being composed of those people who either for traditional social, or modern economic reasons wish to retain communal land tenure on a large scale after transferring to the statutory system, the second being composed of those people who have joined together in order to take over and continue operating as a single unit a large ex-settler owned farm. These two production co-operatives may be discussed separately.

The first type of co-operative was discussed in the report of the Lawrence Mission, principally in connection with the block cultivation of sugar in Central Nyanza,

the traditional land authorities—the *jokakwaro* elders—first agree to allocate an area of land in their *kakwaro* area, ideally not less than 125 acres in extent, exclusively for the cultivation of sugar. A co-operative society is then formed of residents in the *kakwaro* area, which enters into an agreement with a commercial company owning a nearby sugar factory under which the company clears and plants twenty-five acres or more of sugar in the block of land each year over a five year period. Cultivation and cutting of the cane is the responsibility of individual members of the co-operative society who (sic) must sell it to the factory.[8]

Registration of individual titles had begun to take place but there was some feelings, which the Mission shared, that this should not be allowed as it would destroy the sugar cultivation schemes. The Mission accordingly recommended that group registration should be allowed; the group would be the *jokakwaro* in whom the land would be vested, title to the land being in the names of representatives of the *jokakwaro* who would have power to deal with the land including leasing a block of land to the co-operative for sugar cultivation. Apart from small individual plots for subsistence purposes there would be no individual rights in the registered land, and such a system would be a collective farm; the block set aside for sugar cultivation would be owned by a group of people, the *jokakwaro,* who through their representatives would lease it to a co-operative society, the members of whom would be a sub-group within the *jokakwaro,* and would cultivate the block together.

Amongst the Masai too, there was the beginning of registration of individual titles to huge ranches which whatever their contribution to development was considered by the Mission, along with others who had looked at the problem, to pose grave problems of future land shortage in Masailand. Here too therefore, despite the difficulty of discovering what rights groups of Masai might have in any particular area of land, the Mission considered that group registration could be employed, and would have to be if credit were to be forthcoming for the development of such group ranches. It was suggested that existing sections and divisions of the Masai be used as a basis for group registration. Section councils would draw up a list of persons having rights to use the land within the jurisdiction of the section, that land would then be divided up into individual farms and group ranching areas, further lists drawn up of those to have rights within the group area, and "the proportion of interest in terms of livestock of each member of the group"[9] agreed. The group ranch would initially be registered in the name of the county council, but that body would transfer the land to the group when it had properly constituted itself with a managing committee and a defined set of rights and obligations of all members. Here again the nature of the resulting ranch would be a collective farm; no individual rights in the land would exist and all the land would be used and maintained in common. Though the report is none too clear on this point, it seems that individual rights would continue to exist in relation to the income of the ranch; members of the group obtaining income in proportion to the amount of capital (their stock) they contributed to the ranch. From the Masai's point of view therefore the ranch would be more in the nature of a co-operative farm, for cattle are to him what land is to an agriculturalist; the crucial difference between the two types of production cooperatives being whether the individual can as a matter of law identify and take out of the co-operative "his" contribution to it, whether it be land or cattle.

The Kenyan government accepted the analyses and recommendations and implemented them in the Land (Group Representatives), and Land Adjudication Acts of 1968.[10] A group is defined as a tribe, clan, section or family whose land under recognised customary law belongs communally to persons who are for the time being members of the group. Where land adjudication is to take place in any area, and a group within that area wish to retain communal ownership of their land, they may be advised to become incorporated under the Land (Group Representatives) Act. An official known as the Registrar of Group Representatives shall, on the group's seeking incorporation, convene a meeting of the group to adopt a constitution and elect group representatives. This done, the Registrar shall register the group as a corporate body able to hold property and deal with it through the group representatives. These persons, who may be replaced at a general meeting of the group are obliged "to exercise their powers on behalf of and for the collective benefit of all members of the group and fully and effectively to consult all members of the group"[11] on such exercise. The Registrar is given various powers to oversee groups and obtain information on how they are conducting their affairs, including the power to dissolve a group if application is made to him by the required number of members.

It seems that dissolution is the only way that members of a group could obtain individual rights in the land in the area formerly covered by group land; given the examples on the ground which inspired this legislation, this is understandable but it is open to question whether such provisions may not inhibit the use of the institution. A solution to the difficulty is however possible; the legislation could be amended so as to provide that though the group holds the title to the land, so that to the outside world the group owns the land, within the group, as between themselves, members may own interests in the land either as joint proprietors or as proprietors in common, in the latter case they would each have an undivided share in the whole which they could alienate inter vivos or by will. This is not an ideal solution for reasons which have been discussed above, but such provisions would leave undisturbed the core of the co-operative principle—common ownership and use of the land—and the great advantage of group registration, a large area of land can be used for agricultural purposes as one unit, managed by a small number of persons who can combine their traditional authority over land with modern statutory powers.

The second example of production co-operatives is the co-operative run ex-settler owned farms. No special legislation has been passed to provide for these co-operatives; the individuals concerned form a co-operative society in accordance with the Co-operative Societies Act (which is discussed below) and when that society is registered it becomes able to hold and deal with property. Title to the farm is registered in the name of the co-operative, members of the co-operative having interests in the farm (land, buildings, implements, income from produce) in proportion to their contribution of capital to buy the farm. A management committee of the co-operative runs the farm and all members of the co-operative, in theory, contribute their labour.

I say "in theory" because some studies of these co-operatives have shown that practice is far removed from what ought to happen. According to Schiller one of the necessary conditions of success in a production co-operative is that the members of it be a homogeneous group, willing to accept the discipline necessary in fixed planting times, crop rotation, communal tending and harvesting. This condition is rarely fulfilled in these co-operatives which lack discipline and have a high percentage of absentee members. In Schiller's words:

As shown by the experience in ... Kenya, in newly established production co-operatives the danger of a capitalistic deviation from the co-operative conception is quite often present ... Members neglecting the obligation to contribute their labour to the common enterprise and using their membership only to earn through the co-operative society additional income without labour input are no doubt violating the principles on which the idea of the production co-operative is based.[12]

Schiller's solution is that labour should be obligatory as also should living on the co-operative farm, but this surely is to tackle the outward manifestations of the illness without seeking its cause; if these co-operatives are to continue, what needs to be done is to be more selective in the choice of members of the co-operatives for little good will come of trying to insist on civil servants and other city dwellers with jobs there living and working on a co-operative farm.

As a lawyer I am inclined to suggest another contributory factor to the capitalistic deviation of these co-operatives. It is open to question whether the provisions of the Co-operative Societies Act are the most appropriate means of creating a production co-operative. The emphasis in a production co-operative should be on the land and the relationship of the members of the co-operative to the land; members should have or should be able to obtain rights in the land. This is essential in the type of society which exists in East Africa for reasons explained above; the peasant farmer generally is satisfied only if he has land, even abstract interests in the land are a second best. The emphasis in the Co-operative Societies Act on the other hand is on shares in the society, a corporate body which owns the land. Both shares and corporate bodies are abstract notions, as to the nature of which lawyers are in constant disagreement, far removed from the land or interests therein. What is clear however to a layman, is that in a society formed under the Act, if a member puts a lump sum of money in, he has a good chance of receiving an indeterminate sum of money from the society each year in return. A production co-operative formed under the Act in other words is seen as an ideal medium for investment and obtaining unearned income; it is not surprising therefore that absenteeism is high or that capitalistic deviation is taking place. It may be that the only effective solution to this defect (and I should stress that I am not saying that to solve this defect will without more clear up the problem of these co-operative farms) is legislation which is geared specifically to the creation and management of, and rights to land in production co-operatives, but a partial solution would be to transfer these co-operatives to the jurisdiction of the Registrar of Group Representatives under the Land (Group Representatives) Act amended in the manner I suggested above, for this would help emphasise the land aspect of the co-operative and de-emphasise the share and income related thereto aspect.

The difficulties of these production co-operatives in Kenya highlight two fundamental questions, namely to what extent should discipline be imposed on peasant farmers to get them to cultivate in an "approved" manner, and should this discipline be imposed by a farm manager given full powers of management as Maina[13] would prefer, or should it be imposed and management conducted by a committee of co-operative society members, notwithstanding that this might delay the taking of vital on-the-spot decisions? Secondly, to what extent is it likely that peasants will accept a modern form of communal tenure which deprives them of any possibility of individual rights in the land and to that extent involves a fundamental departure from many types of traditional communal tenure? Despite the existence of many reports and much legislation on land tenure in Kenya, the former of which discuss production co-operatives and communal land tenure, the latter of which makes provision for their existence, it does not seem that these questions have really been faced up to, let alone answered. Until they are, and a realistic framework is created for these co-operatives in Kenya, a lawyer, looking at the situation from his perspective, must have serious doubts as to their viability and the government's commitment to them.

These questions exist for Tanzania and Uganda no less than for Kenya, and their legislative and administrative solutions must be looked at as they provide interesting contrasts both to Kenya and each other. We may look at Tanzania first. To put the matter quite shortly, the general land law of Tanzania is in a mess. It is an amalgam of customary land law, as to which little effort has been made to record it, reform it, or provide for land governed by it to be transferred to a statutory system, and a statutory system. This latter consists of (i) pre 1925 English land law (1925 was the date of the great English codification, reformation and simplification of land law), (ii) a land registration law which is based on the English Land Registration Act 1925, (iii) postindependence legislation which had as its objects the acquisition by the state of the title to all land governed by the statutory system and the stimulation of development of the land, (iv) a miscellaneous collection of legislation dealing with specific problems in specific parts of the country, (v) legislation creating a framework for the development of specific land tenure systems, principally communal, for use in production co-operatives. This last group of laws is the one I will concentrate on, but a general point must be made straightaway, not for the first time, that such a maze of land laws is itself a hindrance to the development and administration of the land by officials, co-operatives and ordinary individuals alike, so until these general laws are at the very least simplified and codified, production co-operatives labour under a handicap quite apart from those which may be inherent in the nature of the institution.[14]

There are two pieces of legislation which may be considered here, that providing for the village settlement programme, and that providing for ranches for the Masai, which allows an interesting contrast with the Kenyan legislation. It must be stressed that although the village settlement programme has been virtually wound up, the legislation remains on the statute book and is worth examining in its own right and because it could provide a framework for the tenurial relation of the *ujamaa* villages.

The Land Tenure (Village Settlement) Act establishes a Commissioner for Village Settlement and provided for a right of occupancy for each village settlement, known as a settlement right, to be granted to him in his corporate capacity. It might be free of rent or the development conditions provided for in the Land Ordinance. The commissioner might assign this right to a society, and this is a village settlement co-operative society, registered under the Co-operative Societies Act. The commissioner and the society were required to make provision for the development and use of the right for the purpose of a village settlement on the land concerned. To this end the commissioner and the society, if the power had been delegated to it, might make rules for the development and use of the village settlement, for the use and cultivation of the land therein, for harvesting and marketing of crops, and for the conservation and protection of the natural resources of the village settlement. The rules might cover such matters as rotation of crops, afforestation, buildings and conditions of tenancy and might include the making of schemes for the carrying out of any thing in respect of which rules might be made. The third stage of the tenure system is the derivative right; an interest in the land which is granted to the individual settler, either for a homestead plot, where he lives in the village, or for an agricultural plot, where the farming area is, or both. The derivative right is held subject to conditions which emphasis that the community interest is not lost when individual interests arise. The commissioner or the society might forfeit the right for non-payment of rent (if rent is charged, which is not obligatory), for breach of any express or implied condition, for repeated failure to comply with the rules or with any scheme made under the rules, and for abandonment of the land or the right for a period exceeding six months. The general law of forfeiture is ousted by a provision in the Act, that, notwithstanding any other law to the contrary, neither the commissioner nor the society are required to serve any notice of intention to forfeit, or give the right holder any opportunity of making good his breach or remedying his default. A right holder whose right has been forfeited, however, receive compensation for his unexhausted improvement, the value of which is to be determined by accommittee consisting of two representatives of the commissioner, or where a right of occupancy has been assigned to a society, one representative from the society in place of one from the commissioner, and one representing the erstwhile right-holder.

The rules as to dispositions and succession further emphasis the role of the community. A disposition inter vivos of a derivative right was void unless made with the approval of the commissioner or the society as the case may be. Succession provisions were complicated but the main points, were, first, a person could not succeed to a derivative right unless he was approved by the commissioner or the society as the case may be; secondly, the person who did succeed need not be the person who would have succeeded according to the relevant customary law, but if he was not, then, thirdly, he, or any other person who would have benefited from a succession in accordance with the relevant customary law, might apply to a primary court for compensation either out of the deceased's other property, or if he had none, or it was not enough, out of the derivative right itself, which the commissioner or the society would have been required to pay and claim back from the new right-holder.

Thus the law assumed that the villages would start off as collective farms and later move towards becoming co-operative farms with each farmer having his individual plot within the whole. Practice however was different for at the F.A.O. Land Reform Conference in Rome in 1966, the Tanzanian delegate was reported as saying that "communal land settlement schemes were tried in our country but did not work because of absenteeism, so we had to change our system completely, first ploughing up the land and then dividing it into individual plots. Therefore we have prooved in our country that individual farming is better because people prefer it."[15] It is not clear whether these remarks were made with reference to village settlements or some other programme, but either way it suggests that the third stage of the derivative right of the individual settler had become the basic tenure position in the villages; it would still have been possible however to combine this with a communal approach to cultivation and many other matters including the provision of credit though the legal framework of proprietorship in common is much more complicated in Tanzania than in Kenya for reasons given above. What these remarks also suggest is that Tanzania has discovered from experience that, contrary to President Nyerere's thesis, traditional communal tenure does not predispose peasants to modern collective farms, but is in fact much closer to modern co-operative farms.

Apart from these planned villages where the legal framework for their development attempted to provide both for communal and individual tenure, democracy and efficiency in management, there are other production co-operatives which are of the collective farm variety and are reasonably successful because they have two of the essential ingredients for success, an inspired leadership and an ideology to spur the members on and maintain discipline. These *ujamaa* village co-operatives have become registered co-operative societies under the Co-operative Societies Act but this does not deal with land tenure questions. It is not clear what law governs the tenure

95

position of these co-operatives, customary law (and if so, which one, the law of the place or the law of the parties) the Land Tenure (Village Settlement) Act, or the general statute law which would mean the pre 1925 English law modified principally by the 1962 reforms. This is a matter of real practical importance as some of the following questions will make plain; is it possible for the members to turn their collective into an co-operative farm, in legal parlance, turn their joint proprietorship into a proprietorship in common; what is the position if neighbours wish to contribute their land to and join the co-operative; can the co-operative lease a piece of the land to e.g. an organisation like the National Milling Corporation or to the individual members, an alternative method of turning a collective into a co-operative farm; can the co-operative mortgage the land or a portion therefore to the National Development Credit Agency? Inspired leadership, vital though it is to get these collective farms started cannot provide an answer to these questions of management, yet the growth of self-reliant and prosperous communities, and the continuance of a co-operative spirit may in part turn on satisfactory answers being found. Once again, we see that the lack of knowledge of what the present law is on tenure and the lack of a clear code of modern land law might well hinder the further development of production co-operatives.[16]

The second piece of legislation which provides for production co-operatives in mainland Tanzania is the Range Development and Management Act of 1964, passed principally with the development of the Masai and their land in mind.[17] The Act is designed to create a legal framework for the conservation and development of range areas, specifically so far the Masai district, by range development commissions and ranching associations—co-operatives of stock-owners. A Range Development Commission is established to conserve, develop, and improve the natural resources of a range development area. The minister, after consultation with an R.D.C., may make rules, inter alia, prohibiting and restricting entry into the area, and empowering the commission to issue permits of entry and erect road barriers to control entry into the area. It seems that this is regarded as an essential preliminary move to any effective control of the use of the natural resources of the area. We can the better appreciate this when we realise that the people primarily concerned are pastoral nomads. The commissions are given power to issue general or special (individual) orders prohibiting, restricting or controlling such activities as the use of land for any agricultural purpose, and the construction of buildings, prescribing the method of cultivation of the land, requiring, regulating, or controlling such matters as the protection of slopes and the drainage of land, and declaring land within the area to be a closed area where there may be no occupation or cultivation of the land, or grazing of stock upon it. The commission may take executive measures to ensure that conservation is carried out. All these rules, orders and measures are issued and taken on the basis that customary law still applies to the land in the range development area, but clearly their effect will often be to alter or make redundant some of these rules.

A greater effect on customary law is provided for in that part of the Act dealing with ranching associations. Here a considerable effort seems to have been made to graft a ranching association on to a traditional social organisation, while at the same time the effect on customary land law is drastic. An association may be formed after the prospective members have had an opportunity to examine proposals and been consulted at meetings at which all the details are explained to them. 60 per cent of prospective members must approve the proposals. Once the association is formed it is registered with a commission and becomes a body corporate. It then becomes entitled either to an allocation of land, or to the grant of a right of occupancy for 99 years, subject to conditions not inconsistent with the development of the land for ranching purposes, and when such allocation or grant is made, all customary rights and titles to the land the subject of it shall be extinguished, and all customary rights and titles in any other land within the range development area of any person who is or becomes a member of the association are likewise extinguished. The association may engage in normal commercial dealings with the land, with the approval of the commission, and with such other consents as are required by law.

These commercial dealings will be governed by the ordinary, non-customary law of Tanganyika. The individual members of the association, however, will have exchanged their customary law rights in the land for the right to reside in the ranchlands of the association, to keep and graze stock not exceeding their quota, which is determined by the association on the basis of the quota of stock units fixed for the association by the commission, and to such other general rights of enjoyment of the natural resources of the ranchlands as may be provided by the rules and bye-laws of the association. All these rights are to be exercised in conformity with the rules and bye-laws of the association and such orders of the commission, as are thereafter made to implement a ranch management scheme, and may include such matters as controlling, regulating, and prescribing the use of the lands, waters, and other natural resources of the ranchlands.

This Act then is explicit that customary law is abolished once a ranching association is established, and on this matter therefore the Kenyan and Tanzanian legislation is in agreement as to range development. In other respects the legislation is very different for the Tanzanian Act is much more detailed and explicit on the rights and obligations of the members of ranching associations, and leaves them correspondingly less freedom to evolve in their own style. This legislative approach reflects the Tanzanian belief, evidenced in other actions, that the Masai cannot be left to decide for themselves whether to develop or not, and if yes, whether to develop in a co-operative direction. The danger of such an approach is that the co-operative style or spirit of development is lost sight of by officials charged with the duty of implementing the Act and the co-operative society is seen by both administered and administrators as just another device for exerting increased government pressure on the Masai. Such information as I have, from persons who have some knowledge of how the Act is being administered, suggests that this is what is happening, and as a consequence the ranching associations are not yet very effective. If this is so, then the administration must be criticised for overloading the Act with obligations and sanctions, and making possible a style of administration which will have rendered largely ineffective those parts of the legislation which for all their complexity, do make a better effort than any other in East Africa to come to terms with the peasant's desire to retain "his" property (in this case, stock) and blend it in with the co-operative approach to use and management of the community's resources.

To turn now to Uganda, we may first briefly summarise the general position as to its land law which takes after mainland Tanzania's rather than Kenya's.[18] Most land is governed by customary law, though that law may have been modified by legislation as is particularly the case in Buganda, and that which is not is governed by the Public Lands Act, pre 1925 English law and the Registration of Titles Act 1922 which is based on the Victorian (Australia) Torrens system of registration of title. Legislation does exist whereby land governed by customary law can be transferred to the statutory system under which an individual title will be registered, but little use has been made of it.

There is no special legislation dealing with production co-operatives notwithstanding that there are many group farms in the country. In lieu of a general survey of co-operative land tenure in Uganda therefore, I will look at one group farm in Bunyoro, the subject of research by Charsley,[19] concentrating on the land tenure aspects of the farm, as I understand them from his report. The Bunyoro Land Board, a public authority in which public land in Bunyoro was vested, granted a five year lease of a block of land to a co-operative society. Individuals already on the land were given the option of moving out to other land or joining the group farm; either way it seems that their interests in the land would have to be acquired by the Land Board before being leased to the co-operative. The co-operative society, registered under the Co-operative Societies Act divided up the block of land—just over 960 acres—into 61 fifteen acre holdings. In some group farms, these holdings would not themselves be each in one place for the main purpose of the group farms was to provide a large acreage for mechanical cultivation of cash crops; thus the farm would be further divided into a mechanical cultivation block and a settlement and food crop block, in the former of which a member would not have permanent rights—in legal parlance he would have at most a licence in e.g. 12 acres (a licence confers a privilege to use the land on the licensee but does not confer on him any interest or right in the land, it is much more easily revoked or withdrawn than is a lease)—in the latter of which he would have a sub-lease from year to year of e.g. 3 acres.

In the group farm studied by Charsley, this pattern of tenure was not followed; instead plots were consolidated and "permanently allocated" (a sub-lease from the co-operative to the member?) being laid out "in such a way that strips of single crops could be cultivated continuously across successive strips. One strip in each plot was allocated for food crops and the house site".[20] In theory members of the group farm were to take part in managing and cultivating it, but in practice absenteeism was high, hired labour was employed, and the Farm Manager was left with much of the work of management including maintaining discipline. Charsley considered that one of the problems was that since the overriding policy on group farms was mechanisation, it followed that little initiative could be left to the farmers themselves, who were "little more than ... obedient assistants to the machines",[21] or the committee of the Co-operative which was meant to be running the farm. (An additional drawback was that the group farm was merely one of the co-operative society's interests and the committee running the farm was drawn from the society and not just the farm, and had a minority of farm members on it.) It would seem from his analysis of the group farm that Uganda was falling into the same error as Tanzania appears to be in relation to the Masai ranches, using the co-operative society as a convenient tool to implement a government policy which has little to do with co-operative principles.

It is clear from Charsley's account that group farms had not got off to a very auspicious start in Uganda, and that this had been appreciated in the administration there. Whatever changes may have been made since his research, one which has not is to provide a statutory framework for the development of the farms, geared to the specific needs of peasant production co-operatives. I think that this is a mistake. As the law stands at present, it is not clear what rights of ownership the co-operative society has in the land of the group farm, what rights may be alienated to members, what their rights are inter se, and what part of the general land law governs the whole arrangement or any part thereof. This is not conducive to the formulation and implementation of a clear policy on group farms, to the obtaining of credit and other supplies, or to the commitment of the members to the farms. An Act on the lines of the Land Tenure (Village Settlements) Act of Tanzania would be the most appropriate form of legislation, as this would combine leaving the title to the land vested in the local land board with conferring rights in the land on a co-operative, which should be limited to members of the farm, and on the members via leases and sub-leases, or settlement rights and derivative rights as they are called in the Tanzanian legislation. In this connection, it is worth recalling that at the F.A.O. Land Tenure Conference referred to above, the Ugandan delegate was reported as saying in agreement with the Tanzanian delegate that "even if land is group ploughed, a man must know that his crop is growing on his own land so that he will look after it better ...".[22] Any legislation therefore should be geared to proprietorship in common—co-operative farms—rather than joint proprietorship—collective farms.

It is difficult to escape the conclusion that there has been too much optimism and too little thought given to production co-operatives in East Africa. The basic fallacy has been the equation of traditional communal with modern collective tenure, and the failure to appreciate that for the peasant farmer, there is no adequate substitute for real security—that is, a plot of land. Four observations may be made on this. *First,* traditional communal tenure left a fair amount of individual rights and responsibilities to the member of the tribe, clan, family etc. and these were growing all the while under the impact of the colonial economic order. In collective farms, the members lose their individual rights and decision-making powers in practice; a one-crop collective farm cannot allow much discussion or individual decision-making on such matters as planting, weeding, harvesting and processing. *Secondly,* a modern system of communal land tenure requires a sophisticated system of land law; it is not easy to understand, depending as it does on the separation of rights in the land from the land itself, on the substitution of shares, estates, interests for earth, soil and grass. Suspicion of this by the peasant is hardly surprising, and can only be overcome if the law allows the peasant to "own" a plot of land within the collectivity, however it chooses to describe the resulting relationship, and whatever restrictions it places on the ownership. *Thirdly,* how realistic is it to expect a peasant farmer to make the transition to cash cropping, to modern statutory communal tenure, and to participating in the running of a co-operative society all at the same time? Incidents of absenteeism and moribund co-operative committees suggest that too much is being asked of the peasant, and as often as not, the co-operative society ceases to be one except in name only. *Fourthly,* in so far as the reason for creating production co-operatives is the benefits to be obtained from large scale mechanical cultivation, these can be obtained through other ways, e.g. state farms, or individual farmers forming tractor hire co-operatives.[23] There must be social as well as economic reasons for the creation of production co-operatives, and this means that good leadership and a belief in co-operative principles are necessary to success. A clear legal framework for production co-operatives will not create these but it may allow them to be utilised to the full. All three East African countries have some way to go before it could be said that they have such legislation, but for the reasons discussed in this part of the paper, such legislation is one necessary component of successful production co-operatives.

Controls over and Powers of Service Co-operatives

Compared to production co-operatives, service co-operatives abound in the rural sector of the East African economies. All governments have decided that co-operatives are the best way to bring the rural inhabitant into the modern commercial sector, to cut out the non-African rural trader, to market and process crops, to collect taxes, to channel credit to the farmer, and to stimulate him into political awareness. Task after task has been heaped on to the co-operative movement, more and more primary societies have been established so that it is not surprising that in all the countries by the late sixties the movement was showing signs of strain, and governments were being recommended in reports, and were acting on the recommendations to increase their powers of control and supervision over the movement. In this part of the paper I want to concentrate on two matters which between them raise important issues going to the heart of the nature of the co-operative movement, the extent of government control over co-operatives and the powers primary co-operatives have over their members. I will concentrate on Kenya's Co-operative Societies Act of 1966, making reference where appropriate to the other countries' legislation, and then discuss the problems which arise from the legislation in the context of the general principles of the co-operative movement.

The Act establishes a Commissioner for Co-operative Development who is the Registrar of Co-operative Societies, and Assistant Commissioners, all of whom are responsible for the control and supervision of co-operative societies. All co-operative societies must be registered before they can carry on business and claim the privileges attendant upon that status, and the Commissioner is empowered to refuse registration or cancel a registration. The Act makes it clear that he has a wide discretion in the exercise of his powers here; it states that

a society which has for its objects the promotion of the economic interests of its members through co-operative principles, and which *in the opinion* of the Commissioner is capable of promoting those interests *may* be registered as a co-operative society[24] (my italics).

Even where the Commissioner is satisfied that a society has complied with the preliminaries to an application, chief amongst which are that it have at least ten members (members must be over eighteen) and a copy of its proposed byelaws accompany the application, he has a discretion whether to register or not. Instead of registration, the Commissioner may provisionally register a society if not satisfied that it complies with the pre-conditions to registration, but nonetheless he considers that with due diligence it will ultimately comply. Provisional registration lasts one year. A society may appeal to the Minister against a refusal to register, or a cancellation of registration.

Societies may with the approval of the Commissioner amalgamate with one or more other societies or divide into two or more societies provided that members and creditors are notified of the proposals, are given an opportunity to leave the society or call for the payment of the society's debts, and as to members, two-thirds are present and vote for the resolution to amalgamate or divide, at a general meeting. They may also form co-operative unions. In addition however, the Commissioner may require two or more societies to amalgamate, to join together and form a co-operative union or district co-operative union, and a primary society to join a union. These last two powers are to be exercised where the Commissioner considers it desirable for the efficient functioning of a co-operative union.

The bye-laws of a society including any changes thereto must be approved by the Commissioner and cannot take effect until they are so approved. Societies must keep proper books and accounts and must produce them for inspection by the Commissioner at any time. An officer from his department must countersign all cheques. Accounts must be audited at least annually by an auditor appointed or approved by him. He may of his own accord, and on the direction of the Minister or an application by a majority of the committee of a society or a third of the members, must hold an inquiry into the workings of a society, and he may also direct an inquiry into the books of a society on the application of the creditors of a society. If, after an inquiry he is satisfied that the committee of a society is not properly performing its duties, he may remove the committee and order the society to be run by a committee of two people, whom he may appoint, for at least one year. A variant on this power occurs in Tanzania where the appointment of persons following the dissolution of a committee may be for any period up to four years. Such persons are required to comply with the directions of the Registrar. As an alternative to the above action the Commissioner in Kenya and the Registrar in Tanzania may dissolve a society.

Turning to the powers of the society over its members and others, it may seem strange to approach matters from this perspective, for members each have one vote, can attend general meetings and thus disapprove of the managing committee's plans and ultimately of the committee by not re-electing them to office. But the reality is that many societies were imposed on farmers from above; in those and others members take little active part in affairs, and committees are regularly re-elected by a handful of electors so that from the members' perspective, where the society is at all active, it is an organisation having power over them. There is first of all the general provision that bye-laws are binding on all members who may be fined by the society for breaking them. Secondly, the society is given wide charging powers over members' goods and chattels. A charge is similar in many respects to a mortgage and so what this means is that in the circumstances set out in the Act, a society is given certain rights of ownership in a member's goods and can, by exercising those rights, permanently deprive the member of his goods e.g. by selling them to a third party. The circumstances in which a society is given a charge are first where it has supplied goods, services or credit to a member, there it has a first charge on the things or produce created or produced with the aid of the goods etc. supplied by the society, and secondly, where a member is generally indebted to the society, there the society has a first charge on the member's share in the society.

Thirdly, and perhaps most important from the point of view of the co-operatives' ability to carry out government policy, are the compulsory marketing provisions of the Kenyan and Tanzanian Acts.[25] In both Acts, a society is empowered to contract with its members that they dispose of their produce to or through the society, that they produce a specified amount of produce or pay a specified sum by way of damages for failure to do so. Damages will be charged on the member's property and stock. The contract will also create a charge on the proceeds of sale of all existing or future produce of the member, and the society may pledge the produce of its members as security for a loan to it. Large though these powers are (and they are in fact larger than they appear when it is realised that "contract" is a rather euphemistic description for the way the obligations contained therein are imposed on the members) they may be justified as part of the normal operational framework of a primary society, for members, by joining such a society, accept certain restraints on their freedom of manoevre thereafter, and obligations to support the society; the only way a society can make forward contracts for the supply of produce to e.g. a marketing board, or obtain credit from an agricultural bank for short- or longterm purposes is by covering itself by this type of contract so that it has some assurance that the produce will be forthcoming, and that it can give security for a loan. If there should be criticism of the power thus given to the societies, it is misplaced for it should be directed against the pressure brought to bear, or obligation imposed on farmers to join a primary society in the first place. As it is, these provisions, supplemented in the way discussed below, are the lynch-pin of the two systems of co-operative and state marketing of practically all primary produce in Kenya and Tanzania, and collection of local dues, cesses and taxes from the farmer. How far they are very useful for the obtaining of loans we will consider in the next part of the paper.

Both Acts provide for a further extension of these compulsory marketing powers to cover non-members of societies, as good an illustration as one can find in the law of the wider "governmental" role being conferred on the co-operative movement. The Minister may make an order requiring all the producers of a particular crop in a specified area or throughout the country to dispose of it to or through a co-operative where that co-operative can show that its members produce a certain percentage of that crop in the specified area or throughout the country. (In Kenya the percentage is 60, in Tanzania it is 75 for the two preceding years.) In Tanzania too, the Minister must be satisfied that such an order is in the general interests of the industry affected, must publish a draft order to which objections may be made and must be considered, may revoke the order in certain circumstances and shall revoke it if 75% of the producers of the crop vote in favour of revocation. There are no specific provisions for revocation in Kenya but presumably if the designated co-operative society ceased to produce 60% of the specified crop, the order would cease to have effect. Although these powers have been used there is in Kenya at least, some doubt as to their desirability for the Kenyan Dairy Commission of Inquiry, reporting in 1965 considered but rejected using the power to control all diary produce via the Kenya Co-operative Creameries on the grounds that "it was not practicable nor desirable to vest in a Co-operative Society operating a monopoly full statutory powers of control".[26] Instead, a Kenya Dairy Commission, a statutory marketing and processing body was proposed which would take over these functions from the K.C.C.

The statutory provisions discussed above, allied to the knowledge that membership of many primary societies has been obligatory indicate how far removed are East African co-operatives from the co-operatives of classical theory which requires that membership be voluntary, that decisions be arrived at democratically, that societies be auto-financing, free from government control, and concerned not just with profit but with the moral welfare of their members.[27] Whatever the original hopes of all the governments when they expanded their co-operative movements after independence, policies and practice have gone far to turn them into semi-state organisations. The legislation reflects this, as does the report of the Tanzanian Presidential Special Committee of Inquiry on the Co-operative Movement and Marketing Boards.[28]

This report is worth considering as it provides much of the rationale and justification for strict government control and consequent departure from traditional principles. The movement in Tanzania had been expanded so fast that there were not enough qualified people available to serve as officers in societies, consequently, inefficiency, corruption, peculation, non-collection of debts, and incurring of debt were rife and combining to bring the whole movement into discredit with the very people who were supposed to benefit from it. Co-operatives were and are a crucial part of Tanzania's policy of socialist rural development—indeed to some extent the pre-

independence success and strength of the co-operative movement inspired the policy—so a failure of the movement could
not be countenanced. There appeared no alternative to the
Presidential Committee to greater centralisation of control and
supervision in the Co-operative Development Division of
government, a standardisation of the terms and conditions of
service of co-operative officials via a Unified Co-operative Service run by a U.C.S. Commission on the lines of the civil service
and its Commission,[28a] and compulsory membership by all
societies of the Co-operative Union of Tanganyika which
should itself establish specialised service departments (e.g. a
Systems and Methods Section to advise on efficient ways of
carrying on operations, a Contracts Section equipped to nego-
tiate major contracts) to assist member co-operatives.

These and other recommendations were clearly trying to
preserve some degree of separation between the co-operative
movement and the government, and some degree of democratic
control of the operations of all societies, but the demands
of efficiency and better supervision inevitably tipped the scales
against autonomy and democracy. In addition, the government
in its official comment on the report[29] made it clear that
some government intervention in the movement was necessary
since the movement was necessarily part of the political life
of the nation. The dilemma between democracy and efficiency
in management comes through in page after page of the report and that the dilemma is insoluable is to some extent
borne out by the fact that the co-operative movement did not
approve of the report to the same extent that the government
did, and a certain amount of negotiation was required between the government and the movement before the 1968
Act, based on the report was finally passed.

The governments of the East African countries have got
themselves into a position over their co-operative movements
from which they will have difficulty in extracting themselves.
By building up the movements quickly from above, they have
undermined the spontaneous grass-roots nature of the movements wherein their real strength lies; a fast build up has
meant too few staff and inadequate financial management,
and to correct this, more government control and supervision

is required. Yet this in turn imposes further bureaucracy from above and so further undermines the self-reliance of the movements,—witness for instance the clear lack of confidence displayed in co-operatives by the tight financial control now vested in the Commissioner in Kenya. Nor is a programme of public education on the nature and role of co-operatives as suggested for Tanzania likely to help all that much for while it may stimulate members to take a more active part in the affairs of their societies, it will also inevitably point up the gap between principle and practice in relation to the place of the movement in society. Yet without the growth of more grass-roots commitment to co-operatives, they are unlikely to be as effective as they could be in rural development. Governments would do better to appreciate that the price of a viable co-operative movement may well be a few failures amongst primary societies, and should not seek to eliminate all of them.

This may however be a counsel of perfection, and a more realistic approach for the lawyer would be to ask how can the law be framed so that the Government has the power to act when necessary yet the enthusiasm and democracy of the co-operative movement is not crushed by the ever present threat of government intervention. There are two possible solutions here. First a distinction should be drawn in the law between "ordinary" and "extra-ordinary" government powers. The ordinary powers are those which can be used to assist and help the co-operative movement to supervise itself and they should be so drawn that their exercise takes place as an act of partnership between government and various organs of the co-operative movement—C.U.T. in Tanzania and the District Unions in Kenya as tends to be the practice already in those two countries. Thus the law should be phrased in such a way that the central government may not act until it has been invited to by, or consulted with the relevant part of the co-operative movement. The extra-ordinary powers of regulation and coercion are those which allow the government to intervene on behalf of the state in the affairs of the co-operative movement when supervision in partnership has failed.

Special procedures should be required to be followed before these powers can be activated so as to ensure that they are exercised only for good reason. To put the matter succinctly, the greater the power the governments have over the co-operative movement, the greater the need for procedural safeguards over the exercise of the power and the greater the need to explain and justify the exercise of the powers before it takes place. Although both the Kenyan and the Tanzanian Acts provide for some safeguards, there is a lack of consistency about them, and one may query the desirability of provisions allowing appeals to the Minister from a whole range of exercises of power by the Commissioner or Registrar since such provisions are a constant invitation to the Minister to intervene in the work of the Co-operative Department on no very clear principles at all. Here too, a division should be attempted between exercises of the "extra-ordinary" interventionist power where there are good reasons for ensuring that the ultimate responsibility is on the Minister, and exercises of the "ordinary" partnership power where if formal appeals are needed at all, they could lie to a panel of persons drawn equally from the administration and the co-operative movement. Such a division of powers, clearly set out in the law could do much to restore the co-operative movement's faith in itself and maintain its democratic ethos.

Secondly, governments could establish a system of compulsory co-operative insurance in which all primary societies would pay an annual premium in return for which the members would be covered against loss caused by the dishonesty or gross negligence of staff and/or committee members; naturally a society which had had to claim on the insurance fund would have to pay higher premiums in future so there would be a direct incentive on members to be active in the management of their society and the movement as a whole (for the general level of premiums is fixed by the degree of risk involved in the insurance) which does not seem to exist at the moment where in the final analysis, the government bails out the movement. Such a system might render less necessary the tight administrative control exercised over or proposed for the movement, and that too would help re-awaken members' interest in their primary society.[30]

Co-operatives, Credit and Security

In this part I want to look at one specific problem albeit fairly briefly, that of the provision of credit to, and through, and the giving of security therefore by co-operatives for this is a matter in which the law has a part to play, and which is a crucial determinant of the pace and effectiveness of rural development.

Even where the credit institutions are the purely voluntary rotating credit associations, so prevalent in the developing world, questions of security in case of non-repayment of the loan, and the remedies available to the lender either in the courts or through other, possibly less formal, channels are important. Much more so are they with a co-operative society which may be obtaining its loan from a state or private bank, where the amount of money involved may be substantial and the failure to repay serious both for the society as a whole and its individual members. Co-operatives are generally regarded as being peculiarly suitable to act as lending agencies to peasant farmers; they are close to the farmer and know his needs better than any other organisation, they have facilities for administering the loan and can obtain repayment via compulsory marketing contracts, the group pressure of members acts as a powerful sanction on the potential individual defaulter, and loans to individual small-holders are too risky and costly to administer. Hence all the East African countries use co-operatives for this purpose—in Kenya in fact they have been used to administer the guaranteed minimum return system of agricultural prices—and have provisions in their Co-operative Societies Act dealing with the power of societies to make loans to members and to obtain loans from outside institutions.

Only Tanzania however has created a special network of institutions for the provision of co-operative credit. As apex societies, there is a triumvirate of banks, the National Co-operative and Development Bank, which is a holding company for both the National Co-operative Bank, the banker to the co-operative movement, which "finances the purchase of the crops until reimbursed by the final buyers",[31] and the National Development Credit Agency which handles the development finance; short term loans provide working capital requirements on the farm and medium and long-term loans are offered for production or processing both on the farm and at the primary societies and unions of the co-operative movement. Thus the N.C.D.B. has a comprehensive knowledge of the finance of its customers, and, on the basis of their demands, their respective financial records and assessments of their capabilities, it can appropriately control the flow of funds to the co-operative.[31]

On the receiving end of the loans, in addition to the co-operatives, the Agricultural Associations Act provides for the establishment of associations of agriculturalists, individuals who join together in order to obtain credit for their individual purposes. They do not form themselves into a co-operative, but they must all be personally carrying on the agricultural activity for which the association is formed and the activity must be undertaken in one place or in contiguous places in one area. Loans are made to members of the associations by the N.D.C.A. and secured on their crops, or chattels bought with the loan, in accordance with the Chattels Transfer Ordinance.[32]

Impressive though this framework appears to be, it has been criticised for not being very effective.[33] The machinery is there to cope with long-term planning, overall assessment of needs and funds, and order of priorities, but the will is absent. Insufficient vetting of loan applications takes place at district and regional level because of political pressure to grant societies and individuals loans so that too much time is spent at the head offices dealing with applications for quite small sums. Again the Presidential Committee recorded that political pressure had been applied on the banks to grant unsuitable loans. Thus, the mere existence of a special framework for the granting of co-operative credit is no guarantee by itself that a system of such credit will be properly organised and administered, but it may be an essential pre-condition of a proper system, and both Kenya and Uganda who have at times expressed their intentions of establishing a Co-operative Bank should not be put off by the teething troubles of Tanzania's banks.

Turning now to the provisions in the Co-operative Societies

Acts about loans, generally societies may only make loans to their members, though in Kenya, the Commissioner may authorise loans to non-members. He may also regulate the amount of money which may be lent on the security of a charge on immoveable property, i.e. he might limit such loans to 60% of the value of the borrower's land. Societies themselves however may charge the whole of their property as security for a loan (and it will be recalled they have an automatic charge on members' produce and crops sold to them under compulsory marketing contracts). The charge must be registered with the Commissioner within thirty days of its creation, otherwise it is not effective, and the Commissioner must make his Register of Charges available for inspection to any member, creditor or potential creditor of a society. Where the lending agency is the Agricultural Finance Corporation of Kenya—the main agricultural credit agency in Kenya—it may only lend funds to a co-operative which applies in writing, and of which the officers and committee of the society have been authorised to make the application by a two-thirds majority of the members present and voting at a general meeting. The members of the society are jointly and severally liable to repay the loan and interest thereon, and the Corporation, both before making the loan and thereafter, has a right of full access to the books of the society.

Security for repayment of the loans, upon which the availability of credit depends to some extent, is much more however than a set of provisions about charges, mortgages and who has the personal responsibility to repay. In the small pre-, or barely commercial communities Geertz[34] wrote about, social pressure was usually sufficient to ensure that loans were repaid. This was often supplemented by a simple insurance fund to ensure that the members who had paid in could draw out when their turn came, and court action taken against the defaulter in a local court. In a fully commercial society, where both lenders and borrowers understand the mechanics of credit, and are imbued with the philosophy of the desirability of credit, repayment is again obtained as much through social pressure and "doing what comes naturally" as through fear that the borrower will lose his security—e.g. his house—if he doesn't repay. We are much more concerned about not losing our credit-rating. The laws of mortgages, charges hire-purchase exist and are necessary but the provisions as to the lender's rights to realise his security are, in respect of the vast majority of borrowers, no more than a last resort, a distant threat which never or hardly ever has to be invoked. Indeed, one is almost tempted to say the provisions are a gigantic confidence trick; the availability of credit does not depend on security being instantly and easily realiseable at the first sign of borrowers' difficulties but on national economic policy and the extent to which, in England at any rate, building societies can attract investors' deposits; if it ever became necessary for lenders to realise their security on a large scale because of some dramatic economic downturn, governments would step in and prevent them doing so—this in fact happened in Kenya in the 1930's.[35]

The rural societies of East Africa fall within neither of the above two categories of society, in the matter of credit though they tend more to the former than the latter society, and little effort has been made to adapt the legal framework governing credit or its administration to their needs. The law provides for mortgages, charges, and confers on the mortgagee the traditional remedies of appointing a receiver of the income from the property mortgaged, leasing and ultimately sale of the mortgaged property, (and equivalent remedies are provided in the Chattels Transfer Acts of Kenya and Tanzania in respect of charges over moveable property), yet because the climate of opinion in society does not appear to be geared to the social importance of repaying loans from co-operative societies or banks or governments, borrowers' legal remedies have to be put into the front line rather than kept back as a last resort, and indeed have to be supplemented and made easier to use, a clear indication that they are not seen as a distant threat any more. Another important factor here is that very little credit from private internal sources finds its way via lending agencies like the Tanzanian N.D.C.A. or the Kenyan A.F.C. into agricultural development; most of the funds come either from taxes or external loans, and where the latter are involved, latitude on repayment is severely circumscribed.

But how realistic is it to base a system of security for agricultural credit on mortgages, charges and the possibility of realising them? Is it politically feasible to foreclose on hundreds of smallholders, to sell the property of debtor primary societies, and to bankrupt co-operative unions? Kenya, it is true, has dispossessed farmers in the settlement schemes with temporarily beneficial results as regards repayment of loans, but far fewer farmers have been dispossessed than have been seriously in arrears with loan repayments. In Tanzania, the Presidential Committee reported many cases of societies heavily in debt, but the remedy was always a grant-in-aid from some government fund and a "re-organisation" of the society; at most it might be deprived of credit from the N.D.C.A. and N.C.B. for a period. It seems that in these countries too then, despite a repayment problem and the deliberately easier availability to the lenders of remedies to realise their security, in the final analysis the remedies are not often used, and cannot often be used. Their credibility suffers accordingly. There is too an additional reason why these remedies are less than adequate; they are derived from a law which lays great stress on individual rights in property, yet have been grafted on to a system of co-operative credit with little or no change. A remedy which might be perfectly fair and workable when applied to an individual loan defaulter ceases to be either when applied to a society which because of defaulters amongst its members has difficulty in repaying a loan.

The position on repayment is then that there is no or no sufficient climate of opinion or communal pressure to repay loans, and the existing remedies of lenders fit uneasily into a co-operative framework and in any event are practically unusable through political factors. Can this state of affairs be remedied? There is no short term solution, but one or two possible alternatives to the present arrangement, some of them suggested before by others, are worth mentioning here. First, more care should be exercised at the local level over the vetting of applications for loans; Collinson's suggestion of summary cards (credit-cards?) for members of primary societies on which would be recorded their credit-rating, and which could be used for "'spotting' borrowers at sale time" is a sound one and worth adopting (if it has not already been). Secondly, group pressure to repay might be stimulated by a greater willingness to cut off further loans to a primary society who or whose members were in default with their loan repayments. This has been tried in Kenya, and both Collinson and I in an earlier paper, have suggested it before for Tanzania. One of the difficulties is that "group pressure" is a rather chancy business; if the society is in default because the majority of its members are in default to it, group pressure to repay is a non-starter. Nor is the invoking of the remedies available to the society as a chargee likely to help very much for members could refuse to deliver their crops to the society (the choice before them would be deliver and find a large portion of the price kept by the society, not deliver and find oneself liable in damages) and to seize and sell their implements would leave the debtor even less able to pay his way in future. It might be that where there was a widespread problem of default amongst the members of a society, rescheduling of repayments or a moratorium on repayments would be the only solution, with the lending agency carrying the loss involved. But there should be a firm principle that only in the most exceptional circumstances—e.g. a total crop failure due to natural disasters—should an individual's debt to a society or a society's debt to a lending agency be written off. It will be that much more difficult to create a climate of opinion in favour of repayment if it is known that default on a large enough scale will result in cancellation.

Thirdly, I would repeat my suggestion, made earlier in the paper, that an insurance scheme be devised for the co-operative movement, which could be used to meet some of the losses arising from the giving of credit. The joining together of a mortgage and a life insurance policy is now a recognised lending device in England, and it should not be beyond the wit of insurance experts to devise a system whereby part of the loan to the society is required to be used to make a down payment on an insurance policy payable on final repayment or "final" default and part of each repayment instalment goes as a premium to that policy, which is invested in government stock. On successful repayment of the loan, the policy would mature and be available as an additional loan to the society.

Forthly, a variant of the above could be worked out in conjunction with the mechanism of the revolving credit association which is a familiar lending device in many African societies, is specifically provided for in the law in Tanzania, and is in use on a wide scale in Uganda.[36] A loan could be made to a primary society; a certain percentage of the loan would be retained by the society in its account in the N.C.B., this would represent a two-way insurance element both for repayment purposes and for later lending to members if the revolving credit mechanism broke down. The bulk of the loan would be made available to a certain number of members, but all members who wanted a loan, whether they then received one or not, would commence paying monthly or quarterly instalments to the society to build up loan reserves. When those reserves had reached the size of the original loan, less a further insurance and repayment element, they would be loaned to some more members and so on until all the members in the scheme had had a loan and paid it back. The cycle could then recommence; indeed payments into and out of the fund could be set at such a level that after the initial loan, the society was more or less self-sufficient as regards loans at the same level. If any default was made by a member in payments, other members' contributions would be raised, and the defaulting member cut out of the cycle. If default was made after a loan had been received, the member's plot and farm tools should be vested in the society, and he and his family be paid a small living wage for working for the society until such time as the loan is paid off with the income from the plot and its produce. (The defaulting member would not necessarily continue to work on his own plot, he might be employed in general labouring work and his plot might be leased out to a fellow-member to cultivate.)

The basic advantages of using a variant of the revolving credit association are first, that one would be using a credit mechanism which was rather similar to a well-known traditional one, and as Geertz has pointed out such an "intermediate institution" can be used to help people make the transition from "a traditionalistic agrarian society to an increasingly fluid commercial one", as the institution "is essentially then an educational mechanism in terms of which peasants leran to be traders, not merely in the narrow occupational sense, but in the broad cultural sense; an institution which acts to change their whole value framework from one emphasising particularistic diffuse, affective and ascriptive ties between individuals, to one emphasising—*within economic contexts*—universalistic affectively neutral and achieved ties between them".[37] Secondly, with the exception of the small number of first borrowers in the cycle, all the members of the association would have a clear financial stake in the system of credit from its commencement, and this should operate to increase their willingness both to keep paying in themselves and bring community pressure to bear on defaulters. Thirdly, by maintaining and constantly increasing an insurance reserve, the society is in a better position to repay the loan to the lending agency. Fourthly, such a system would help put the individualistic remedies of the "English" law of security back where they belong; very much a last resort, and applicable only to individuals.

Whether these suggestions are taken up for further consideration or not, it cannot be urged too strongly that some reconsideration and reform is needed in the law of agricultural and co-operative credit in all East African countries, for the present system is not working very well. Ideally the law ought to be geared far more to the needs, problems and special characteristics of the co-operative society and the peasant farmer, than it is at present. Even where, as in Kenya particularly and Uganda, credit is given to individuals direct, with their land titles taken as security, consideration should be given to increasing the range and type of remedies available to the lending agency, so as to increase its flexibility of response to the problem of defaulters. Equally important too both for co-operative and individual credit law reform is to try and redress the balance of the English-derived law so that the interests of the borrowers are at least as well protected as those of the lenders. This applies to all three countries, Uganda and Tanzania because their general land law, which includes law on mortgages etc., is derived from English law stemming from a period when the balance was not very even, and Kenya because since independence, legislation has been introduced which deliberately takes away certain rights of the borrower in default.

This paper has been concerned to look at co-operatives and rural development in East Africa from a broad legal angle, concentrating on those atters which have a high legal content. The overall impression derived from such a survey is that on these matters, the creation and implementation of the law has suffered from an absence both of originality, and of sufficient specifically legal considerations—these would include such matters as the extent of a society's or a member's rights in the land, the need for a simple and workable legal code on land law and credit transactions, and the need for procedural safeguards on the exercise of governments' powers over the co-operatives.

To such a generalisation, there are obvious exceptions in all countries, but there is equally no denying that the co-operatives in all countries are not as strong as government policy would have them, and this may have the result of finally turning government away from them, as appears to be the case in Kenya, or turning the peasant farmer away from them, as the Presidential Committee reported was happening in Tanzania. The defects of the co-operatives cannot be corrected overnight by the passage of a law, but they can be exacerbated by the hasty passage of an ill thought-out law and set on the road to amelioration by a well thought-out law. There is ample scope for such laws in all three countries.

On the question of originality, apart from the need for a uniform code of land law in Tanzania and Uganda to provide a modern general law, there is much to be said for adopting a fairly experimental, almost piecemeal, approach to legislation in this area and not relying on foreign models of dubious relevance. If the problems of the co-operatives in the settlement schemes in Kenya are different to those in the areas of consolidated and registered land, then the law governing them should be different too. This approach is in fact already adopted in respect of production co-operatives where tenure problems can more easily be seen as being different but there is no reason why, if the situation requires it, it should not be extended to service co-operatives. In sum, the most important message of this conclusion, and indeed of the whole paper, is that governments should be more aware of the creative potential of law and legal techniques in their own right; lawyers should not, in other words, be brought in at the end of a policy discussion, given a brief and told to turn it into law nor, alternatively, should they be told to "draft a law about co-operative credit" without being given any brief as also happens; rather they should be in on the discussion from the beginning, able to contribute their distinctive approach, and if you like, biases. In this way, at least an adequate framework, for the co-operative movement might emerge, and that is a *sine qua non* of its further development.

Poul W. Westergaard

Co-operatives in Tanzania as Economic and Democratic Institutions[1]

In the development of human resources the focus must be on motivation, involvement, participation and self-help ... Co-operation provides its own motivation under conditions in which it is sometimes extraordinarily difficult to enlist interest and active participation. It appeals to the self-interest of the rural producer in a way that he can understand and demonstrates, through tangible results, how he can pool his efforts and resources with others in a similar situation, in order gradually to lift himself out of poverty and stagnation. By enrolling him as an active participant in decision-making, the co-operative form of organisation stimulates initiative and gives him the will and the means to shape his own future.[2]

The belief expressed in this statement in the suitability of the co-operative form as a prime mover in rural development is shared by the Tanzanian Government, which in *Government Paper* No. 4 of 1967[3] stated:

There is no other type of organisation (than co-operation) which is so suited to the problems and concept of rural development ... It would be impossible for the Government administrative machinery to deal with numerous individuals requiring Government assistance and services ... Without the use of co-operatives the number of people wanting Government help will make dissemination of Government services and assistance financially very expensive and administratively almost impossible. Self-help will be difficult to organize, and changes in attitudes so essential for bringing about required structural changes are likely to take much longer than if co-operatives are effectively organized, emphasizing production. The revitalisation of the co-operative movement in Tanzania is therefore vital to any programme of rural development.

The co-operative movement has played a major role in the rural development of Tanzania and its role will be even greater in the future.[4] Not only are co-operatives regarded as being suitable as development agents, but the co-operative form is also regarded as being fitted for the implementation of the socialist policy of Tanzania: "The co-operative is basically a socialist institution ... The co-operative movement in Tanzania is a source of considerable strength for the growth of socialism ..."[5]

A co-operative is an economic organisation with certain economic functions, but it is also an institution which is supposed to be run according to certain principles: "Co-operation is at one and the same time a commercial enterprise and a democratically controlled popular movement."[6] The suitability of the co-operative movement to act as a development agent is, indeed, because of these co-operative principles. The degree to which the co-operative movement succeeds in playing its role as a development agent, as described above, depends on the degree to which the movement succeeds in implementing the co-operative principles—and the ideas behind these principles—in practice.

The paper is divided into four parts. The discussion in this part will be centred on two main themes, efficiency and democracy. I shall try to relate this discussion, where appropriate, to the general discussion of the same themes which has taken place under the auspices of the International Co-operative Alliance (ICA). There are two aspects of the problems of democracy in the co-operative movement: one with respect to the relationship between the management of co-operatives and the members; the other with respect to the relationship between the co-operative movement as such and the government. The two problems are, of course, interrelated. The main interest in this section is in discussing "the rules of the game" with respect to the autonomy of the co-operative movement vis-à-vis the government.

Co-operative problems cannot be fruitfully discussed in a vacuum. A discussion must be based on a knowledge and understanding of how the co-operatives actually operate, of the institutional framework within which the co-operatives operate and of the historical background of the co-operative movement. I shall therefore, in the following, look at the present co-operative set-up. The purpose of that section is to provide a background, but also to provide information about what co-operatives in Tanzania actually "look like" as a point of interest in its own right.

A fruitful discussion about co-operative problems must not only be based on a knowledge of the institutional framework in an economic sense, but also on a knowledge of the political framework. The third section therefore reviews the role which the co-operative movement is supposed to play in the socio-politico-economic development of Tanzania. It would be going far beyond the scope of this paper to treat this subject at any length. That section is therefore very short and should only be regarded as a reminder.

The peculiarities of the present co-operative set-up can be better understood if it is seen in a historical perspective. The first section therefore gives a review of the development of the co-operative movement in Tanzania. It is not intended to be a comprehensive account of the development of the co-operative movement in Tanzania (this account has still to be written) but has the more limited scope of describing certain facts which should make the present set-up more understand-able. The section is heavily biased towards a description of the relationship between the co-operative movement and the government and is far from doing justice to the contribution of the co-operative movement itself to the co-operative development in Tanzania. This bias should be kept in mind.

The general bias of the paper—apart from being written by an economist—is towards an emphasis on agricultural marketing co-operatives to the neglect of other types of co-operatives. This bias, however defendable, is primarily, of course, because of the overall theme of this seminar. But even without the emphasis in the theme of the seminar on *rural* development, a paper on co-operatives in Tanzania would deal mostly with marketing co-operatives, simply because these are the backbone of the co-operative movement in Tanzania (as in the other East African countries).

The Development of the Co-operative
Movement in Tanzania before Independence

There are two types of co-operatives which are especially related to the rural development of Tanzania: marketing co-operatives and *ujamaa* villages (i.e. a co-operative or collective farming system in some respects similar to the kibbutz in Israel). I shall, however, have very little to say about *ujamaa* villages as such. I shall attempt to justify this omission later. The legal foundation upon which the co-operative movement in Tanzania is built was laid in 1932, when the first law was passed to make provision for the registration of co-operative societies. The *Co-operative Societies Ordinance of 1932* empowered the Governor to appoint a Registrar of Co-operative Societies and stipulated that "... a society which has as its objects the promotion of the economic interests of its members in accordance with co-operative principles ... may be registered under this Ordinance ...".[7] The Registrar may refuse to register a society if he is of the opinion that it is not viable. The function of the Registrar, besides the act of registration, is to supervise the co-operatives. He shall audit—or cause to be audited—the accounts of every registered society at least once a year and he has powers to enquire into the financial conditions of a society and to prescribe rules relating to the management of a society.

The "unofficial" birthday of the co-operative movement in Tanzania was in 1925, when the Kilimanjaro Native Planters' Association (KNPA) was formed

... primarily with the object of benefitting all members by instituting co-operation and assisting in the proper control of coffee-planting and sale of produce, to guard against diseases and pests, to circularise to all members information and proper methods of cultivation and preparation,

as it was stated in the rules.[8] The main function of the Association was the marketing of coffee grown by its members. Coffee was introduced in the Kilimanjaro Region by missionaries at the end of the 19th century and soon taken up as a cash-crop by the local people, the Wachagga. By 1916 there were about 14,000 coffee-trees owned by Chagga growers. The colonial administration encouraged the coffee-growing and also the formation of the KNPA in 1925. When the Co-operative Societies Ordinance was enacted in 1932, the KNPA was split into 16 primary societies and one secondary society, the members of which were the primary societies, and these societies were registered under the Ordinance. The name of the secondary society was the Kilimanjaro Native Co-operative Union (KNCU), which exists to-day under the same name.

One of the rules of the KNPA was that the sale of coffee should be controlled by the association. This applied to coffee grown by members, but the association had no control over coffee grown by non-members. This caused considerable trouble and it was soon found that control would have to be exercised over all coffee. To enable this to be done, the following rules were made under the Native Authorities Ordinance and came into force on April 1st, 1929:

> All native planters of coffee shall be members of KNPA; but no subscriptions shall be payable by members of the Association. Every native planter of coffee shall market his crop through the Association . . .[9]

The marketing monopoly of the KNPA was transferred to the KNCU and led in 1937 to a revolt among the members against the Union.[10] The coffee prices were low, due to the Depression, but the growers held the Union responsible for the decline in prices. "In their eyes the co-operative society was more a government institution—the management was put in by the government (the manager of the KNCU was a European)—than a self-help organisation . . .". The revolt was suppressed by the government, but the marketing monopoly of the KNCU was formally repealed. In October of the same year an *Ordinance to make provision for the control of the native coffee industry and the marketing of the products thereof* was enacted. The Ordinance gave the Governor powers to establish native coffee boards in any district of Tanzania. One of the powers given to such native coffee boards was ". . . to order that all producers of native coffee in the area specified in the order shall sell such coffee to the Board or through such agency as the Board may direct ..."[11] In November 1937 the Moshi *Native Coffee Board* was established and the board appointed the KNCU to be its agent for the purchase of coffee from the growers. The Moshi Native Coffee Board was later dissolved and its functions taken over by the KNCU. In 1962, the Tanganyika Coffee Board was established, and since then has arranged for the sales of coffee at auctions in Moshi.

The growth of the KNCU has been very spectacular. In 1935, around 22,000 producers with an estimated total acreage of 9,380 acres under coffee, sold through the KNCU 1.5 million tons of coffee. By 1961, the number of producers had increased to 50,000, who cultivated 34,000 acres and sold a total of 7.4 million tons of coffee. Coffee is an important cash-crop, not only to the Wachagga but also to the nation. The relative importance of coffee has declined somewhat over the last few years as a result of the decline in the world market prices, but even in the 1960's, the export of coffee accounted for between 10 and 20 per cent of the total value of domestic exports. Of the total output of coffee, between 20 and 30 per cent is marketed through the KNCU (coffee produced on estates accounted for around 25 per cent of total production, coffee marketed through the Bukoba Co-operative Union for between 25 and 30 per cent, and the balance was marketed through other co-operative societies than the two mentioned).

The KNCU has engaged in other activities than those relating to the marketing of coffee and the supply of farm inputs. In a pamphlet issued by the KNCU on Independence Day in 1961 one can read:

The Union has its own printing press which produces some fine books, and in its new headquarters there is a handsomely equipped library with 6,000 books. The building also (contains a hotel with) .. well-equipped bedrooms ... a restaurant, a laundry and 14 fine shops ... The KNCU is spending considerable sums in promoting education. These sums are willingly subscribed by the members, who recognise the need for further education. Some years ago the Union built a Middle School and this was followed by the College of Commerce; and there is now in the course of construction a Secondary School which will be completed next year at a cost of over £100,000 ...[12]

The KNCU is the pioneer of the co-operative movement in Tanzania, but other co-operatives grew up to equally impressive positions, especially in the years after the second world war, when the colonial regime actively promoted the establishment of new co-operatives. The interest of the administration in encouraging the co-operative movement was expressed in the appointment, in 1951, of a Commissioner for Co-operative Development. The function of the Commissioner is to make active attempts to foster and promote the co-operative movement, as distinct from the Registrar's merely legal function of registration, audit and financial supervision. In practice the functions overlap, so much the more as the offices of the Registrar and of the Commissioner have, since the first appointment of a Commissioner in 1951, been vested in one and the same person.

By 1940 there were only 40 co-operative societies registered in all Tanzania, including a few Indian and one European society. By 1952 the number of registered societies was 172 and in 1961, the year of Independence, the number was 857. The two most important registrations took place in 1950 and 1953. In 1950, the Bukoba Co-operative Union (BCU) and 48 affiliated primary societies were registered (there are to-day 73 primary societies affiliated to the BCU). The main crop handled by the BCU is coffee. In 1953, the first unions, which in 1955 joined together in the Victoria Federation of Co-operative Unions (VFCU), were registered. The main crop handled by the VFCU is cotton. In 1959, the VFCU was appointed the sole agent in the Lake District of the Lint and Seed Marketing Board, which was established in 1952. By the end of 1960, the VFCU comprised 19 secondary societies (unions) and 360 primary societies. Other important registrations were of co-operatives handling coffee and tobacco in the Southern Highlands.

On the eve of Independence a total of 34 co-operative unions were registered (of which 19 were grouped together in the VFCU). The unions and their affiliated societies were typically based on the marketing of cash crops for export and confined to those parts of Tanzania where these cash-crops, especially coffee, cotton and tobacco, were grown. Like the

KNCU, the other co-operatives engaged in other activities than those relating to marketing and the supply of farm inputs, and the co-operatives became to an increasing degree involved in the political struggle for Independence.

The Development of the Co-operative Movement after Independence

At independence, the co-operative movement was very popular with the political leadership of the country. In the foreword to a booklet on *The Co-operative Movement in Tanganyika,* published in 1961, the Minister for Agriculture, Mr. P. Bomani, who had been the General Manager of the VFCU in 1955–60 said:

The coming of independence and the birth of a nation was thought to be a most appropriate time to record the history of the Co-operative Movement in Tanganyika. On this happy occasion I would like to acknowledge the part played by the Co-operative Movement in the struggle for the liberation of our country—a part which will go down in the annals of Tanganyika's history. In the moulding of our people into a nation, the Co-operative Movement has had and will continue to have a most important role to play. Already it has paved the way for our peasant farmers, who form the majority of our population, to take their rightful place in the nation's economy. It has been a school for democracy, a spearhead in the war against poverty, ignorance and disease, and I am sure it will be one of the principal pillars in the future of our new nation ...[13]

The co-operative form was seen as being "well suited to the African setting and to the achievement of independence in the economic sense: control of the economy by the indigenous people rather than by expatriates and others non-African in origin".[14] The government embarked upon an urgent programme for organising co-operatives in those parts of the country which had until then been largely untouched by the movement, and the number of registered societies rose dramatically from 857 in 1961 to 1,362 in 1964 and 1,518 in 1965. In 1969 there was a total of 1,737 registered societies.

In 1962, an *Agricultural Products (Control and Marketing)*

Act was passed by Parliament, which gave the Minister powers to establish marketing boards which would have exclusive rights to market scheduled crops and rights to appoint agents. The most important of the marketing boards established under this act is the National Agricultural Products Board (NAPB), which started operations in 1963. The crops handled by the NAPB are maize, cashew-nuts, paddy, groundnuts, sunflower seeds, simsim, copra, cassava and a few others, all of which are relatively low-value crops, compared with the "traditional" cash-crops, coffee, cotton and tobacco, and most of which had not been handled by co-operatives before the establishment of the NAPB, but rather by private traders, in so far as they were marketed at all. The NAPB appointed co-operative unions and their affiliated primary societies as its agents. Where the crops mentioned were grown, but no co-operative societies existed, such societies were hastily established. The power of the Registrar to refuse registration of a society if he was not satisfied as to its viability was not used; co-operatives were organised from "on top" under considerable political pressure.

The rapid increase in the number of co-operative societies was not without its problems. The enthusiasm of the first few years after Independence gave way to criticisms. There were complaints of inefficiency in the management of the societies and cases of misuse of funds and corrupt practices were reported. In January 1966, the President appointed a *Special Committee of Enquiry into the Co-operative Movement and Marketing Boards* with the following terms of reference:

> To review the staffing and, where necessary, the organizational structure of the Co-operative Movement and Marketing Boards in order to recommend what steps should be taken to strengthen them for the maximum benefit of producers and consumers alike.

The Special Committee reported in June 1966 and later the same year, the government published a response to the report of the Special Committee.[15]

The Special Committee found that the general structure of the agricultural co-operative movement was sound,[16] and that the defects of the co-operatives were problems of growth. The Committee listed five basic defects:

(1) *Uninformed membership*

There are a great many societies whose members are uninformed about the nature of co-operatives, how they are supposed to function, the duties of the Committee of the society and the powers and responsibilities of the members assembled in the general meeting. Even less is understood about the relation between the Union and the various marketing boards and between each layer and the government. The whole structure thus rests, in many places, on a weak foundation; without an informed membership co-operatives cannot function soundly.

(2) *Shortage of appropriate manpower*[17]

... There are two aspects of the shortage of appropriate manpower, although they are interrelated: dishonest employees and inadequately trained employees ... The common thread in the manpower situation is the fact that the employees of co-operatives do not adequately regard themselves as a professional group, with ethical standards to live up to, with career possibilities and with opportunities for growth into situations of greater responsibility. On the contrary, they generally feel that they are at the mercy of uninformed and sometimes corrupt committee-men, who have the unrestrained power to employ, fix the terms of service, and discharge all employees of the co-operatives. At times the roles are reversed and a too-clever employee feels free to run the committee, playing on his literacy and greater knowledge, and secure against control by others.

(3) *Lack of democracy at union level*

... In a great many instances the farmer does not regard the union as belonging to him. Often it is thought of as an arm of the government. ...
The Committee recommended that there should be direct election of union committee-men by the farmers.

(4) *Lack of skilled people in the movement with specialist knowledge*

(5) *Susceptibility of the movement to political interference*

... We have already mentioned the political decision to accelerate the growth of the co-operatives; this decision, however sound in intent, has been misinterpreted so as to justify exaggerated demands for the premature registration of societies, a root cause of the present problems ...

The Special Committee made two major recommendations. It proposed the creation of a *Unified Co-operative Service,* which would be responsible for the engagement, discipline, terms of service and dismissal of all employees of registered societies. The engagement and dismissal of employees would thus be removed from the legal control of the committees of the co-operatives. At the same time it was recommended that the upgrading of existing personnel and training of new personnel should be accelerated. The other major recommendation of the Special Committee was that as a temporary measure —until the Unified Co-operative Service became effective— the Registrar should be given emergency powers to terminate the employment of any person appointed by the committee of a society to administer and manage the affairs of the society, if the Registrar was of the opinion that such a person was not performing his functions satisfactorily.[18]

In its response to the Special Committee's report, the government endorsed the five basic defects listed by the Committee with the exception of No. 3—lack of democracy at union level. The government saw nothing basically undemocratic in the procedure of electing union committee-men from delegates from primary societies, who were themselves democratically elected. With respect to the fifth defect—political interference —the government remarked that:

... it must be agreed that by their very nature and by the role they play in the economy of the country, the co-operatives cannot be isolated from political life and must therefore be subject, from time to time, to political considerations. The term "political interference", however, requires to be defined, as many instances of such "interference" have proved to be completely beneficial, while others have proved to be equally disastrous ... As it is government policy to employ the economic arm of co-operation to achieve the political aim of socialism, it is inevitable and also necessary that the two should meet and overlap from time to time ...

131

The two major recommendations of the Special Committee were accepted by the government and incorporated in subsequent legislation. The *Unified Co-operative Service Act of 1968* follows the proposals of the Committee, except that the Act only refers to national and secondary societies, not to primary societies (at least not for the time being). In the new *Co-operative Societies Act of 1968*, the Registrar was given powers as recommended, except that they were made permanent. Already in 1966, however, the Minister used his powers under the Co-operative Societies Ordinance of 1963 to dissolve the committees of 16 of the weakest co-operative unions and their affiliated primary societies (about 400). The supervision of the management of these societies was taken over by government personnel (regional and district co-operative officers). In most of these societies, new committees have now been elected.

The Special Committee believed that the performance of society secretaries and perhaps of union managers could be considerably improved if they were given an incentive to run the societies with maximum efficiency, and therefore proposed that a system of incentive payments to employees of co-operatives should be established. This was accepted by the government and the Co-operative Societies Act now expressedly allows the use of the annual net surplus—or part of it—to staff incentive bonus schemes, whereas the old Ordinance was tacit on this point. I shall later discuss the remarks of the Special Committee with respect to the relationship between the co-operatives and the marketing boards.

As a means of strengthening the co-operative movement, an agreement was signed in 1968 between the Government of Tanzania and the Governments of Sweden and Denmark on technical assistance to co-operatives in Tanzania. Under this agreement the two Nordic countries make available an assistant regional co-operative officer in each of the 17 regions in Tanzania, plus teachers at the Co-operative College, plus some staff in the co-operative headquarters in Dar-es-Salaam. Another part of this agreement concerns the financing of the Co-operative Education Centre (CEG). The activities of the Centre are now financed partly by the Co-operative Union of Tanganyika (CUT), partly by the Nordic governments. The CUT is to take over all the financing by 1972. The CEC was established in 1964 by an agreement between the Government of Tanzania, on behalf of the CUT and the Tanzania Nordic Co-operative Consortium, representing national co-operative organisations in Denmark, Finland, Norway and Sweden. This agreement has been superseded by the new agreement of 1968, which expires in 1971.

The Present Co-operative Set-up

As at 1st January 1970 there were a total of 1,737 registered co-operative societies. Of these, there were national organisations: the Co-operative Union of Tanganyika, established in 1961 as the apex organisation of the co-operative movement; the Savings and Credit Union League, established in 1964 as an apex organisation for the credit and savings societies, which are also affiliated to the Co-operative Union of Tanganyika; and the Co-operative Supply Association of Tanganyika (COSATA). The COSATA was established in 1962 as a wholesale supplier to consumers' co-operatives, but soon ran into trouble. The functions of the COSATA have now been taken over by the State Trading Corporation, and the COSATA now esists only as a name.

There are 1,369 societies, the main functions of which are to provide marketing facilities. Twenty-nine of the societies are unions (secondary societies) and 1,340 are primary societies affiliated to any of the unions (447 of the primary societies are affiliated to the Nyanza Co-operative Union). There are 44 consumers' societies (corresponding to 3 per cent of all registered societies) and 233 savings and credit societies (13 per cent of total).

Eighty-eight primary societies (5 per cent of the total) are not affiliated to any of the secondary societies; they are more or less active in a variety of trades, such as the tailors' or carpenters' societies, charcoal societies, transport societies, etc. In the following description of the present co-operative set-up I shall confine myself to the marketing societies, which account for 79 per cent of all registered societies.

The Functioning of the Marketing Co-operatives

The marketing system. In order to understand the functioning of the marketing co-operatives, it is necessary to understand the marketing system as such. The agricultural marketing system is typically organised as a pyramidal three-tier system, with the primary societies at the bottom, secondary societies in the middle and a marketing board at the top. The marketing function of a primary society is to buy produce from the farmers and store it until it can be transported to the premises of the marketing board. The co-operative unions do not handle produce in a physical sense but are essentially service organisations for primary societies. The unions' marketing responsibilities are typically to organise transport of the produce from the societies' stores to the godown of the marketing board; to provide the societies with gunnybags and with crop finance; to have the crop and cash insured and to collect money from the marketing board on behalf of the primary societies.

The marketing boards. There are all together 12 marketing boards in Tanzania. Some of them have very limited functions and do not themselves market the crops under their jurisdiction. The most important marketing boards, as far as the co-operatives are concerned, are the Lint and Seed Marketing Board (LSMB), established in 1952; the Tanganyika Coffee Board (TCB), established in 1962, and the National Agricultural Products Board (NAPB), established in 1962. There is a fundamental difference between the TCB, on the one hand, and the two other boards, on the other. The TCB is an agent of the coffee co-operatives (and of the Tanganyika Coffee Growers Association, a society whose members are coffee-estate owners). The board sells, at auctions, the coffee on behalf of the co-operatives and the proceeds are passed back to the co-operative societies. When the growers deliver their coffee, they receive 75 per cent of the estimated sales price at the auctions minus various deductions. The total price will depend on the actual sales prices at the auctions, i.e. the growers are directly exposed to the conditions on the world market for coffee.

In contrast to the TCB, the LSMB and the NAPB are owners of the produce once it has arrived at their premises and has been paid for. The growers are paid only once, at the time they deliver their produce to the primary societies and the co-operatives are paid only once by the boards. The co-operatives are the agents of the boards, not the other way round. The growers are thus not directly exposed to the fluctuations of the market in any given year, which only has an impact on the trading surpluses or deficits of the marketing boards. The two boards operate price-assistance funds, which are intended to smooth out fluctuations in the growers' prices, which over the years are supposed to follow the price trend in the free market.

In the early years of its existence, the LSMB accumulated large surpluses, which were put into the price-assistance fund. At 1959 the balance was over 105 million shs. During the 1960's the price-assistance fund was brought down to a balance of 37 million shs in 1968. At the end of the financial year 1968–69, the NAPB had total (estimated) trading reserves of 55 million shs, of which 36 million shs were in the Cashew-nut Export Trading Equalization Fund. In addition to the trading reserves, the NAPB had a general reserve (estimated) of 24 million shs. The NAPB took over from its predecessor in the southern regions, the Southern Region Cashew-nut Board, net assets worth 5 million shs, which had been accumulated in the 1962–63 and 1963–64 seasons.

The price-fixing procedure. The growers' prices, i.e. the prices which are paid to the growers when they deliver produce to the primary societies, are announced in advance of each season. (In the case of coffee it is the advance payment which is announced.) In principle, the growers' prices are calculated by subtracting from the estimated sales prices the estimated marketing costs and other deductions, regard being paid to the position of the price-assistance fund (if any).

Coffee handled by the KNCU. In the case of the 43 primary societies affiliated to the KNCU, each society makes its own deductions to cover the estimated costs of the society and deductions for other purposes, such as appropriations to an education fund. The deductions must be approved by the

135

Registrar of Co-operative Societies. As a consequence of differences in the quality of the coffee and hence in the final sales price, and as a consequence of differences in costs and non-marketing deductions, the total price received by members of the KNCU societies may differ from society to society.

Cotton handled by the LSMB.[19] The prices paid for cotton by the primary societies are the same (for the same grade) all over Tanzania in any given year. The primary societies and the unions receive fixed levies to cover their costs of marketing cotton. Since the 1966–67 season, the society levies have been on a sliding scale, based on the turnover of the society. It is the responsibility of the LSMB to recommend to the Minister the prices to be paid to cotton farmers in the forthcoming season. After review and possibly modifications, these recommendations are sent to the Economic Committee of the Cabinet for review and approval.

Cashew-nuts handled by the NAPB.[20] In the case of cashew-nuts, the main crop handled by the NAPB, the growers' prices were originally calculated in two steps: the NAPB sould first calculate the into-store prices, i.e. the prices which would be paid by the NAPB to the co-operatives on delivery to the NAPB godowns. Then the co-operatives would calculated the growers' prices by subtracting from the NAPB into-store prices the co-operatives' marketing costs and other deductions. Since the marketing costs varied as between districts, there would be a number of different growers' prices. In 1968 it was decided that with effect from the 1968–69 season, the growers' prices for cashew-nuts would be the same all over Tanzania (for the same grade), and the price-fixing procedure is therefore now similar to the one for cotton.

Other Functions than Marketing

The main function of a marketing society is to provide marketing services, but most societies are engaged in other economic activities as well. The typical subsidiary activities are the supply of fertilizer and insecticides and other farm inputs to the farmers and the channelling of agricultural credit from the National Development Credit Agency (NDCA) to the farmers. Besides these activities, which are to some extent connected with the basic marketing function, some unions have in recent years gone into wholesale distribution. The unions have been granted selling monopolies in their respective regions for the commodities distributed by them.

An Illustration: The Marketing Margin for Cashew-nuts

I said above that the growers' prices are, in principle, calculated by subtracting various deductions from the sales prices. These deductions are of two kinds: deductions relating to the marketing activities of the marketing organisations and deductions which are not related to the marketing activities. These non-marketing deductions can be regarded as taxes imposed upon the growers through the marketing system—some of the non-marketing deductions are indeed directly identifiable as taxes. The marketing margin, i.e. the difference between the final sales price and the growers' price, thus consists of a variety of deductions. I shall illustrate this by considering the marketing margin for cashew-nuts. It should also be mentioned that in all the co-operative unions there is an education secretary whose job it is to organise and carry out co-operative education for staff, committees and members.

I shall look at the marketing margin in 1967–68 and 1968–69 for cashew-nuts produced in the Coast Region, which is the second most important region as far as cashew-nut production is concerned. The composition of the marketing margin is shown in the table on page 138. The calculation of the figures is based on a number of assumptions and is partly based on (estimated) historical costs and deductions and partly on deductions made before the season to cover estimated costs. We need not bother with this here.[21]

In 1968–69, the NAPB's actual average sales price for cashew-nuts from the Coast Region was 1,235 shs per ton (see the second column in the table). Part of the sales of the NAPB

The marketing margin for cashew-nuts from the Coast Region in 1967–68 and 1968–69 (shs. per ton purchased by the NAPB).

	1967/68		1968/69	
NAPB actual sales price		812		1 235
Subsidy to local processing industry		48		35
NAPB potential sales price		860		1 270
Growers' price		700		736
Marketing margin		160		534
Marketing deductions:				
NAPB costs	47		61	
Co-operatives' deductions	197	244	215	276
Non-marketing deductions:				
Subsidy to local processing industry	48		35	
Export tax	16		42	
District Council cess	35		37	
NAPB surplus	− 213		144	
Union's tractor levy	10		−	
Co-operatives' special levy	20	− 84	−	258
Marketing margin		160		434

Source: **cf. ref. 21.**

was to the local processing industry at subsidized prices below the world-market prices. The subsidy amounted to 35 shs per ton of cashew-nuts purchased by the NAPB. If the NAPB had sold all cashew-nuts at world-market prices, it would have obtained an average price of 1,270 shs per ton, which was the NAPB's *potential* sales price in 1968–69. The growers received on the average 736 shs per ton; the marketing margin was therefore 534 shs per ton. The deductions for marketing costs amounted to 276 shs per ton. 258 shs per ton was deducted for non-marketing purposes, as specified in the table.

The growers actually received 736 shs per ton of cashew-nuts in the 1968–69 season. It would however, have been possible to pay the growers more than that without the marketing organisations suffering any loss, if only the marketing costs and not the non-marketing deductions had to be covered by the marketing margin. The non-marketing deductions are, as I have already pointed out, taxes. The sum of the actual growers' price and the total tax burden can be called the *potential* growers' price. The potential growers' price was 994 shs per ton in 1968–69. The tax incidence, i.e. the tax burden expressed as a percentage of the potential growers' price, was 26 per cent in the 1968–69 season.

In the 1967–68 season, the actual growers' price was 700 shs per ton (see the first column in the table). The potential growers' price was 616 shs and less than the actual growers' price. The growers thus received a subsidy in the 1967–68 season which amounted to 14 per cent of the potential growers' price. It will be seen that the cost of this subsidy was "borne" by the NAPB, which had a deficit on the Coast Region crop in 1967–68 of 213 shs per ton. This deficit was matched by a similar surplus on the crop from Mtwara Region and the NAPB almost broke even on the total trade in cashew-nuts in 1967–68. The surplus of the NAPB in 1968–69 on the Coast Region crop (and a surplus on the Mtwara Region crop) was carried over to the Cashew-nut Export Trading Equalization Fund after allocations had been made to the NAPB's general reserve.

It should finally be mentioned that with effect from June 1969 the District Councils no longer collect produce cesses. This decision was made in connection with a general shift of the tax burden from rural areas to urban areas (at the same time a sales tax was introduced, the incidence of which is higher in urban areas than in rural areas).

Future Tasks of the Co-operative Movement

When Tanzania became independent in 1961, the political philosophy adopted was one of "African Socialism", a phrase used by so many countries of different political outlooks that it has become virtually meaningless. This phrase had, however, some real content in Tanzania, as far as the agricultural marketing system was concerned. We have seen how the private traders were squeezed out of the marketing system by giving (indirectly) monopolies to the co-operatives. But it was not until 1967, the year of the Arusha Declaration, that Tanzania started to follow a general policy which was socialist not only in name but also in substance. Important sectors were nationalized and at the same time the emphasis was placed on rural development, which had to some extent been neglected in favour of urban, industrial development. I do not intend to review the new policy of *Socialism and Self-Reliance* but would only refer to the two policy documents of most relevance to the co-operative movement: *Government Paper No. 4 of 1967* (1) and *Socialism and Rural Development.*[14]

The co-operative movement is supposed to play a major role in the economic development of Tanzania. This role is best described by quoting from *The Second Five-Year Plan 1969– 74,* which was published in 1969. In chapter III (on the rural sector) one may read:

A central part in the development of rural socialism in Tanzania must be played by the co-operative movement; for it to fill a progressive role, however, it must be revolutionized. Two changes are required: (1) the societies must become production-oriented ... (2) the increased democratic participation of the membership in the control of all co-operative activities.

The last paragraph in the section on co-operative development reads:

In summary, the second five-year plan will represent a transitional period during which the traditional marketing functions of the co-operatives will be made more efficient, for the benefit of the farmer, while new growth will be shifted sharply in the direction of production and multi-purpose societies ...

A Discussion of Some Issues Arising from the Previous Sections

"The co-operative movement ... must be made more efficient, both in management and in its democratic machinery." This quotation from the policy document *Socialism and Rural De-*

velopment by the President, Mwalimu J. K. Nyerere, sums up two main points arising from the previous sections and will be taken as the starting-point of the following discussion. First, I should, however, indicate the limits of the discussion. There are two types of co-operatives which are of special relevance to the rural development of Tanzania: marketing co-operatives and *ujamaa* villages.

One of the themes I want to discuss is the problem of democracy in the co-operative movement. It is maintained that this problem—as well as the problem of efficiency—is substantially different in an *ujamaa* village and in a marketing society, simply because of the differences in the scale of operation, including the geographical distance between the members of each of the two types of co-operative organisations. The problem of democracy in an *ujamaa* village may be more suited for a sociological analysis than for an economic one.

There are two aspects of the problem of democracy in the co-operative movement: one with respect to the relationship between the management of co-operatives and the members and the other with respect to the relationship between the co-operative movement, as such, and the government. The two problems are, of course, interrelated. I shall deal mostly —but not only—with the second aspect.

The main interest in this section is to discuss the "rules of the game" with respect to the autonomy of the co-operative movement *vis-à-vis* the government. The first aspect mentioned above has been dealt with by others during this seminar.

Two Main Problems: Democracy and Efficiency

It should be clear from the previous sections—and it is well expressed in the above quotation—that the co-operative movement in Tanzania faces two major problems: efficiency in management and efficiency in its democratic machinery. I shall first discuss these two problems under separate headings. The problems are interrelated and I shall therefore in a following sub-section discuss the two problems together. First of all, I would, however, like to point out that Tanzania is far from being the only country facing these two major problems. Indeed, it is probably true to say that the two problems are faced by all co-operative movements all over the world. They have been the subject of many discussions under the auspices of the International Co-operative Alliance (ICA) and I shall attempt to link the discussion to that which has been carried on under the auspices of the ICA.

Problems of democracy. It is appropriate, first of all, to ask ourselves what is meant by democracy in a co-operative movement? We may rephrase this question by asking: what are the co-operative principles?

At the 1963 congress of the ICA, it was decided to set up a Commission on Co-operative Principles, the terms of reference of which were to make a review of the present relevance of the "Rochdale Co-operative Principles", as they had been defined by the ICA congress in 1937, and to recommend—if deemed necessary—a new text or texts. The Commission reported at the 1966 congress (in which Tanzania participated). Its report and recommended re-formulations of the co-operative principles was adopted by the congress by show of hands by an overwhelming majority. There are six "new" principles. The most important principle in the context of this paper is No. 2, which reads:

Co-operative societies are democratic organisations. Their affairs should be administered by persons elected or appointed in a manner agreed by the members and accountable to them. Members of primary societies should enjoy equal rights of voting (one member, one vote) and participation in decisions affecting the societies ...

In the comments on the second principle the Commission discussed the two aspects of the "democracy problem", the relationship between management and members and the relationship between the movement and the government. With respect to the latter, it was stated that:

There is no doubt in the minds of the Commission that democracy in the management of co-operative organisations necessarily implies autonomy in the sense of independence of external control, apart from the obvious obligation of co-operative societies to bow to the same general laws as all other business undertakings and accept the discipline imposed by the State or the planning authorities. In a fully developed co-operative unit the management must rest in the hands of the members and all decisions be taken by the co-operators themselves, with no external interference. Autonomy is therefore a corollary of democracy.

The Commission admitted, however, that in a number of developing countries the co-operative movement may need some government help and that therefore the government has a legitimate right to exercise a certain control over the co-operative movement.

It must be admitted that the present system gives the co-operatives in Tanzania a rather limited influence on their own affairs. The dilemma of the Tanzanian leadership can be stated in something like a paradox: because the government has been dissatisfied with the democratic content of the co-operative movement (i.e. the relationship between the management and the members)—and with the economic efficiency of co-operatives—it has interfered so much with the autonomy of the co-operatives that their democratic content—which is desirable—has been severely limited. The dilemma, from the point of view of the co-operative movement, can be expressed in a paraphrase (with opposite sign) of some lines in a Danish music-hall song: "He has my sympathy, but he has nothing to have it in". The government wants us to be democratic, but we have been left with very little to be democratic about.

I shall now *first* attempt to show that, even within the present framework, it seems possible to give more meaning to what is left of the autonomy of the co-operatives. I shall argue that, though the present *external* rules of the game—i.e. the law and the institutional framework—are not preventing this autonomy from being exercised, the present "*internal* rules of the game"—i.e. the practice followed by the co-operatives—are not such as to encourage the exercise of autonomy. *Secondly,* I shall discuss the—very controversial—issue of the relationship between the co-operative movement and the marketing boards. I shall argue that it does seem possible to formulate the "external rules of the game" in such a way that both the government and the co-operatives will be satisfied.

Democracy under the present system. If we think of a primary society handling cashew-nuts or cotton, we find that both the levies (the incomes of the societies) and the growers' prices (the most important "cost element") are determined externally and are outside the influence of the committee or the management. But still the society is left with something which is under the influence of the management and hence the management committee and hence the members who elect the committee. The handling and administration costs and the cost of shrinkage of produce are—as I shall point out later—to a certain extent determined by the efficiency of the management. The surplus of a society is the difference between the income and the cost. If the cost can be kept down, the surplus will be greater than it would otherwise be.

There is, however very little in the present "internal rules of the game" which focusses attention on this piece of autonomy. I shall return to this subject later when I discuss the dual problem of democracy and efficiency.

Democracy is not only a question of having something to be democratic about. It is also a question of information. Information may not give the members of co-operatives more real power, but it may increase their understanding of the marketing system and may therefore satisfy their criticisms or, at least, direct their misgivings into the relevant channels for complaints. A frequent complaint of co-operators relates to the surpluses of the marketing boards, especially the NAPB. Co-operators are aware of these surpluses (but less aware of the deficits)[22] and feel that the marketing boards are exploiting the co-operatives. They maintain that the trading surpluses belong to the growers and blame the marketing boards for keeping these surpluses.

The relevant information here is to explain (1) how the price-assistance funds of the boards are supposed to operate (2) that it is Parliament, not the marketing boards, which should be blamed if any institutions are to be blamed at all, and (3) that if the farmers want to complain about the marketing policy of the government, there are democratic channels for lodging such complaints.

The co-operative movement and the marketing boards. The

144

terms of reference of the Presidential Special Committee of Enquiry were to look into not only the co-operative movement but also the marketing boards. I shall here refer to those parts of the Special Committee's report which dealt with the relationship between the co-operative movement and the marketing boards.

The Committee observed that the many marketing boards are of different types and that therefore it is difficult to generalize about them. One function which most of the boards have in common is that they arrange for the final sale of the crop or of the crop after primary processing. The manner of sale differs because the markets are different and it is therefore necessary to employ knowledgeable people in the marketing of the various crops. But "it does not follow that one needs independent boards. The specialists could as well be employed by a co-operative".

The Committee argued for and against the price-assistance funds. It admitted that it could be argued that the price-assistance funds perform the valuable function of accumulating capital. The Committee, however stated in paragraph 216:

In any case, however, the funds are invested, there is no special reason why the function of capital accumulation cannot be performed by deliberate decision of the co-operatives, rather than incidentally and covertly by the boards ... if this function is performed within the co-operative movement the farmers will tend to have the feeling, and quite legitimately, that the capital is theirs, whereas the fund in the hands of an independent board is not the farmer's property, and is even beyond his effective influence.

The Committee remarked, however that:

Although, as we have seen, there is no inherent reason why the functions of the boards could not be performed by co-operatives, it does not follow that this must now be done. So much of the national income, and especially the foreign exchange of Tanzania, is derived from the sale on world markets of Tanzania's agricultural products that there is an over-riding governmental interest in the operation ...

These remarks of the Committee were accepted by the government, which added:

... The stage at which some, or all, of the present functions of boards could be passed to and undertaken by co-operatives will depend on the progress made in the implementation of the Committee's other proposals regarding the improvement of the functioning of co-operatives and the merging of some, or all, marketing boards. The overriding interest of Government in the proper and efficient conduct of marketing is stressed.

It seems to be implied both in the report of the Special Committee and in the government paper that there are only two alternatives with respect to the relationship between the co-operatives and the marketing boards: *either* the present system *or* a system in which the functions of the marketing boards are completely and solely under the control of the co-operative movement. It seems, however, that there is a third alternative, in which the functions of the marketing boards would be undertaken by co-operatives but under the overall control of the government. The government's overriding interest in the proper and efficient conduct of marketing is acknowledged.

For the reasons expressed in the second part of the quotation from paragraph 216 in the Committee's report (see above), it seems desirable to pass the functions and responsibilities of the boards to the co-operative movement. The relationship between the Committees of the marketing boards—which would then be owned by the co-operatives—and the government could be regulated according to sections 109 and 110 of the Co-operative Societies Act of 1968. The relevant parts of these sections read:

... The Registrar may ... appoint special members to the committee of any registered society if such society is in receipt of financial assistance from the Government or if the Registrar considers such appointments to be necessary in the public interest ... A special member of a committee ... shall remain a member of the committee until his appointment is determined by the Registrar. Where the Registrar has appointed special members to a committee, any such member may require that any decision taken by such committee shall not have effects until the approval of the Registrar has been obtained and, where any such requirement is made in respect of any such decision, the decision shall be of no force or effect and shall not in any way be acted upon until the Registrar has signified his approval thereof.

There seem to be at least two great advantages in having the functions of the present marketing boards exercised by the co-operative movement (under the overall control of government). One is that much of the non-constructive dissatisfaction of co-operators would die away. The other is that having these functions exercised by co-operatives, which are directly responsible to the farmers rather than to persons who are essentially civil servants, might increase the efficiency of the boards, because there would—or at least could—be a strong popular pressure on the management. I am not saying that a take-over would automatically make the boards more efficient[23] but it seems that by a take-over the "external rules of the game" would be formulated in such a way that there could be a much stronger pressure on the boards for efficiency than at present.

Efficiency of co-operative societies. In a competitive economy, in which co-operatives compete with private traders, the efficiency of the co-operatives may be judged by whether they succeed in surviving or not and, if they do, by the surplus they realise, regard being given to the services rendered to the members, including the growers' prices. Under a compulsory one-channel marketing system, as in Tanzania, no competition exists and the efficiency of the co-operatives can therefore not be judged by whether they survive or not, as in a competitive regime. The efficiency of any one marketing organisation can be judged, however, if there are many other organisations in similar conditions. The performance of one primary society can be compared with the performance of other societies with similar turnovers and similar locations and if it is seen that there are differences in performance (measured by, e.g., the cost level), it can be concluded that there are differences in efficiency.

Quite a few comparative studies of the marketing costs of primary societies have been made in Tanzania in recent years[24] and they do confirm that there seem to be differences in the economic performance of co-operatives which can only be explained by differences in the efficiency of the management.

147

It it is believed that differences in marketing costs can be attributed to differences in management efficiency, the question then arises how the economic performance of the badly managed societies can be improved. In those cases in which inefficient management is due to lack of skills and training, education is clearly one of the ways to improve the situation. This is, of course, realised and the Co-operative College and the Co-operative Education Centre in Moshi are running extensive educational programmes.[25] Another way of helping to keep the costs down is to increase supervision and control by co-operative inspectors and this way is also being followed at present. A third way in which management efficiency could be improved would be to introduce incentives for the management. This is, of course, not an alternative to the two other methods but rather a supplementary measure. We have seen that the Presidential Special Committee of Enquiry recommended the introduction of incentive payments to employees of the co-operative societies. The recommendation was accepted by government and section 56 of the Co-operative Societies Act now explicitly allows such payments to be made.

An effective incentive system would relate the incentive payments directly to the economic performance of the societies. Rather than a fixed sum of money payable under certain conditions, the incentive payments to the management should be a certain percentage of the annual net surplus. (This percentage may vary with the size of the surplus: the higher the surplus the lower the percentage. By such a system the bonuses would not be excessive, but the incentive to reduce the costs as much as possible would still be effective.) Any specific incentive system should take into consideration the specific conditions of the society and should exclude from the formula factors over which the employees have little control, such as the size of the co-operative and freight rates.

Incentives need not only be a question of money. Incentives could also be of a "moral" nature and it seems that it would be relevant to study the systems of "moral incentives" in other socialist countries.

Democracy and efficiency. I have stated earlier that the co-operative movement in Tanzania is far from alone in facing the problems of efficiency and democracy. Also these problems have been discussed under the auspices of the ICA. In his inaugural address to the 1966 congress, the President of the ICA stated:

Co-operation is at one and the same time a commercial enterprise and a democratically controlled popular movement. It has, therefore, to meet a double requirement. Firstly, it must represent the highest economic efficiency in an competitive economic setting. But, secondly, it must also maintain its character of a democratically controlled self-help movement, for and by and through the people. The double task of fulfilling these two main criteria has certainly confronted co-operative organisations in practically all countries with problems which are both formidable and urgent.[26]

The problem—as stated above—is that, if a co-operative movement is too democratic, it may be too inefficient as a commercial enterprise and may therefore not be able to survive in a "competitive economic setting". If a co-operative is to survive the competition, it must be very efficient, but, if it is so, the risk is that it may lose some of its democratic content, as expressed in the second ("new") co-operative principle (on democratic administration).

The way the dual problem of democracy and efficiency is stated above is, however, not relevant in the Tanzanian case and this is, of course, due to the fact that the above statement refers to a "competitive economic setting", while co-operatives in Tanzania have a monopoly position (this is, of course, only true with respect to the marketing societies). One could actually make the point that a co-operative society in Tanzania *could* be both undemocratic *and* inefficient and still survive, because the survival is guaranteed by the institutional framework within which the co-operative operates.

The problems of democracy and efficiency, as stated by the ICA, are interrelated and the same problems are faced by Tanzania, but—it seems—in a more fortunate way than in a competitive economy. I have already quoted the Presidential Special Committee, which pointed out that without an informed membership co-operatives cannot function soundly and I have also pointed out that an important aspect of democracy is information. Growers to-day complain about low prices (as

149

growers have probably always complained in any country). Why is the government taxing us by collecting an export tax? Why did the NAPB have a surplus on cashew-nuts in 1968–69? (They seldom ask why the NAPB had a deficit on the Coast Region crop in 1967–68.) These things should be explained to them and they should be told that there is nothing they can do about, e.g., getting rid of the export tax, except by lodging their complaints through the democratic channels open to them. They should also be told, however, that, if they really want to get more money from the co-operative society, there *is* one way of getting it which is to some extent under their influence and that is a lowering of the handling and administration costs of their society and hence an increase in the surplus. It should be demonstrated to them that there are some societies which are apparently managed less efficiently than they could be, judging from the performance of other similar societies. It should be suggested to them that they could decide to pay the management incentive bonuses out of the annual surplus as a means of lowering the costs of the society.

By linking the incentive bonuses directly to the surplus, there would be a built-in mechanism which—one hopes—would increase the understanding of the members of "the nature of co-operatives, how they are supposed to function, the duties of the committee of the society and the powers and responsibility of the members in the general meeting" —to repeat a quotation from the report of the Presidential Special Committee.

It seems that with proper information, as indicated above, the members would at one and the same time be given a better understanding of how the system works *and*—by focussing their attention on those elements of the marketing margin which they can (indirectly) exert some influence on—pressure would be put on the management to be as efficient as possible, even more so if the pressure were combined with an incentive system. An incentive system could, of course, be introduced both at the primary society level and at the union level.

The fortunate thing about the interrelated problems of

democracy and efficiency, as faced by Tanzania, is that it seems possible to formulate the "internal rules of the game" in such a way that the democratic machinery of the co-operative movement can be made more efficient at one and the same time as the management is made more efficient. The common denominator of an increase in management efficiency and efficiency of the democratic machinery is information, relevant information. How the relevant information can be transmitted to the members is a practical problem which should be seriously studied and experimented with.[27]

The co-operative movement has been given a very important role in the marketing and distribution system of Tanzania and an even greater role has been allocated to the co-operatives in the years to come. Organising marketing and distributive services (and production) on a co-operative basis is regarded as being very suitable for achieving the socialist aim of Tanzania. It can be argued that, in present-day Tanzania, the rationale for basing marketing and distributive services on co-operatives cannot be stated only in terms of efficiency and the need to avoid exploitation. Many of the existing co-operatives have in the past played an important role in fighting exploitation by private traders, but in a socialist country the aim of avoiding exploitation by middlemen can be achieved by state marketing and distribution organisations, set up and controlled by the government, which—by definition—represents the peasants and workers of the country. This point emphasizes that an essential part of the rationale for basing marketing and distributive services on co-operatives in present-day, socialist Tanzania must be that co-operatives have a certain "democratic content", which a state trading system would not have.

The co-operative principle of democratic control is reflected in section 35 of the Co-operative Societies Act 1968: "The control of the affairs of a registered society shall be vested in the general meeting ..." Democracy in a co-operative movement has two aspects, which are interrelated: the *internal* relationship between members, committee and management and the *external* relationship between the co-operative movement and the authorities. In this paper I have focussed attention on a description and discussion of the *external* relationship and we have seen how the autonomy of the co-operative movement is limited in certain respects. I have argued that even within the present framework the co-operatives have something to "be democratic about" and I have discussed how this piece of autonomy could become more meaningful. I have also argued that it does seem possible to define the relationship between the co-operative movement and the present marketing board in such a way that both the government's legitimate interest in keeping control over the marketing system *and* the co-operatives'—understandable—interest in performing *all* the marketing operations can be satisfied.

O. Okereke

The Place of Marketing Co-operatives in the Economy of Uganda

As countries aspire towards development, especially low-income countries, co-operatives are looked upon as one of the institutional means of allocating scarce resources, of stimulating economic growth and of enhancing the economic and social status of the community. In his policy statement in Parliament, the Minister of Marketing and Co-operatives aptly described the Uganda co-operatives as "the People's Economic Movement",[1] an organisation the government considers will help "the common man to fight that enemy known as poverty".[2] These motives for co-operative development stem from the potential advantages of co-operative organisation.

Advantages of Co-operative Enterprise, with Particular Reference to Agricultural Marketing Co-operatives

Some of the potential advantages which have prompted the formation of agricultural co-operatives in Uganda are as follows:

(1) They provide opportunities for earning higher farm incomes. It is assumed that by combining as co-operatives, peasant farmers can provide themselves with processing and storage facilities which they cannot own individually, without outside aid, and by handling their members' produce, they may be able to obtain increased supply and reap some economies of scale which would reduce marketing costs and result in higher returns to the members.

(2) They are a way of replacing the middlemen and therefore, passing on the growers the profits that would otherwise go to the middlemen, thus improving the bargaining position of the growers.

153

(3) They provide a useful channel for propagating ideas for the improvement of methods of cultivation and marketing. This is especially so where co-operative societies consist of "progressive farmers" whose influence is likely to bear upon other Co-operative members.

(4) They serve as a useful means of extending credit to farmers and thereby enforcing programmes of technical assistance and advice. Due to the urgent credit needs of the farmer both for capital investment and working capital, co-operative societies are a powerful means of channelling the efforts of peasant farmers towards co-operative practices. Credit extension by Government, for example, to co-operatives, for distribution to their members, is contingent upon the societies and members fulfilling certain obligations, such as sale of crops through the societies by the members, and the societies keeping accurate accounts and records of members' crop deliveries to them.

(5) Where co-operatives are linked to a marketing board set up for the purpose of overseas sale of the cash crops handled by the movement, it may be possible to raise the prices obtainable from such crops to the benefit of growers if such crops form a large part of world supply to the extent that their prices can be raised by withholding output.[3] However, it is possible that such higher prices obtained may be withheld from farmers through a series of deductions, such as export tax, cess, and payments into a buffer fund or a Price Assistance Fund for the purpose of cushioning/subsidising prices of such commodities in the event of a fall in the world market. Such was the case in Uganda with coffee and cotton which fetched high prices in the 1950's on the world market, but growers however, received lower prices. When the world prices of these crops fell, growers were paid higher prices, until the funds were exhausted, and they were exposed to the vagaries of the world market.

Historical Background to the Development of Agricultural Marketing Co-operatives in Uganda

In the past, agricultural marketing was in the hands of non-Ugandans. Until the post-war period, restrictions were put in the way of Africans to participate in agricultural processing and other economic activities by the British Colonial Administration. It was in order to counteract the powerful alien business interests which controlled the country's economy that the Ugandan peasant farmers began to organise themselves as Co-operative Societies as early as the 1910's.[4]

Hence Galbraith's hypothesis that the existence of market power creates an incentive for the development of a countervailing force[5] which neutralises it, has found expression in the action of the Uganda peasant farmers. But these early farmers' Co-operatives could not effectively organise themselves as a powerful countervailing force, not only because of weak leadership, but also because of government's opposition to Co-operative endeavours.

The persistent agitation by the peasant farmers to be given a chance to participate in economic activities led to a change of attitude on the part of the government. This changed attitude began to be noticed in the 1940's, with the passage of the Co-operative Societies Act in 1946, an act which legalised co-operative activities.

However, although government attitude at that time had changed in favour of co-operative development in the country, the British Colonial Administration's policy was merely that of increasing the share of the Ugandans in economic activities through Co-operatives. In sharp contrast to that half-hearted measure, the present national government, since independence (1962) has adopted the movement as one of the instruments of public policy, not merely to increase the people's share in economic activities, but as a major means of Ugandanization in the agricultural sector.

This has been done through a series of legislative and statutory measures which have entrenched the movements' position in the country's economy. From about 75 primary societies registered in 1946, the movement has, by 1969, grown to nearly 2,000 primary societies with over half a million members, 31 district unions, and 3 apex organisations namely, the Uganda Co-operative Central Union; the Uganda Co-operative Alliance, and the Uganda Co-operative Bank. So, we see the co-operative movement emerging from an era of inhibition and insecurity to an era of domination and security.

The Market Structure and Co-operatives

In this analysis, three areas of agricultural marketing are considered, namely, cotton marketing, coffee marketing and finally, the marketing of secondary crops.

Bain has defined market structure as the

... organisational characteristics which determine the relations of sellers in the market to each other, of buyers in the market to each other, of the sellers to the buyers, and of sellers established in the market to other actual or potential suppliers of goods, including potential new firms which might enter the market.[6]

In other words, for all practical purposes, what determines market structure is the way the market is organised as "to influence strategically the nature of competition and pricing within the market".[7]

Clodius and Mueller have further amplified the term by stipulating a number of its structural variables. The most emphasized characteristics of market structure can be summarised as follows:

(1) The degree of seller concentration in terms of the number and the size distribution of sellers in the market.

(2) The degree of buyer concentration similarly considered.

(3) The condition of entry to the market, i.e., the relative ease or difficulty with which new sellers may enter the market, "as determined by the advantages which established sellers have over potential entrants",[8] and

(4) The degree of market knowledge or information—its distribution among buyers and sellers and its adequacy in terms of sharpening prices and reducing risks and uncertainty about the future.

Market structure, therefore, states specifically the precise structural conditions under which a commodity or a factor is actually sold or purchased.

The Market Structure in the Cotton Industry

There are two basic features of the structure of cotton marketing and processing in Uganda, namely, (a) the sheltered position of co-operatives and, (b) the cost/plus formula and the price structure.

Sheltered Position of the Movement

The movement, since 1968, has become virtually the sole ginner of raw cotton and the sole seller of lint to the Lint Marketing Board. Private ginners gin for the co-operatives as much as the latter give them, on contract basis. Thus, co-operatives have been given an assured market in the cotton industry with a virtual absence of competition. Opponents of the system correctly argue that with competition between ginners, their services would be offered at the lowest practicable price; ginners with high cost will be forced to leave the industry. This is hardly the case in the industry now, especially since cotton zoning limits the co-operative ginners to their respective zones. The case for competition in the cotton industry was argued by the commissioners inquiring into the industry in 1962,[9] as the only way by which the efficiency of the industry could be maximised and so, the only way of minimising the ginning costs in order to pay the grower maximum price for his crop. The 1966 Cotton Committee, on the other hand, did not consider that full competition, was consistent with "the highly desirable aim"[10] of encouraging the co-operative sector of the industry. The theoretical argument[11] in favour of this monopoly arrangement hinges on the fact that certain projects need large capital outlay, and so, in order to induce a potential investor to make an investment, he needs some protection from competition—"infant industry argument". Government, therefore, steps in and grants monopoly rights to the investor on the assumption that such protection will encourage high quality of output from the production units and allow a reasonable return on capital invested. Since 1963, co-operatives have, systematically been granted an increasing share of the cotton market, until they became the sole ginner of the crop.

Due to the co-operatives' increased share of the cotton quota, the amount of cotton ginned in co-operative ginneries has, correspondingly increased since 1962/63.

Table 1. *Co-operative Share of the Cotton Market, 1962/63–1967/68*

Zones	1962/63	1963/64	1964/65	1965/66	1966/67	1967/68
1. West Nile and Madi	100	100	100	100	100	100
2. West Acholi	Nil	65	70	80	100	100
3. East Acholi	Nil	60	100	100	100	100
4. Lango	20	60	75	90	90	100
5. Teso	Nil	35	60	65	65	100
6. South Teso (Segregated)	Nil	Nil	Nil	Nil	Nil	100
7. Usuku	Nil	Nil	Nil	Nil	Nil	100
8. Mbale	41	55	60	70	70	100
9. Busoga	35	50	55	60	60	100
10. Mengo/Entebbe	15	25	28	40	40	80
11. Mengo/Buruli	–	–	–	–	–	100
12. Mubende	15	35	46	60	60	–
13. Masaka	Nil	65	70	100	100	100
14. Bunyoro	50	78	85	100	100	100
15. Singo/Mubende Mwenge/Kyaka	–	–	–	–	–	100

Sources: Cotton Amendment Act No. 2, 1962; Legal Notice No. 229 of 1963; Statutory Instrument, 1964, No. 256; *Cotton Commission Report,* 1966; Statutory Instruments, 1966, No. 128 and 1967, No. 95.

1. * There have been mergers and shifts in the cotton zones, e.g. for the 1967/68 crop year, Mengo/Buruli was carved out of Mengo/Entebbe zone.

2. ** Other areas were added to Mubende zone in the 1967/68 crop season to form Singo/Mubende/Mwenge/Kyaka zone

3. In the 1968/69 crop year, Mengo/Entebbe zone's share was increased to 100%, thus completing the take-over.

The policy of protection is self-defeating, at times, because such investors, being assured of protection, may do nothing to improve the quality of their output or ensure the efficiency

Table 2. *Amount of Cotton Ginned in Co-operative Ginneries,
1962/63–1966/67.*

Year/ Season	Country's Total No. of Bales produced	Union ginneries Total Production (Bales)	Union ginneries' production as a % of country's production
1962/63	358 476	97 062	27
1963/64	379 413	147 527	39
1964/65	437 931	224 656	51
1965/66	444 629	265 951	60
1966/67	426 677	271 994	64

*Sources: Annual Reports of the Department of Agriculture; Reports
of Committee/Commission of Inquiries into the Cotton Industry of
Uganda (1962 and 1966); Annual Report of the Department of Co-
operative Development; Annual Reports of the Lint Marketing
Board.*

of their production units, while doing everything in their
power to maintain their monopoly position. There is, therefore, a strong argument against granting investors monopoly
power, on the grounds that such a power may last longer
than it is necessary. Protection ought to end when the organisation so shielded from competition is able to stand on its feet.
The problem, however, is the determination of the time when
the "infant" is mature enough to fend for itself.

On the other hand, it is arguable that the promotion of
African participation in the processing industries is incompatible with unrestricted competition which results in the
crowding of the industries with "surplus and uneconomic
factories". African entrants with small capital are unable to
compete with big businessmen having large capital resources.
The 1962 Cotton Commission had to admit the merit of the
system to a limited degree, in enabling the co-operative movement to enter the cotton industry, and to some extent, to
grow.

Without the financial aid available to them from the Price Assistance Fund at sub-market rates of interest, the co-operative ginneries would not have been able to establish themselves as soon as

they have done, or perhaps at all; and without their guaranteed pool shares it is possible that, at least, in the early stages they might have been squeezed out by private ginners.[12]

Government's decision, since 1963, not to introduce free competition in the cotton industry has been welcomed by the Uganda Co-operative Alliance on similar grounds that "free competition would make it difficult for new entrants in the industry to operate";[13] that experience has revealed the use of "ruthless and unethical methods in free competition".[14]

Co-operative unions, on their part, favour being granted monopsony rights in their respective areas as a means of ensuring greater use of their ginning capacity. This system, however, deprives growers not belonging to co-operatives in those places, of getting the benefit of higher prices inherent in situations of competitive buying, especially, as such growers are not in a position to get such other benefits as bonuses from the processors, unlike the co-operative members. By this one-channel marketing measure, the co-operative ginneries are assured not only of an increase in their throughput, but also of a greater access to the source of raw material.

The "status quo" has been altered. Yet to replace one set of monopolists/monopsonists with another set does not alter the basis of the argument against monopoly power. In this connection, the market structure has a racial element. It would appear that the motivation for this privileged position in which the co-operative movement has been entrenched is political, rather than economic, in terms of the economic arguments for monopoly power, and it seems to be a measure to redress the imbalance of the past. The restrictions placed, in the past, by earlier colonial Administration in the country, on African entry into trade and commerce, have been a source of grievance and agitation.[15] Co-operatives are therefore, now being used by the indigenous Government, as an institutional framework to Ugandanise the agricultural sector and thus, serve as a vehicle for the redistribution of income and economic power.[16]

A view widely held is that the granting of the movement this monopoly power can only be justified if it is for a limited period—during the formative years of the movement—otherwise, Government becomes a kind of "Godfather" for an indefinite period, and that may stifle the initiative of the movement.

Within the movement itself, competition between the co-operative union ginners would give all growers the advantage of higher prices, but since the cotton price is fixed by law, this is hardly the case.

The Cost/Plus Formula and the Price Structure in the Cotton Industry. The cost/plus formula is considered to be one of the major factors that affect the efficiency with which the ginneries are operated. It is a pricing system under which ginners are guaranteed a certain margin of profits, after taking into consideration the operational costs of the ginners, determined on the basis of certain available data. Up to 1961, the margin of profit allowed the ginner was Shs:24/- per bale of lint (i.e. 6 cents per pound of lint), plus quality incentive bonus of Shs:45/- per bale (i.e., about 11 cents per pound). The costs allowed the ginner are usually not those actually incurred, "except by accident". Such a system is likely to produce super profits for some operators. The system "is considered to be a disincentive to changes and hence, against improvements. It is an incentive to load costs and it enables the relatively inefficient units in an industry to survive, when under some other system they might go under".[17] Since 1965 however, the price formula has been revised and the profit margin cut. In the 1964/65 season, the quality premium ranged between 2 cents and 5 cents per pound.[18] Hence, the 1966 Cotton Committee suggested that a new formula should be evolved and "must be one which encourages efficiency in ginning, discourages inefficient ginners or those ginners who cannot get enough seed cotton to gin, so that in future, only a few large and efficient ginneries would be operated".[19] On the other hand, the recent report on co-operative unions is of the opinion that the present price structure and low profit margin allowed the ginner is detrimental to co-operatives, especially "as they are suffering under a number of handicaps", being late comers in the industry. It holds the view that ginning costs have increased considerably and "have largely negatived recent increases in efficiency within the co-operative sector, which should otherwise have been rewarded with substantial profits".[20] The committee has recommended a recalculation of ginners' margin of profit in favour of co-operatives, simultaneous to their being granted 100% take-over of cotton ginning.[21] This recommendation tends to perpetuate the very system that has come under severe criticism—and is hardly consistent with incentives to efficiency. Because of the cost/plus formula, there are no risk elements for the movement on the buying and selling sides in the cotton industry.

The Structure of Marketing in the Coffee Industry. The system prevailing in the coffee industry until 1969 was that co-operatives competed side by side with private traders and associations[22] of growers in Robusta coffee and in Arabica coffee outside Bugisu, Sebei, West Nile and Ankole districts. Since last year, however, as in the cotton industry, co-operatives have acquired the sole right of coffee processing in the dry-processing sector. Coffee processed by co-operatives is sold to the Coffee Marketing Board, which has now been entrusted with the responsibility of overseas sale of all Uganda coffee,[23] thereby ending the differentiation between the "free side" and the "controlled side" of the industry.[24] In the Arabica coffee industry, co-operatives now process more than 90% of the coffee crop because competition in many parts of the Arabica producing areas has been barred.

There have been many complaints from the movement about the persistence of competition in the industry, some of which have even featured in Parliamentary debates. A member of the Uganda People's Congress (UPC) for Central Busoga, once complained about traders "going into Busoga and paying 53 cents a pound plus gifts of glasses, plates and saucepans for kiboko coffee, instead of the minimum of 48 cents a pound".[25] Government was, therefore, urged to stop the practice, because "if the grower can see a better price, he will run away and sell his coffee there".[26] By such incentive schemes, the private traders intended to increase their throughput. That there was, until 1969, in the coffee industry, where Government allowed some measure of competition, a good number of non-co-operative organisations of peasant farmers, indicates that growers themselves welcome competition in marketing.

The case of the Bugisu Co-operative Union and the Bugisu Coffee Marketing Association (BCMA) in 1962, is one evidence that without Government intervention, overt or covert, rival organisations are likely to emerge to challenge the dominance of the movement where the latter is in a monopsonistic position, in order to establish competition. The result of the competitive structure of the robusta coffee industry, until recently, is that co-operatives have not been able to process up to 50% of the total crop.

Table 3. *Quantity of Coffee Robusta Processed by Co-operatives, 1962/63–1965/66.*

Year/ Season	Country's Total Qty. of Kiboko produced (tons)	Qty. Processed in Union factories (tons)	Union Factories' production as a % of country's total production
1962/63	153 104	44 206	29
1963/64	171 400	62 495	36
1964/65	118 600	49 484	42
1965/66	145 400	42 954	29

The rejection, by the 1967 Coffee Committee, of the movement's demand for further monopsony rights in the coffee trade, is a recognition of the merits of competitive market situation in the coffee industry. Although Government allowed competition in the industry, at that time, thus giving growers the choice of alternatives, yet it had to declare its intention to transfer all coffee processing to co-operatives in future.[27] *The Structure of Marketing in the Secondary Crops Trade.* There are far more numerous private traders in the secondary crops trade than there are in the coffee trade, because of the more liberal licensing regulations in respect of the former. There is, therefore, far greater competition in these crops marketing than in coffee marketing. Before 1960, Government's statutory marketing arrangements did not affect secondary crops trade, hence no category of these crops was under

Government's control. Since then, by declaring buying seasons and fixing minimum grower prices for certain scheduled crops, the Secondary Crops trade has become a controlled industry. Until the new Produce Marketing Board takes over the responsibility of overseas export of all scheduled produce, the prevailing arrangement is that co-operatives and individual traders buy the crops from the growers and, either resell them in the internal market, or on the international market themselves, or through intermediaries—produce dealers—based in the main towns. At the moment, amongst the scheduled minor crops, it is only in the case of tobacco that overseas sale is channelled through the Board.[28] The tobacco crop is now coming on very well as a foreign exchange earner.

Government has directed that co-operative unions should be agents of the Board in the marketing of secondary crops. This is an attempt to expand co-operative participation in the trade. As it was in the coffee trade, the movement is faced with the risk of paying higher grower prices than the statutory prices, which they usually cannot realise from their sale proceeds, with the result that most of them have had to sustain losses in their minor crops trading accounts. Nor is there the complicated system of cost/plus formula to offset any probable losses by assuring them a measure of profit on their outlay.[29] When the necessary machinery has been completed, the Uganda co-operatives will become the sole buyers of secondary crops as well.[30]

The Impact of the Market Structure

The results of the present marketing structure in the cotton and coffee industries can be summarised as follows: (a) possibility of loss in efficiency, (b) lower grower price and a limitation in the growers' market, and (c) excess capacity in the Processing Units.

Possibility of Loss in Efficiency. The protection afforded the co-operatives would seem to encourage inefficiency because the management has no incentive to reduce processing costs, having been assured of a margin of profit (in the case of the cotton industry) and protection from competing firms. Nor has it any incentive to make improvements, since it has the assurance of patronage.

Under most statutory schemes, a processor has an allotted share of the market; his buying and selling are usually determined in a manner which guarantees his costs by reference to an average (or possibly minimum) standard of efficiency. Management in such cases, so far as marketing is concerned, becomes chiefly a matter of sticking to the rules; discretionary action being rather small.[31]

Examples of how efficiency could be lost as a result of such statutory marketing schemes as tend to be paternalistic in nature could be seen in the cases of two unions—the Busoga Growers' Co-operative Union and the Bugisu Co-operative Union.[32] The Busoga Growers Co-operative Union, up to 1962, had a reputation for efficiency and production of good quality lint for which it earned considerable premiums. It was able to hold its own in the face of competition from the private sector. It seemed that deterioration in the management of the union set in since 1963, when co-operative ginners began to enjoy a large measure of protection, and a committee of inquiry had to be appointed to probe its affairs in 1964. In spite of the 1962/63 crop year being a good cotton year, the union's surplus fell from £39,860 it was in the previous year, to £3,776, instead of rising. This was an indication that all was not well with the union. Many bales of lint were left outside and were damaged by rain. Such a case of negligence could not be afforded by one not assured of some measure of profit margin for his business, however badly managed. The estimated loss of damaged bales at the union's ginneries at Namwendwa and Nakirumbi was of the order of £55,225. Consequently, it was unable to pay anything as cotton bonus with such a small surplus, to its member societies, and only managed to pay them 4% interest on shares, instead of the statutory 5%. However it is pertinent to point out that under the law a co-operative society can declare as much dividend as it is able to do so long as it does not exceed 5%.

The Bretton Inquiry into the Bugisu Co-operative Union in 1958 revealed that "there is much inefficiency, enough to make a strong case for discontinuing the monopoly and exposing the union to the necessity of proving it is better than the alternative of other types of marketing".[33] Yet the Uganda Government's statement on the report added that the Government "intends to continue to give the union a monopoly of processing, grading, and exporting all Bugisu Arabica coffee for so long as it shows itself capable of discharging this responsibility efficiently".[34] Thus, although the union had demonstrated it was incapable of discharging the function efficiently, government's concern was protection of the union and a further encouragement of inefficiency by continuing to shield it from competition.[35] For the brief period in 1962, when the union competed with its rival, the Bugisu Coffee Marketing Association, it had a trading loss of over £60,000 in its coffee account caused by the fundamental fault of its paying growers more than the world price for their coffee, in order to forestall its rival. Having had no competition in the past it would appear that the union lacked the ability to figure out risks and contain them.

In defence of the monopoly rights enjoyed by the movement, there is a school of thought that argues that protection is not a disincentive to efficiency. A typical example is the Okoro Coffee Growers' Co-operative Union, which was granted the sole right of Arabica coffee processing in the West Nile district in 1963. Since then, it has been doing well, doubling its turnover and surplus every year, in spite of the fact that its primary societies were processing their coffee with hand pulperies before Government agreed to provide the union with a processing factory. They thus demonstrated the fact that "efficient market method is better than the prestige of owning a factory," and that protection need not promote inefficiency.

The Twena Tubehamwe Growers' Co-operative Union, on the other hand, is a classic example of a union "which has been terribly hit as a result of severe competition from private coffee traders".[36] It has not been able to attain the estimated breakeven tonnage of 250 tons of parchment coffee per annum since its registration, and has been making losses.[37] It has, however, been found that society members of the union have some grievances against the union, one of which is under-payment for their cherry deliveries (24 cents per lb. to societies who then pay 1 cent less to their grower members). Dissatisfaction among the members "encourages the private buyers to disuade, with great success, the members from delivering cherry to the union".[38] Government, has, accordingly, accepted the recent Committee of Inquiry's recommendation that the union should merge with a nearby union and be granted a complete monopsony right in its area of operation as a means of salvaging it from its present predicament.[39]

The conclusion one can draw is that the union's difficulty does not stem from the so-called severe competition, but from administrative problems which have cost it the loss of confindence of its member societies. The Masaka Growers' Co-operative Union is in competition with adept private coffee buyers, like Baumann & Co. Ltd., and yet, has been able to hold its own.

Thus, protection could be a contributory, not a decisive, cause of inefficiency on the part of any union.

Lower Grower Price and a Limitation in the Growers' Market. The impact of the monopoly rights granted the movement in the cotton industry is seen, not only in loss of efficiency in some unions, but also in the limitation of the growers' market and payment of lower prices to the producers. For example, in the cotton industry, a free market would have given the grower the choice of any ginnery to which he is disposed to sell his seed cotton. But because of the zoning system which gives the co-operatives rights over the zonal crop, the grower is compelled to sell his crop to the only ginnery in his area, which has acquired a monopsony position. Consequently, the grower is denied the right of an alternative outlet for the sale of his crop. Being given a monopsony power, the co-operative ginner may abuse his monopsony position and be tempted to show less concern in maintaining the loyalty of his members, knowing that, in the circumstances, the growers will have no other choice than to deal with him. For example, there have been cases of non-payment of growers for their cotton for months by some co-operative unions.[40] When payments for the growers' crop are so delayed, such deferred payments amount to a reduction in the price of the commodity, considering the producers' rate of time preference. Growers' prices for seed cotton are usually fixed by law and gazetted. Co-operatives, because of the absence of competition in the cotton industry, do not usually pay growers prices higher than the statutory price.

On the other hand, in the coffee industry, when competition (mainly Robusta) was in operation, growers had, in many cases, been paid prices above the minimum because of the system of declaring minimum prices. The recent Committee on Co-operative Unions is of the view that "the system has worked to the detriment of, not only the co-operative unions, but also of the majority of growers,"[41] and has recommended fixed, rather than, minimum price for coffee. It is the author's view that while co-operative unions that pay a price above that justified by market situation, may lose, growers will benefit from getting a higher price, although it is also possible that the growers may suffer as a result of reduced bonus, in the event of a union making a small surplus, due to payment of a higher price. A typical example is the Masaka District Growers' Co-operative Union, which, because of competition from the private traders, paid growers 46 cents a pound of Kiboko, 1965/66, when the minimum price was 40 cents per pound. This risk element arises from the fact that the co-operative unions, after paying higher grower prices than the statutory prices, may be unable to recover what they have paid out, from their sales of clean coffee to the Coffee Marketing Board. But where the movement has acquired monopsony rights, this risk element is minimised.

Unlike in the cotton industry, the cost/plus formula is not applicable to the coffee industry. The profits a processor has to make will largely depend upon his business acumen and his ability to bear risks.

Excess Capacity. The present arrangement whereby co-operatives, due to inadequate processing facilities in some cases give part of their crop to private processors to process on contract has the effect of perpetuating excess capacity, making some of the processing units in the whole industry less utilised. As a result of that, the unit cost of processing is likely to be higher, because the fixed costs have to be borne by a small output.

In the cotton industry, when the market was shared between co-operatives and the private sector, it was found that in some zones, there were more ginneries than were required for the ginning of the crop, and as such, not all the ginneries would be required to process the whole crop. The average throughput of 2,400 bales per ginnery per annum is now considered sub-economic, and an efficient ginnery is considered to be one with a standard capacity of 4,000 bales a year. Judged on this criterion, most of the ginneries, especially, the private ones, were "inefficient". But, whereas most of the private ginneries, when they were operating, were working at excess capacity, most of the co-operative ginneries now work under abnormal pressure, "some ginning as much as thrice the amount of cotton they are designed to handle". This is because the co-operatives have been assigned more cotton than they can process, although, before the movement's share of cotton ginning was increased to 100%, most of the union ginneries were operating at excess capacity, owing to the statutory pool arrangement which made it obligatory for them to

Table 4. *Throughput of Cotton Bales in Six Co-operative Ginneries, 1965 to 1967*

Union	Ginnery	Output: (Bales)		
		1965	1966	1967
Busoga Growers'	Nakivumbi	10 062	10 701	9 084
Co-operative Union	Kaliro	9 231	10 299	11 119
	Balawoli	4 761	3 406	4 339
Lango Co-operative	Odokomit	7 722	7 507	7 255
Union	Aloi	—	6 970	6 627
Uganda Growers'[a]				
Co-operative Union	Kawembe	5 325	5 882	—

Source: Annual Reports, Department of Co-operative Development, Co-op. Unions' Files.

• This union was split into three separate unions in 1968.

reallocate a certain proportion of cotton collected by them beyond their due share, to other ginners. Some co-operative unions are now known to be ginning over 10,000 bales of cotton per annum. (Table 4)

In the coffee processing sector, there is also "serious over-capacity". In the 1964/65 season, average production per dry-processing factory (excluding hulleries) was below 1,800 tons.[42] Only about 33 $1/3$ % of the factories were found to have attained "this modest average", while over 20 % of the factories produced below it. In a number of cases, "performances in the 1965/66 season were even worse".[43] Similar over-capacity exists in the wet-processing sector.

But, judged, on the basis of 1,800 tons of parchment coffee per annum, considered to be the average production per factory, a number of unions were well above the average. The major cause of the existence of "extensive dry processing capa-

Table 5. *Throughput of Clean Coffee Production from Seven Co-operative Union Factories, 1965–1967.*

Union	Factory	Tons 1965	1966	1967
Banyankole Kweterani G.C.U.	Bushenyi	3 491	2 753	4 459
Bugisu Co-operative Union	Mbale	3 372	10 751	6 204
Tuwena Tubehamwe G.C.U.[a]		153	191	64
Sebdi/Elgon Co-operative Union	Mbale	288	702	352
Bwaru Mpologoma G.C.U.	Seyange	4 392	4 187	1 215
Masaka District G.C.U.	Kyabakawza	5 095	3 065	3 847
Mubende G.C.U.	Bakubye Kakumira	1 704	1 545	854

Source: Dept of Co-op. Dev. Ann. Reports., Co-op. Unions' accounts files.

[a] Now merged with the Banyankole Kweteram G.C.U.

city", it would appear, is due to "faulty factory licensing policy",[44] which does not take into consideration the need of an area for any proposed factory, before a licence is issued. Thus the desire to increase co-operative share of coffee processing as a prelude to the movements' final control of the industry now partially achieved may be the reason for this "faulty licensing system". But, the danger may outweigh the potential benefits, by perpetuating idle capacity. The transfer of all coffee processing[45] to the movement may also be fraught with some political difficulties.

Drawbacks of Co-operatives[1]

In spite of the potential advantages of co-operative enterprise, co-operatives all over the world are faced with a number of problems. In the performance of their functions, the Uganda Co-operatives have faced a number of difficulties which constitute their drawbacks, namely, maladministration, inadequate capital resources, conflict between management and board members and disloyalty of members.

Mal-administration. The efficiency of the movement, to a very large extent, depends upon the efficiency of the staff running it. Investigations into the affairs of most co-operative unions have shown that there is a large measure of mismanagement in them. The standard of management in the movement is poor owing to a number of factors:[47]

(*a*) unsatisfactory recruitment policy, whereby mediocre local personnel is preferred to outside expertise, (*b*) insufficient locally trained and experienced managerial staff to run the unions and societies, (*c*) limited training facilities for co-operative personnel, (*d*) growing size of the unions as business units being out of proportion to the available calibre of management, (*e*) lack of effective control from the Department of Co-operative Development over the movement. The recent establishment of the Ministry of Marketing and Co-operatives is aimed at increasing the supervisory role of the Government.

It must however be borne in mind that since entry by Africans into commercial and industrial activities was restricted in the past, it is not surprising that managerial experience is not yet developed as it should. Hence mistakes are made in running the Co-operative movement in Uganda. It is for that reason that the Uganda government has embarked upon a wide range of training programmes for co-operatives, such as management training courses, as well as courses dealing with accounting, book-keeping and marketing methods for Co-operative office bearers and board members.

Inadequate capital resources. Apart from lack of people with adequate business-know-how to manage the affairs of the movement, Co-operatives have insufficient capital of their own. Because of that, they depend, to a large extent, upon the government for funds. For example, in buying cotton ginneries and coffee factories, the Government lends the movement 90% and $66\,^2/_3\%$, respectively, of their capital costs. In the group farm scheme, funds for credit distribution to members come largely from government. For example, in the 1966/67 crop season, the movement was only able to raise 10% of the finance from its own sources, to lend to members. This financial problem is exacerbated partly by the inability and unwillingness of members to pay their dues promptly, and partly by misuse of funds in certain cases.

Conflict between the management and Board members. Due to inadequate knowledge of their rights and responsibilities, board members, in some cases, tend to interfere unduly in the running of the business of the movement. Board members are supposed to confine themselves to policy-making, while the management executes policy, but in some cases, board members want to do what the management is expected to do, such as employment of workers. Such a cleavage mars the smooth running of a society or a union. Such was the case with the Bugisu Co-operative Union, thus leading to a lot of wrangling, with a consequent fall in efficiency.

Disloyalty of members. The question of members' disloyalty is tied up with the insufficient monetary benefits they get from their societies and unions, such as lower prices, delay in payment for crop deliveries and instances of embezzlement of funds by the officials of the movement. In such situations member's loyalty has been severely strained and they tend to sell their crops to private traders for higher monetary rewards.

For example, one of the reasons for the defection of the members of the Kigezi District Growers' Co-operative Union in 1965 was the fact that the Union was paying its member societies a lower price for their coffee deliveries than they could obtain from private buyers. The remedy for this disloyalty has been seen to lie in giving the movement the monopsony of crop marketing in the country.

Prospects for the Co-operatives

The question that may be asked is, have the Uganda Co-operatives any future? What prospects have they in the rapidly changing economy of the country?

In recent policy statements, government's intention to put into the hands of the Co-operatives the control of agricultural marketing, and Ugandanise other sectors of the economy, through Co-operatives, and through other institutional arrangements, has been re-iterated.[48] Co-operatives are now in "the forefront of Uganda's Move to the Left" and the movement is now the biggest business owned and run by Ugandans. This is so, because we see:

(a) That co-operatives are now in control of cotton ginning. Since 1969, it has become the sole ginner of raw cotton, thus constituting a one-channel, marketing system in the cotton industry, (b) They are now in control of all dry coffee processing; and plans are on foot for them to take over the marketing of secondary crops, (c) they are stepping up their share of retail trade through consumer societies which are to be given government financial aid and technical assistance, (d) the 1970 May Day Presidential announcements have further given co-operatives a stake in the distributive services.[49]

Through co-operatives, a sizeable number of Ugandan peasant farmers have entered the money economy. As long as Co-operatives are in this sheltered position as an act of public policy in the programme of Ugandanisation, their future seems assured. But in the face of competition, it is difficult to see, in the light of present evidence, how they can survive as an economic proposition, unless attempts are made to improve their operation in a number of ways:[50]

(*a*) The skills of the movement can be strengthened by appointing men with experience and the requisite technical know-how and qualifications to run it. This in turn, requires strengthening the staff of the Department of Co-operative Development, (*b*) Improving the member's understanding of their role in the movement through better educational schemes, so that member's loyalty to the movement is ensured and conflicts between management and members are minimised, (*c*) Increasing the protection of the members from abuses by office bearers. This can be done through increased supervision of the societies and unions by Co-operative officers so as to check any tendency towards abuses, such as embezzlement of funds, provided that such supervision does not jeopardise the exercise of initiative by the office bearers of the movement, (*d*) Adequate support of co-operatives by their members through regular payment of their dues, so as to build up sufficient capital funds for their projects.

In this paper, the importance attached to co-operative development as an instrument of economic and social change has been analysed and the position occupied by co-operatives in the agricultural marketing structure has been demonstrated. The central theme running through the whole of this paper is that co-operatives have been adopted by the Uganda government as an institutional framework to promote economic and social transformation.

An attempt to expand the market for co-operatives by statutory measures means that co-operatives, which, in the absence of state action might turn their resources to alternative uses, in the face of competition from the private sector, are induced to stay in business. Artificial barriers placed in the way of private traders deprive them of a large part of the market and result in most of their plants lying idle, while most of those of co-operatives are largely fully utilised. The working to full capacity of some of the co-operatives' processing units should, by definition, result in lower unit costs and consequently, bring greater financial rewards to the co-operative members. Similarly, as the marketing boards are under obligation to buy all crops processed by co-operatives for sale in the world market, they have therefore taken over from these marketing co-operatives marketing risks inherent in overseas sale of agricultural commodities. But whether, in the absence of this secure position in which the Uganda co-operatives find themselves in agricultural marketing at present, there would result maximisation of the net revenue of the members and greater improvement in the services offered them is outside the purview of this analysis.

Having achieved the major objective of income redistribution and the transfer of economic power to Africans, the Uganda co-operatives are now faced with the problem of adapting co-operation to the needs of a rapidly developing country in reconciling economic objectives with social ends. Changing social and economic circumstances make it imperative for the co-operatives to adjust themselves to new conditions.

Co-operatives are legitimately considered one of the suitable means of Ugandanisation in the development effort. The transfer of an alien business to peasant farmers evokes in the latter a sense of enthusiasm which, if properly directed, can lead to a more efficient utilisation of resources. Policy-makers are here faced with a dilemma, namely, to have a low rate of economic growth through a greater indigenous participation in economic activities, or a high rate of economic growth through alien control of the economy, since these immigrants possess the technical-know-how. The transfer of economic power to an inexperienced group inevitably results in a decline in efficiency at the initial stages and consequently slows down economic growth. But this is a short-run problem.

The contributions that the Uganda co-operatives have made to economic growth have largely been due to government's deliberate efforts in increasing their share of crop marketing at the expense of the private sector. The danger in their getting so much of government support is that they may lose their independent character which is a feature of the co-operative movement in other countries.

One could argue that economic development necessitates equality of opportunity for all in the country, so that the full potentialities of the people could be tapped. To quote Bauer and Yamey,

It is the function of the state to widen the range of opportunities for its people and facilitate access to them, and it is for the members of society to choose among alternative opportunities open to them and develop them with the aid of their personal endowments.[51]

If therefore, co-operatives are granted a monopsony of crop marketing, one would depose that the individual peasant farmers' choice of alternative outlets for their crops is being curtailed. On the other hand, it is equally plausible to argue that if co-operatives are to be effectively used as an instrument of public policy, it is difficult to see how they can operate without government intervention and protection from

The Structure of Agricultural Marketing in Uganda

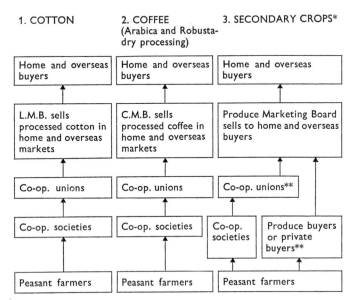

1. COTTON

2. COFFEE
(Arabica and Robusta-dry processing)

3. SECONDARY CROPS*

Home and overseas buyers	Home and overseas buyers	Home and overseas buyers	
L.M.B. sells processed cotton in home and overseas markets	C.M.B. sells processed coffee in home and overseas markets	Produce Marketing Board sells to home and overseas buyers	
Co-op. unions	Co-op. unions	Co-op. unions**	
Co-op. societies	Co-op. societies	Co-op. societies	Produce buyers or private buyers**
Peasant farmers	Peasant farmers	Peasant farmers	

* The chart illustrates what the position will look like when all the overseas sale of secondary crops is channelled through the Produce Marketing Board.
** A greater part of the produce is sold by co-operative unions and private produce dealers in the home market.

competition. As an instrument of public policy, the Uganda co-operatives inevitably tend to be tied up with the political power structure.

However, with the gradual emergence of an economic elite and a leadership core imbued with a sense of responsibility and entrepreneurial ability, government intervention in co-operative development may be relaxed and the movement stand on its own feet.

The difficulties that the Uganda co-operatives are now facing can be considered as teething problems. In the longrun, having acquired considerable experience, they are most likely to improve upon their efficiency and fulfil their members' legitimate expectations of increased economic returns and enhanced social status.

Nelson Kasfir

Organizational Analysis and Uganda Co-operative Unions

The importance of co-operatives in Ugandan economic life developed steadily during the last decade of colonial rule and has grown enormously since independence. Under the Protectorate Government co-operatives grew from 401 primary societies and 5 unions representing 36,620 farmers in 1951 to 1,662 registered primary societies belonging, in the main, to 21 unions with a membership of 252,378 farmers in 1961.[1] By the end of 1967 over half a million farmers were enrolled in 1,920 agricultural primary societies themselves members of 31 producers' unions.[2] More spectacular has been the acquisition of processing units. The first ginnery to be operated by a co-operative union was leased to Uganda Growers in 1949. The first licence for a coffee factory was issued in 1954. In 1962 14 ginneries and 7 coffee factories and pulperies were co-operatively owned.[3] By 1967 48 ginneries and 15 coffee factories and pulperies were being operated by co-operative unions.[4] The imposition of a 100% processing monopoly in cotton in 1968 and a dry-processing monopoly in coffee (covering 80% of the crop) in 1969 further increased the production brought under co-operative control. In this fashion collection and processing of Uganda's two major sources of export earnings have been placed in the hands of co-operatives. Unions also handle maize, tobacco, millet, groundnuts and tea. They run cattle ranches, consumer shops and a variety of other enterprises.

Thus, co-operative unions have grown in both size and complexity over the past two decades. It is both interesting and important to find out what sort of organisations they have

178

become, and how they have performed. Some unions have produced surpluses consistently, while others have lost money virtually every year and ended up under direct (though temporary) government control. A third group started off making surpluses and rapidly expanding the number of productive units under their control only to meet with disaster a few years later. How can these differences in performance be explained?

Certain factors are constant for all unions. Most important of these are the price paid by the union to the grower for each raw crop and the sales price paid by the government to the union for the processed crop. These prices are set by the government and do not vary from one union to another, though they do vary in terms of the type and quality of the cotton or coffee. Risks in the ultimate overseas sale of Ugandan crops are assumed by government marketing boards.

Not all the factors affecting performance that vary between unions are under the control of the unions themselves. The quality of the crop grown may differ from one area to another. Weather conditions and disease may create problems in one union and not another. Local political or religious disturbances may overwhelm the effective operation of a particular union.

However, the most important cause of effective or ineffective performance is widely assumed to be good or bad management. The Department of Co-operative Development reported that

Management problems continued to face the movement. ... Five Co-operative Unions operated under supervising managers (i.e., they were directly controlled by government).
Some of the others remained shaky and a few had good and stable management.[5]

In discussing inefficiency and bureaucratic dishonesty in Tanzanian co-operatives, President Nyerere suggests that "the problems of co-operatives are practical ones, which must be worked out and dealt with by better and more skilled management and commercial machinery".[6] Improve the management, it is felt and unions will produce surpluses for their members.

To examine this proposition, it is necessary to inquire more closely into what is meant by the use of the term "management".

Approaches to the Study of Organisations

The general view of management holds that it is a technical and rational approach to accomplishing goals involving the work of men and machines. A former member of the Co-operative Department in Uganda recently defined management as "Getting the job done by planning, directing, co-ordinating, controlling and motivating from facts obtained".[7]

This view of the organisation grew out of the "scientific management" school originally developed by Frederick Taylor fifty years ago and refined by Luther Gulick and Leonard Urwick. The exponents of this school emphasised the achievement of efficiency through careful building of the formal organisation. The basic intention was to find the most scientific techniques to achieve the organisation's goal. This required seeing men as extensions of the machines with which they worked. Thus, Taylor developed time and motion studies of workers and Gulick and Urwick worked out a series of propositions for better management based on division of labour, unity of command and the appropriate span of control. These propositions tend to acquire both a universalistic and an exhortatory character as their proponents usually press them forward as the best possible way to achieve effective performance from any organisation.[8]

Efforts to refine some of these propositions began to run into trouble, as investigators discovered that both workers and administrators had more complicated motivations than was implied by the mechanistic approach of the scientific management school. If workers were entirely rational, they ought to respond more productively when their money wages were raised. Instead, it was discovered that workers were sometimes more interested in what their fellow workers thought of their actions than in what management wanted them to do. In other words the social group formed by the accident of having been placed on one work site produced an informal organisation that exercised powerful influence on the behaviour of workers. The most striking illustration of the operation of informal organisations is the well-known phenomenon of "restriction of production". Workers determine for themselves what a fair day's output will be and then enforce this standard on their compatriots.[9] In addition members of this school (often referred to as the human relations approach) pointed out the necessity to know about the social background of the members of the organisation in order to learn why certain patterns of behaviour were characteristic of certain organisations and not others. Thus, human relations students reversed the emphasis of the scientific management school by making their studies specific to the particular context in which the organisation functioned and by focusing on social and informal variables instead of the formal organisation. For them the basic problem of establishing effective organisations was social, not rational.[10]

An attempt to integrate the insights of both of these schools was made by Herbert Simon and James March. They pointed out that the most important activity of any organisation, as an organisation, is to make decisions. The trouble with the propositions put forward by the scientific management school is that they are not scientific at all, since the conditions under which they apply have not been specified, and the propositions contradict one another.[11] The human relations school, on the other hand, ignores the formal organisation and purposes towards which the organisation is—more or less successfully—attempting to bring together the activity of its various participants. In order to find out how organisations actually work, then, investigators must study the process of decision-making in the organisation. Social factors, communications patterns, the distribution of authority, and efforts to gain adequate information on which rational decisions can be based are important.[12] These factors will vary between organisations, naturally, so that the process of decision-making—and presumably the level of performance—may also be expected to vary.

About the same time another approach based on what the individual gave to and received from the organisation was

181

formulated by Chester Barnard. In his view it was important to examine the contributions that an individual made to the organisation and the incentives that the organisation had to make available to him in order to secure his continued participation. When contributions outweigh incentives, individuals either modify their participation or terminate their membership in the organisation.[13] In addition to discovering whether the organisation has ample incentives to provide to its members, it is possible to distinguish between different incentive systems operating in different organisations. For example, some organisations depend on ideological incentives to keep members satisfied, others on social incentives, and the remainder (the vast majority of organisations) depend largely on material or money incentives.[14] Co-operatives use all three, though in varying combinations.

Each of these schools of organisational analysis have contributions to make to the study of co-operatives as organisations. For most people involved in co-operative work the scientific management school still contains the basic ideas of what are the important factors for running an organisation. As a result in the discussions of organisational problems of co-operatives, the range of decision-makers whose activities should be examined is greatly restricted and the relevant motivations to be taken into account are significantly narrowed. The roles of other important figures—members of the union's board of directors, officials of primary societies, junior staff, and delegates to the annual general meeting—are either downgraded or regarded as obstructive. This bias follows directly from the assumption that running a co-operative union is a highly technical matter in which there will be one decision which is more rational than any other.

The human relations approach suggests that a far wider range of people affect the output of the union, and in ways that escape the attention of those who concentrate on top management. The decision-making approach tends to correct an over-emphasis on social factors to the exclusion of the formal organisation by focusing attention on communication patterns and the distribution of authority. An analysis based on the incentives available in a union requires an examination of the various kinds of organisational participation of those involved in the union's operation and ways in which the union rewards them. Few of the research possibilities indicated here have been explored in studies of co-operatives anywhere.

Still, one problem with these different schools is that each gives an incomplete view of the organisation, and ignores significant patterns of behaviour, which affect the decisions taken. Some of the most important recent studies of organisations suggest that looking at the groups and individuals within an organisation in terms of their interests and their differential access to power to achieve them may provide far more understanding of behaviour within the organisation.

Power, as a specific research problem, has not been isolated in earlier work on organisations. One logical consequence of the assumptions of some of the earlier approaches was that power, independently exercised, could not exist in the well-run organisation. The scientific management school treated members of the organisation as extensions of the machines on which they worked. Thus, the problem of power and conflict could only arise in a poorly organised factory or association and should be eliminated by the institution of better management techniques. The human relations approach implied that if workers can be made happy, they will be highly productive and the problem of power and conflict will disappear. But, as Michel Crozier points out, "a human being ... does not have only a hand—as implied by the scientific management school and a heart—as implied by the human relations school. He has also a head, which means that he is free to decide and to play his own game".[15]

To use a power approach requires that the researcher view the organisation as an arena in which small subgroups employ a variety of strategies in order to protect themselves and weaken their opponents. To determine who the antagonists are requires a close examination of the particular organisation as the situation is likely to vary from one to another. Not all formal members are actors, as access to knowledge is one of the important resources in any power struggle. Thus, unscrupulous commercially-oriented farmers have often effectively aggregated power on the basis of county, tribe or religion in order to get rich at the expense of their less knowledgeable compatriots. In addition while the rules which make up the formal organisation must be seen as weapons in the struggle for the resources available and consequently an important factor to consider, the boundaries of the formal organisation must not be taken as fixed. Many institutions and individuals who, by formal definition, belong outside the organisation turn out on closer examination to be important actors in the power struggle. In Ugandan co-operative unions, for example, the co-operative officer and the co-operative department play important roles in order to promote what they regard as important interests.

To put the argument in another way, the power approach uses a "transactional" perspective to relations between members of the organisation.[16] But instead of seeing each of these relations between an individual or a group and the organisation itself, as Presthus suggests, this model forces the investigator to determine whether particular groups lie behind the "organisation" and are conducting the transaction. Thus, in a co-operative union one must examine relationships between primary societies and the union committee, between the workers and senior staff, between the committee, the secretary-manager and the co-operative officer. In theory the list is endless; in practice the researcher must identify the most salient relationships.

Two significant books that have self-consciously employed this approach are Melville Dalton's study of six American business firms, and Michel Crozier's examination of two French government agencies.[17] Dalton was actually employed, though not to do research, by several of the firms on which he reports, which meant that he could get the "feel" of struggles between groups from the inside. He found an almost bewildering variety of informal cliques that banded together either within a department or across departmental lines in order to achieve a purpose. When that situation was resolved, the cliques would break up and re-form around another issue. The most effective leaders at various levels in the organisation were those who had political talents and could get people to work together for their purposes. Such men could take decisive action, but were able to compromise where necessary. Not all managers would do this, however. Some were flexible and moved far beyond their formal role, while others shrank from action and hid behind it. The resultant "slack" was often an invitation for encroaching action by the head of a rival department.

One major reason for power struggles in these firms was to acquire extra resources in order to enhance one's prestige and the possibility of promotion, to ensure employment of friends, to hold in reserve for possible emergencies, or to use to make subordinates (engaged in their own power games) more willing to co-operate. Attempts to control auxiliary programmes, particularly those that were jointly shared by several departments, provided a fertile field for power struggles. For example, two groups of operational managers were in conflict over whether the front office or the managers should control the maintenance programme. Control was useful to the more aggressive managers for a variety of side benefits they could derive from using maintenance men. The other weaker managers wanted front office control so that they would get equal access to maintenance men when they needed them. Meanwhile, the front office had to find some way to keep some sort of control over maintenance without sustaining reduced production in departments whose managers offered "persuasive" reasons for decentralising maintenance activities.

One of Crozier's case studies concerns a government industrial monopoly in France. It is a relatively simple productive system using a small number of personnel who are divided into groups of production workers, maintenance workers, lower supervisors, technical engineers and top management. As it happens, each group is fairly well-insulated from the others by virtue of the highly routinised operation and a plethora of rules. However, various alliances and competitive relationships have grown up between different groups. The production workers accept an alliance with the maintenance workers, and cover up for them, even though this means production workers accept an inferior position in the relationship. They do it, because the support of maintenance workers is crucial in making a strike successful, and because maintenance workers who are males tend to act as social leaders for the production workers who are mainly females. However, the maintenance workers cannot go too far in lording over production workers. If they overstep well-understood norms, they may be subject to pressures and blackmail by the production workers.

The basic tactic of the maintenance workers is to prevent anyone else from handling the machines. No explanation of a repair problem is ever given to a production worker or a lower supervisor. Blueprints and maintenance directions from the ministry always disappear from the shop. New maintenance recruits learn how to make repairs on the job and not by reading manuals. In this way the maintenance workers maintain virtually absolute control over machine stoppages.

The lower supervisors have very little power, since they are kept out of maintenance concerns, and are not strongly supported by top management when they try to control other areas. As a result they tend to avoid involvement with any other group's problems and to minimise their contribution to the organisation. Note that they have a higher position within the official hierarchy than the maintenance workers, but far less power.

The technical engineers, like their subordinates the maintenance men, attempt to keep the tasks under their control free from outside interference which would diminish their power. As a result they tend automatically to reject technical changes and improvements. The top management takes the reverse position. Because he is hedged in by many rules, the director of the plant has little actual power. He can increase his influence mainly by planning and constructing new buildings and additions to existing shops which force changes in the routines of other groups. He also derives some power from his position as arbitrator of disputes of groups underneath him. However, Crozier indicates that he can only become master of his plant when there is a large-scale transformation of its activities. Consequently the top managers favour change in most situations.

Thus, both Crozier and Dalton find that individuals and

groups attempt to use the uncertain areas which the rules do not cover to enhance their power and thus gain control over additional resources of the organisation. A major difference between Crozier and Dalton is that the latter discovered that the coalitions which fought together were highly fluid, while the former found them to be relatively rigid and based on occupational categories.[18] Crozier sums up the approach by asking

What is the common thread among these diverse strategies? Each group fights to preserve and enlarge the area upon which it has some discretion, attempts to limit its dependence upon other groups and to accept such dependence only insofar as it is a safeguard against another and more feared one, and finally prefers retreatism if there is no other choice but submission. The group's freedom of action and the power structure appear clearly to be at the core of all these strategies.[19]

While there are very few studies of co-operatives or African organisations which emphasise conscious subgroup activity towards accumulating organisational resources, there are some promising indications. In a study of British co-operative retail societies, G. Ostergaard and A. Halsey call attention to the formation of "political" groups (that is, groups promoting particular policies they want the organisation to adopt) within the retail society.[20] They suggest that these appear first as cliques, which are followed by pressure groups and then organised political parties. Cliques are hard to investigate due to their secretive nature, but pressure groups, that is, the guilds, have played an important public role in influencing co-operative society policy. Today, they feel, the role of guilds has declined and the most active group are the employees of the society. In a small number of English societies political parties have developed, while in a few a multi-party system has been institutionalised.[21] For the most part, however, the development of parties remains shadowy, because of the widespread feeling that they must be contrary to co-operative ideology with its stress on common purposes shared by all members. They discovered that in those societies in which parties were publicly acknowledged and fought society elections, the general level of participation in co-operative affairs was significantly higher (though still a small fraction of the total membership) than in other societies. They argue that further development of political parties would give new meaning to the idea of self-government which is central to co-operative ideology.[22]

A case study of the Nigerian Coal Miners' Union also focuses on power struggles and conflict, but as they are carried out in a particular African setting.[23] Internal conflicts were acknowledged by participants to occupy a major portion of the time and interest of those in the union. The basic causes included a sharp split between those who came from the area around the coal mines and "strangers", and between surface and underground workers. The chance for promotion into the staff of the state corporation that ran the colliery also reduced union solidarity. Furthermore, the leaders tended to model the union after national party and government institutions (with "ministers", "foreign relations", and "back-benchers") a policy which encouraged development of factions, as did the desire of many union members to become officers in order to get into national polities, the national labour movement, or to gain access to union funds. Strategies were adopted by those who gained power to prevent their opponents from unseating them. This tendency resulted in centralising the administration of the union and keeping most of the rank and file in the dark about union programmes and even rules of procedure. Thus, a knowledge of power struggles is essential for understanding the NCMU.

However, one might get the impression that organisations consist of nothing but power struggles and backdoor deals or compromises to resolve them. While this is the impression that Dalton's study suggests, Crozier warns us that no organisation could possibly survive, if the groups within it pressed their advantages to their logical conclusions all the time.[24] Power struggles within every organisation are limited by the fact that members join in order to achieve certain common goals. Some measure of progress towards these goals must occur if the organisation is to survive. Herbert Simon points out that "the process of organising involves, among other things, securing acceptance by the organisational members of a *common model* that defines the situation for them, and provides them with roles and expectations of the roles of others, and with commonly accepted classificatory schemes".[25] The degree to which a common model is accepted can vary from one organisation to another (for example, within co-operative unions) or could be imposed (for example, by requiring all farmers to join a primary society). But a minimal level of acceptance of common purposes and common procedures (generally emphasising hierarchy) is certainly necessary. Thus, studies from the perspective of the power approach can fill gaps in our knowledge of significant organisational behaviour, but will not displace other approaches.

Thus far I have used the term "power" without offering any definition for it. There is, however, an important ambiguity in how the concept can be used in organisational studies. Is power a relationship of groups within the organisation, or is it an attribute—or, more precisely, a potential—of the organisational system itself? Most students explicitly employing a power model use Robert Dahl's "intuitive" definition of power—the ability of A to cause B to do something he would not have done otherwise.[26] In attempting to state precisely the power relations between A and B, the researcher must indicate (1) the probabilities that A will affect B's action slightly or greatly (weight of power); (2) the range of persons or groups represented by B (domain of power); (3) the range of issues over which A can affect B (scope of power); and (4) the reasons why B does what A wants (bases of power).[27]

However, Dahl's definition of power limits the researcher's imagination to zero-sum relationships between the participants in the organisation. It focuses attention away from the impact of power relationships on the performance of the organisation itself. Yet, if the power struggles are significant, they should have an impact (which might be either positive or negative) on the effectiveness of the organisation. It is interesting to note that neither Crozier nor Dalton report what difference the various strategies employed by cliques and occupation groups made in terms of the output of the businesses involved.

A different sort of approach to power highlights the issue

of organisational effectiveness. In Parsons' definition power is viewed as the capability of the system to mobilise resources in order to achieve its goals.[28] Determination of what the goals are involves examination of the relative strength and strategies of particular subgroups within the organisation. Discovery of the mobilisation potential of the organisation also requires close examination of relations between groups. So, the research implications of Dahl's definition are not missing from Parsons' approach. Parsons, however, is able to pose questions that are beyond the reach of the zero-sum model. Since his definition is posed in terms of systematic capabilities, it directs the researcher to look for individuals or groups who are building coalitions and concentrating organisational resources in policies that meet organisational goals.

However, some of the conflicts in the organisation might be overlooked, if the researcher concentrated exclusively on those which helped (or hindered) organisational goals.[29] There is no neat resolution to this problem, as it involves examining patterns of behaviour at two different levels—that of the individual or subgroup and that of the organisational system. But nothing prevents the researcher from investigating the patterns at both levels, and particularly the interconnections between them. In doing so, he must examine the strategies that subgroups employ, whether these strategies are rationally related to the goals of the subgroups, and what impact they have on the organisation as a whole and its goals. The ambiguity, then, simply imposes a dual task upon the investigator.

Furthermore, the researcher cannot assume that conflict within the organisation is necessary detrimental to it—whether or not it advances the fortunes of subgroups or individuals within it. As I suggested above, the detrimental effects of conflict are emphasised by both the scientific management and the human relations approaches. But, while certain kinds of conflict can hamper or even destroy the effectiveness of the organisation, other kinds may enhance it.[30] The most important positive function of conflict is to clarify the alternatives to a policy decision which the organisation must make, and the intensity with which these alternatives are held. As we shall see later, a subgroup within a co-operative union may use the ultimate threat of secession to bring its position to the attention of other power-holders. Failure to heed intensely held positions may spell trouble for the continued effectiveness of the union later on. The advantage of conflict is that it permits other members to evaluate the importance of the issue to the most affected subgroups. Conflict may also increase the solidarity of the organisation by indicating more clearly the types and degree of common purpose held by the conflicting members. In addition the manner in which conflicts are resolved may increase solidarity to a level higher than that which existed before the conflict developed. Also, conflict may initiate "search behaviour" in order to find a new alternative that will satisfy all subgroups involved in the dispute.[31]

Finally, leaders who are sensitive to the kinds of conflict existing in their organisation and the reasons for the strategies used by subgroups and individuals are more likely to be able to weld together coalitions of subgroups to achieve the larger organisational goals. This is what Parsons has in mind when he talks of mobilising resources as the critical aspect of power in organisations. Dalton points out that cliques can be "interlocking action centers", though they may either attempt to promote or resist change.[32]

Some interesting studies in American factories and unions support the argument that those who hold power can often promote organisational goals more effectively. An early study of the role of supervisors in creating high morale among employees of a large American public utility found that those supervisors with influence on their own superiors (and skill in human relations) tended to have satisfied employees. Those who lacked this sort of power had low morale in their employee units, whether or not they were adept at the art of human relations.[33]

In an investigation of four American union locals a significant relationship was found between the effectiveness of the local in bargaining for advantageous contracts and the amount of power various official echelons (that is, the president, the executive board, the bargaining committee, and the membership) had over individual members. Unions with more control at each level (even though it was distributed in either a more democratic or a more authoritarian fashion depending on the local) were more effective. Their members were more likely to vote in union elections, go out on strike, man the picket line than unions with less organisational control over their membership.[34] A similar study of a large business with 31 geographically separated production units revealed a strong direct correlation between the amount of power and the level of productivity within the units.[35]

If the amount of power which can be mobilised is a critical variable in the effectiveness of the organisation, then close attention must be paid to individuals who (no matter what their formal role happens to be) are in a position to concentrate the resources of the organisation on its goals. Simon refers to this type of person as the "organisational entrepreneur", the man who induces others to form or continue in an organisation.[36] As I mentioned above, such men must have considerable political talents in order to bend factional struggles to larger purposes.[37]

We should also consider the problems involved in the use of the term "effectiveness", before we turn to the application of a power approach to Ugandan co-operative unions. Effectiveness, or performance, can only be meaningful in terms of the goals pursued. Effective with respect to what end? is the question that must be asked. Thus, use of the concept of organisational effectiveness requires us to be clear about the goals the organisation and subgroups within the organisation are attempting to achieve.

The use of a power struggle perspective alerts us to expect that the goals of subgroups and the organisation are likely to differ. What is effective in achieving the organisation's goals may be dysfunctional for individuals within the organisation and vice-versa. Naturally, the most effective organisations are those which manage to find a high degree of overlap, or even better, reinforcement, of the goals of both level.

However, it is worth asking whether the organisation can have interests or goals which are different from its members. Can there be an organisational interest which is not the personal interest of some members? The danger here is either to give added legitimacy to the goals of a subgroup ("*L'Etat, c'est moi*"), or for the researcher to reify interests which do not actually exist. It seems to me that organisations do have interests of their own, though these must always be carried out by its members. For example, there is a tendency toward organisational self-maintenance and survival, and a bias in favour of achieving either its original goals or new ones that have replaced them. In addition, as Philip Selznick has argued, "... it is essential to think of an organisation as a dynamic conditioning field which effectively shapes the behaviour of those who are attempting to remain at the helm".[38] The nature of the interests individuals have is changed by their entry into the organisational arena.

Using the Power Approach in Uganda Co-operative Unions

For a variety of reasons the power approach provides an attractive framework for the investigation of co-operative unions in Uganda. In the first place the formal emphasis on democracy within co-operative unions enlarges the range of tactics open to the growers and their representatives. At the same time a co-operative is a business and is subject to the same kinds of stresses as any small business hiring 50–500 employees. The possible tactical alliances between subgroups of employees and members of the committee or primary societies in a certain area are capable of infinite variation.

The heavy involvement of the Uganda government further complicates the power possibilities. The government has decreased the margin of union funds required for loans for capital expansion (in some cases the government has put up 100 % of the loan). So, it must look after its investment. In addition by putting heavier responsibilities for processing agricultural produce into the hands of the unions, the government has introduced a new factor into the problem of maintaining a high level of export earnings. Most importantly, the government was responsible for the initiation of most unions and has guided their development ever since. If a

13 – 704520 *Widstrand*

union gets into real trouble, the co-operative department will step in and attempt to straighten it out. Thus, it would be sheer formalism to regard the government as anything other than an active member (or several members in some situations) of each union with self-conscious strategies for maintaining power to achieve its particular interests.

In addition Ugandan co-operatives are still extremely new organisations, particularly when we consider the sudden expansion in their activities over the past decade. They are organised in the same format as co-operative societies in Great Britain though environmental conditions are obviously different in Uganda. They engage in relatively complex business operations. All of this is rather bewildering to the average grower who has little education and few precedents to help explain why he should belong to a co-operative. The consequence is to radically reduce the understanding of the different responsibilities a member may hold, and the sense of common purposes for which the co-operative is intended to work. The uniform perception of a "common model" is relatively weak. Consequently, growers who find themselves in co-operatives feel free to engage in an extremely wide range of tactics to achieve personal goals at the expense of those of the union. One expects to find a bewildering variety of fluid *ad hoc* alliances, though not necessarily a rapid turnover in the persons holding the most powerful positions.

This tendency toward conflict and power struggles is abetted by the extremely low annual income of the typical grower. In their world the amounts of money required by a small or medium-sized business are beyond comprehension. Who can lose, if some is siphoned off the top?

A further factor creating sharp differences between groups within a union is the extremely uneven understanding of commercial practices among the members (including the staff). Some are "cosmopolitans" in this respect, while others remain "locals". Traders and ambitious farmers have been instrumental in the establishment of co-operatives and have been quick to recognise the possibilities for self-enrichment.[39] In a way this limits the number of power seekers active in the organisational arena, though leaving open the possibility of manipulating the support of the more apathetic members or in a few cases the possibility of a spontaneous uprising against a particularly unpopular policy.

Finally, intensely held local attitudes towards religion, national parties, and tribal membership have often created important conflicts among groups within co-operative unions. Subgroups have different goals they want the union to adopt (or permit) and different ideas about the means that should be used to achieve them. Thus, extremely significant patterns of organisational behaviour would be ignored, if we failed to examine conflict and power strategies in the unions.

Where, then, are the likely points of conflict between subgroups? The first one concerns the problem of persuading members to join the union (via a primary society). The task involves convincing farmers to buy shares in a not yet existing union in the hope of building a factory or buying a ginnery. There is usually a group of "founders" who take on the task of convincing growers who live near them to join. Often the co-operative officer in the area is in close contact with the founders and can promise more than matching funds (or a guarantee for a bank loan) against the amount they collect. The growers are often attracted by the idea of receiving a bonus, but more importantly by having an alternative to being cheated by private middlemen. It is worth keeping in mind that few farmers who are convinced to buy shares automatically give up the idea of selling their produce to private traders at some future time when the latter offer a higher price than the union or when the traders offer immediate cash payments.[40] Later the secretary-manager (the top paid official), the committee and the co-operative officer (through the educational facilities of the co-operative department) use co-operative ideology as one weapon to try to convince the growers to remain loyal to the union in spite of the attractions of its competitors.

The basic contact between most growers and the union comes in the sale of raw coffee, cotton or other crops. The primary societies act as collection agencies and then hire transport (or use union lorries) to convey their produce to the factory. To do this the farmers must have gunny bags in which to carry their crop. One of their most universal complaints is that the union does not provide them with enough bags. Here a committeeman from the local area can play an important role by either bringing the problem to the attention to staff, or by bringing pressure to have more bags sent to a particular society. He will then be in a position to demand favours from one or the other. The strongest weapon the farmers have (or had up to the establishment of the processing monopolies) is to boycott a union. A successful boycott is the ultimate weapon. At least one union in Uganda was forced to cease operation (and merge with another one) due to a successful boycott lasting several years. Another union, which had a local monopoly on coffee processing before the national monopoly was instituted, was forced into a relatively ineffective performance by extensive smuggling of coffee out of the district by primary society officials.

The purchase of cotton or coffee raises another delicate problem for the staff—what to do about substandard produce. If they accept too much of it, the union will make substantial losses when it tries to sell processed coffee or bales of lint to the marketing boards. On the other hand, they are under extreme pressure to accept the farmers' crop, if the growers are to pay their poll taxes and children's school fees. Here there is a struggle between the staff and the farmers for the loyalty of the committee-men. The latter are expected to try to raise crop standards so that the union will improve its performance, but they must also stand for re-election at the next annual general meeting.

Most committee-men view their position as a source of wealth. In small remote unions the allowances for subsistence and attendance at meetings form a substantial portion of a man's yearly income. This is also the reason why 90–95% of the primary society delegates come to the annual general meeting.[41] Similar meetings in England attract from 0.27–3.06% of the members.[42] In some unions expenditure on committee travelling and allowances has sometimes got out of hand, as larger and larger amounts for more and more committee meetings are sanctioned each year.[43] The degree to which committee-men use their positions to gain extra resources (some of which may be ploughed back into election campaigns) varies startlingly. In some unions the committee does not try to divert monies intended for union programmes, in others members of the committee can effectively be checked only by a government take-over of the union.

Where committee-men do take advantage of their position, they divert crop finance into other uses, often "loans" (with no expectation of repayment) to their own primary societies or private businesses. They may use union lorries for their own businesses, or to help out those to whom they have family ties, or who may vote for them at the next union election. They have proposed extravagant projects and then accepted one of the higher tenders for constructing the project.[44] In some cases they have engaged in outright theft. A critical question for researchers is to try to determine why this practice grows up in certain unions, but not in others. What combinations of opposing forces can prevent a committee from becoming corrupt?

The declaration of a bonus is a potential point for conflict, though surprisingly the way in which it is divided often fails to attract the attention of the growers. The declaration of a bonus is the single most important factor in maintaining the satisfaction of farmers all over Uganda.[45] Generally, the union's auditors will suggest how much of the surplus should be declared as the bonus, and what portion of the bonus should be capitalized to provide for paying off the union's debts or for future expansion. This often becomes the "rational" position as opposed to the "political" interests of the growers who want as much money in the short term as possible. A second issue arises when the union processes two crops or two varieties of the same crop (for example, arabica and robusta coffee). Generally, one will have done much better than the other and delegates at the annual general meeting representing that crop may demand a larger share of the bonus. In one union this issue was one of the major reasons leading to the secession of a group of societies which then formed their own union.

Within the staff of the union a variety of conflicts may also arise. The hiring of porters and senior staff raises antagonisms and often requires "political arithmetic" to achieve the proper balance—sometimes at the expense of qualified employees. Members of the staff of coffee factories or ginneries sometimes make arrangements with representatives of primary societies to overstate the deliveries of produce and then divert the difference to their own pockets.

Some of these potential conflict points (and there are many others) may be more prominent at one point in a union's development than at a later or earlier time. Changes in the size, complexity and degree of specialisation of the union and its staff may alter the power alignments. Variations in the incentives which are offered by unions at birth, in their youth and at maturity also result in changes in relative power positions. The committee is generally the most powerful body in the union in the early days. One of the critical developments for the union's performance concerns whether the senior staff can emerge as an independent force in the next stage or not. In any case it is important to examine the history of the organisation in order to understand why certain factions emerged, while others remained relatively powerless.

The Comparative Performance of two Unions

A brief examination of two fairly large co-operatives will illustrate the wide gap in performance that exists among the unions in Uganda. Demonstration of this gap will permit us to look for differences in the distribution and use of power by members of each. The two unions contrasted here are Uganda Growers (UG) and Ranyankole Kweterana (BK). The former is the oldest union in Uganda, having been formed 25 years before it was registered by the co-operative department in 1948. Though a small and ineffective organisation prior to registration, it was the first to operate a processing unit and grew into one of Uganda's largest unions. It was so deeply ensconced in debt by 1967 that the government took it over and split it into three smaller unions.[46] BK was founded much later (1957) and only recently has begun to approach the size and complexity of UG in its heyday. Since its first year of operation, it has always produced a surplus.

Little financial information about UG is available for the pre-1948 period (and no balance sheets have been found prior to 1953/54). In the years before 1950 UG was primarily involved in the collection of raw cotton and maize for sale to middlemen and private processors. Its surplus when it had one, was in the 5–10,000 shilling range, and it owned virtually no property except its head office in Katwe—near Kampala, acquired in 1938. It was in direct competition with the Federation of Uganda African Farmers (FUAP) run by Ignatius Musazi. FUAF engaged in both co-operative economic ventures and anti-colonial political activity until it was proscribed by the protectorate government.[47]

In 1949 the Buganda Government purchased Ngogwe ginnery in East Mengo district and leased it to UG.[48] In the following year sales of cotton reached three million shillings and the surplus rose to Shs. 90,000. By 1954 UG had acquired two more ginneries and had begun to erect Kawempe coffee factory.[49] Turnover was now about nine and a half million shillings, though surplus remained about Shs.100,000. The crop balance, which is a potentially important basis for formation of subgroups, was about 20% maize and 80% cotton. From a low of 18 primary societies belonging to the union in 1949 there were 186 member societies (individuals must join primary societies and are only indirectly members of the union) in 1954.

Kawempe coffee factory opened in 1956 and by the following year three-quarters of the sales of UG were processed coffee. UG now owned 5 processing units (4 ginneries and one factory) and achieved its first million shilling surplus on a turnover of Shs.26,200,000. The union stopped handling maize in 1958. Coffee continued to grow in importance until it amounted to 88% of turnover in 1960. The surplus that year amounted to a little over two million out of a turnover of 40 million shillings. This was the high point.

For the next seven years there was a fairly steady decline in turnover (particularly coffee) to one-third the level of 1960. Surpluses turned into deficits which reached two million shillings in 1967, UG's last year of independent operation. Interestingly, cotton began to supplant coffee as the major crop of the union in its last two years. Part of the problem lay in the enormous capital expansion undertaken by UG after 1960 and the consequent organisational problems which were thrust upon the union in rapid succession. A coffee grinding mill and a wholesale shop proved to be losing ventures, and the latter was eventually sold. By 1967 the management of UG was responsible for eight ginneries, two coffee factories, two pulperies, two mills and several stores. Over 300 primary societies belonged to the union, but many were weak as farmers had not received a bonus for many years. At this point the banks refused to extend any more credit and the government was forced to take over.

An analysis of the economic performance of Banyankole Kweterana makes pleasant reading by comparison.[50] It enrolled 45 primary societies in its first year and raised Shs. 100,000 towards the erection of a coffee factory. The protectorate government guaranteed a loan of 67% of the cost of building the factory in 1959. The factory began to process coffee in 1961 and incurred a small deficit of Shs 20,000 on a turnover of slightly less than two million shillings.

In every year since, BK has made a surplus, and has turned in the leading performance in the country in 1965/66 and 1966/67. Its turnover rose to eleven and a half million shillings in 1963/64, but has not been much higher since. In 1964/65, however, its turnover declined by two million shillings, while its net surplus *rose* to its highest point of Shs. 1,800,000. It suffered a drastic decline in its surplus in the year ending in March 1969 due to the unwise payment of an advance bonus to the farmers, and the sudden drop (at the height of the season) in the price offered for processed coffee by the marketing board. However, turnover in 1969/70 is expected to be close to thirty million shillings with a healthy surplus of over two million shillings.

The number of members has grown steadily to 134 with many additional groups awaiting registration. Its pattern of acquisition of processing units and other enterprises has been somewhat slower than UG. Its second factory opened in 1966 and two pulperies were added by the beginning of 1969. As a result of the coffee processing monopoly BK acquired a

Surplus or Deficit as a Percentage of Turnover

Year	Uganda Growers %	Banyankole-Kweterana %
1953/54	1.1	
1954/55	0.3	
1955/56	(figures unavailable)	
1956/57	4.0	
1957/58	3.8	
1958/59	3.0	
1959/60	5.1	
1960/61	0.5	− 1.0
1961/62	2.2	7.6
1962/63	− 1.4	6.6
1963/64	0.5	13.1
1964/65	− 3.4	18.6
1965/66	− 3.3	14.2
1966/67	− 14.1	11.9
1967/69 (18 month year)		0.6
1969/70		7.5 (estimated)

third factory. It ran a canteen for its members for two years, but leased it when it failed to show any profit. A cattle ranch was begun in 1964/65, a petrol pump the following year, and minor crops were purchased for the first time in the year after that. These enterprises have expanded rapidly. During the past year a consumer shop (in which BK holds shares and has provided staff on a temporary basis) has been opened up in Mbarara, capital of the district.

Sales of processed coffee have remained the major business of the union, however. BK buys two different kinds of coffee —arabica, which commands a higher price per pound, and which is grown mainly by farmers in the northwestern part of the district, and robusta, which is grown by farmers in the south. Arabica farmers have contributed from 19% to 39% of the union's coffee sales, depending on how stiff the competition was from private traders and a second union in the district. The other union (Twena Tubehamwe) failed, and has now merged with BK. Since the merger arabica growers have produced 35 % of the coffee turnover. It has only been in the last year or so that the arabica farmers have become aware that payment of a bonus solely in terms of weight of coffee sold to the union gives a disproportionate share of the surplus to growers of the less valuable robusta.

The difference in performance between UG and BK can be compared directly by considering net surplus or deficit as a percentage of turnover.[51]

A full explanation of the difference in performance of these two unions is beyond the scope of this paper. But a brief indication of some important aspects suggests that strategies to improve an individual's or subgroup's power may influence important union decisions.

As in most Ugandan unions the committee was the most powerful subgroup in Uganda Growers during the early years. However, unlike the case in some other unions the salaried staff never managed to define a sphere of activities in which their actions would not be challenged by the committee. The committee ran the union without a secretary-manager until 1955, (each ginnery had a manager and a staff), even though the union was already a nine million shillings business with three ginneries.

The chairman of the committee had made a bid in the early 1950's to establish himself in the top managerial role. Other members of the committee complained that he acted like a chief (he was the son of an important chief) and re-fused to consult with them before taking decisions. He was accused of using lorries and iron sheets belonging to the union in his private business. In 1954 he attempted to move from his uncertain position as union chairman into the vacant manager's position at one of the ginneries. The committee refused to accept his application. An implied threat to burn down the ginnery gave the committee sufficient leverage with the delegates from the primary societies (at a special general meeting) to force him out of the chairmanship.

The man who replaced him had been the vice-chairman, and came from a different county. The co-operative department urged that a general manager be appointed, particularly as

the union would soon open a large coffee factory. The committee agreed and the new chairman was selected to go on an
overseas course in preparation for this position. It was a point
of pride in UG, as in most Ugandan unions, that a local son
who has already been prominently connected to the union be
in charge of operations. In fact, the path through the committee is one of the best defined channels of recruitment into
a salaried position on the union staff.

During his period as the general manager he was acknowledged as a popular leader. He spent little time in his office,
preferring to visit primary societies and factories, listening to
complaints, and settling minor problems. He also tended to
make decisions without consulting the committee, even in the
case of the acquisition of a pulpery. A series of unexplained
cash shortages led to his downfall. The main actor in the
struggle to secure his dismissal was the co-operative department. This problem was complicated, as the general manager
had been appointed originally by the delegates in the annual
general meeting (and not by the committee—the more usual
procedure), and remained popular with them in spite of the
losses the union had suffered. The department managed to
have the position abolished, and thus removed him from the
union staff. A few years later, however, he was re-elected to
the chairmanship.

Over the following five years two men occupied the new
top management position of secretary-manager (both were appointed by the committee, subject to the approval of the co-
operative department). Each lasted a short time. Neither was
able to control the committee, and the first was forced to
resign when a large coffee transaction with a neighbouring
coffee union turned out to have peculiar features.

The members of the committee had long since discovered
that among the advantages of making policy for the union
was the possibility of diverting resources to their own societies, doing favours for societies whose coffee was rejected for
inferior quality or who failed to get enough gunny bags for
transport, and dipping into the till for "loans" to societies
that actually went into their own pockets.

Reaching the union's committee and remaining on it could

be an extremely lucrative opportunity, so it is not surprising that committee-men were anxious to ensure their continued tenure. This was not easy to accomplish, as the union was spread out over East and West Mengo, making communication difficult. Furthermore, there was a strong prohibition against open campaigning for the union committee, partly because the co-operative department has always been against mixing politics and co-operative affairs (campaigning for union office has not been perceived as a different sort of activity from campaigning for national or local governmental office). Another reason inhibiting open union campaigning may have been the strong feelings of the Baganda that it is improper for a man to promote himself directly.

However, there were a number of campaign activities in which a member of (or aspirant to) UG's committee could engage. He could encourage his friends to spread his name about in connection with union office. If he was a committee-man, he could personally present bonus cheques to primary societies or listen to their grievances. He might arrange social gatherings of delegates just before the annual general meeting. An extremely important tactic, particularly for those not yet on the committee, was to make points in the general meeting that would embarass the incumbents.[52] One's skill in speaking was carefully noted.

Finally, a number of shadow organisations grew up after the union became big business. They were called "subunions", were entirely informal as far as UG was concerned, and were organised on a county basis for the purpose of getting one or more men from that county onto the union committee in the hope that the next pulpery, ginnery or coffee factory would be sited in their area. With their own man on the committee they also had a chance for loans for society projects, more crop finance and personal consideration when they brought their produce to the ginneries or factory. Formation of the later subunions seems to have been stimulated by the success of the first one. These subunions charged each primary society that joined relatively nominal dues. In one county only about a quarter of the societies actually joined. The subunion elected its own officers and held committee meetings irregularly. Its members formed a caucus, in effect, to support particular candidates for the union committee and to influence particular union policies.

In Banyankole-Kweterana the committee played an important formative role in the establishment of the union, though it was organised with the help and guidance of the co-operative officer in Ankole district. By contrast to UG (in which the committee antedated the department) the co-operative department has always taken a significant part in decision-making in BK. The original manager of the coffee factory was a Pakistani hired on the recommendation of the department. The chairman of the union was selected to become his assistant a little while after operations began, and replaced him two and a half years later. Like the general manager of UG he has been a popular manager and has spent much of his time keeping contact with the societies and production units scattered over the district.

After some fairly heated discussion the union decided to site its first coffee factory in Bushenyi, which is located in Igara county, even though there were no banking facilities or electricity in the town until the factory was established. Many of the founders, including the present secretary-manager, come from Igara, which has long been one of the more highly developed counties in Ankole.

A few years later the head office for the union was established just outside the district capital of Mbarara. This location was more convenient for making trips to Kampala to see representatives of the coffee marketing board, the co-operative department, or commercial suppliers. At this point the union installed a new factory manager and made the original chairman the secretary-manager in charge of all operations. This remains his position today.

The committee generally accepts the suggestions of the co-operative officer and the secretary-manager (both of whom attend all committee and general meetings). Originally, committee-men were fearful and suspicious about almost every expenditure the union made, and wanted to hire as few employees as possible, but they have grown to trust the managers as the union has prospered and the farmers have received bonuses almost every year. The union has managed to avoid making loans to its societies and thus has not had to worry about the bad debts that seem inevitably to follow such loans. The secretary-manager is able to make emergency decisions on his own, and is rarely faced with opposition from the committee, and virtually never by the primary societies and delegates to the general meeting.

However, one important case illustrates that when a subgroup of growers have strong feelings, they can force the union to accept their position in the face of the combined advice of the secretary-manager and the co-operative department. This issue arose over the siting of BK's second coffee factory. In 1962 the primary societies in Rwampara, a comparatively underdeveloped county in Ankole, formed their own informal organisation (within BK) and began saving funds towards building a coffee store to cut down on the cost of crop transport to the far-away Bushenyi factory. The union management decided not to support this store to the great irritation of members of the subgroup. The Rwampara primary societies resolved to continue to collect money to build it.

The issue simmered for a year and a half and then flared up over the question of where the union's second coffee factory should be located. The Bushenyi manager said that his factory could not handle all the coffee the union was purchasing. In addition the union lost the chance to buy a large amount of the district's coffee because of high transport costs to Bushenyi in the northwestern corner of the district. Private traders could pay more and process the coffee in nearby locations. The secretary-manager and the co-operative officer felt that the new factory should be placed near Mbarara. They argued that this was the most "rational" place for it, because it would then be close to an existing source of power, banking facilities, suppliers whose shops were in Mbarara, and because in this location transport to the railhead at Kasese would be cheaper for the union.[53]

In response the farmers of Rwampara insisted that they had helped pay for Bushenyi factory and now it was their turn to be rewarded. Their area was now the richest coffee producing area in Ankole. They wanted a factory near their farms, and one which would hire their sons. They also wanted the coffee husks (usually discarded in dry processing) for fertilizer.

They enlisted local politicians in their crusade, including the present secretary-general of Ankole. In addition they sent a delegation to see the minister of agriculture, forestry and co-operatives to request permission to secede from BK and start their own union. They also demonstrated that members from Rwampara alone could raise one-third the price of a new coffee factory.

The secretary-manager decided not to press his case aggressively, fearing that if he won, his victory might be met with a boycott. He knew that the other Ankole union was currently facing a serious boycott as a result of management problems. So he kept quiet.

The only other subgroups that might have strongly opposed the Rwampara organisation were the primary societies in the area of the secretary-manager's proposed site. However, the societies in this area were weak, while those near the alternative site in Rwampara were extremely vigorous.

The minister produced a Solomonic decision by agreeing that the factory should be located at the Rwampara site, while giving the franchise for it to BK. The decision was accepted without further disturbance or recrimination and the factory began operating in 1966/67. The absence of a supply of electricity meant that the union had to purchase a diesel engine, which broke down for a time in the first year of operation. However, after it was replaced, the factory ran smoothly.

Conclusion: Power Struggles and Performance

These short descriptions of a few conflicts that confronted BK and UG are not sufficient to permit a full analysis of the importance of power and conflict in co-operative union affairs. However, they do suggest organisational considerations which are usually neglected. The "ordinary" members of most organisations are assumed to have the least amount of power in day-to-day affairs. While the "iron law of oligarchy" is supported by a vast number of studies, the Rwampara case in BK demonstrates vividly that when aroused farmers can become a potent subgroup, and must be regarded as an important *political* factor in resolution of union policy.

The most difficult problem, which has been barely touched on here, is to develop the links between power struggles and productivity. The Rwampara factory-siting case suggests the importance of conflict in permitting leaders to take into account the intensity with which certain positions are held. On the other hand, the more individualistic strategies found in UG had the reverse effect on productivity.

Other schools of organisational analysis, particularly the scientific management and the human relations approaches, have developed many propositions linking aspects of organisational behaviour and productivity. For example, propositions about techniques for information processing and efficient division of labour attempt to relate management and productivity. Similarly, arguments of the human relations school for more worker participation in decision-making have the same relationship in mind. Some of these propositions probably will have to be modified as we learn more about organisations, particularly in developing countries. One way to do that is to expand the range of behaviour we take into account by examining the subgroups that develop within the organisation and the strategies they use to try to improve their positions.

Raymond Apthorpe

Some Problems of Evaluation

Since I am at present engaged in some social studies of agricultural co-operatives in Africa, it is a particular pleasure to have been invited to Scandinavia to discuss some of the problems involved. I am thinking less of its co-operatives, however, than of its social science and especially the work of the Department of Social Anthropology at the University of Bergen. Fredrik Barth and his colleagues there are developing an approach to the study of social change that departs significantly from social pre-requisites' approaches.[1] To paraphrase a point of view from the Bergen studies of entrepreneurial activity and social change and to apply it to the subject of the present conference, evaluation of co-operatives should focus less on "what makes co-operatives" than on, "what co-operatives make". Co-operatives of various types exist. What have their consequences been thus far in relation to their stated aims? What follows will explore one aspect of this, in one instance.

Introductory Remarks

Any internationally and historically complex social organization with spiritual as well as practical ramifications that have become ends in themselves tends, frankly, to defy "evaluation" as in "project evaluation". One may like or dislike "the Catholic Church", or be agnostic about it, depending very often upon one's purely personal circumstances of the individual or those of the group to which one belongs. In many ways the problem about "the co-operative movement" is not very different. Certainly it is not much easier. The functional and administrative activities which are known under this name are intermixed, sometimes seemingly inextricably, with complex moral and political policies. Sometimes, indeed these are considered as more important than the economic dimension.

It is necessary to state this at the outset although the small study that follows will be mainly confined, in its particulars, to some reflections on one ostensibly merely technical organizational detail of but one kind of marketing co-operative in one country, Kenya, in the mid 1960's. This had, in a context of many other factors, serious economic consequences. This encourages me to make it the focus for this study. The economic performance of co-operatives may be among even their least important features, for those in government for instance, who recommended that they be set up for the benefit of poor people living from the land in rural areas. *For the intended beneficiaries themselves,* however, the economic implications of the new organization tend to be crucial.

This immediately brings us to a general theme that students of social policy must keep in mind when considering co-operatives in Kenya and other countries with similar characteristics. There were in the colonial period, and also today, enormous gulfs in social distance, social communication and social identification between the planners of the movement and those they plan for. This is true very often even when plannistrators and peasants come face to face at the local level. The Commissioners and Registrars of Co-operatives, for instance, may have little if any personal experiences themselves as ordinary members of the organizations they recommend for others with by-laws that, among other things, exclude members of the co-operative department from membership. Certainly their own economic and educational circumstances bear little if any comparison with those of poor peasants. Social scientists from the Universities may have little real experience of the problems of government which they are invited to comment on from time to time. But, as between officials from Governments and the ordinary farmers, the situation is often not much better.

A second observation by way of introduction has to do with definitions, never a very satisfactory subject to discuss adequately, but one that cannot be left aside altogether. The analytical problems for co-operative studies are elusive enough.

They are not made any the less so when terms of reference speak of co-operatives in nothing less then cosmological essentials. "Co-operation" being of all words in the vocabulary of public policy the sweetest, it sugars many a pill and is put to a huge variety of other uses in addition. Co-operation has been invited or exported to Africa as, for example, something that transcends both capitalism and socialism as well as being an instrument for the one and as an enemy of the other. "Co-operation" has also been held to be one and the same policy that has brought social change in Africa as well as in Europe, in the colonial as well as in the post-colonial period, for marketing and production and consumers societies willy nilly (not to mention educational and industrial associations) and regardless of whether—to mention just a few points —the crops concerned are for home or export consumption, sold in raw or manufactured form, are of high value or low, or perishable or not.

"Co-operation" affirmed in such general terms, even when limited to an agricultural or rural sector, belongs to that same order of illusions as the idea of a perfectly free and equal utopia. This may serve the interests of demagogues and tyrants, and of a bureaucracy whose salaried members depend on the continuance of the *status quo* for *their* incomes and security which bear little direct relation, at any rate, to the vagaries of ordinary farming and structural changes proposed for the agricultural sector. For the individual producers of a crop in a rural district, on the other hand, the effects of the introduction of a co-operation into a region where previously there was actually or potentially a different organizational infrastructure, may be real and significant. Our study must reach down to this aspect of co-operatives.

Finally, by way of introduction, it is to be noted that co-operatives, like other rural development policies in Africa at the present time, owe their respectability very often to the fact that they have been recommended by expert or professional third parties invited by government bodies to advise them. In practice the terms of reference accepted by these policy-recommenders tend to be so limited that there is a virtual guarantee that the pattern of policy on which judge-ments have been sought will not be changed very much. Co-operative policies are, characteristically, reformist or administrative approaches even to problems which have been defined as being in need of radical attention. This is true very largely, I believe, both of co-operatives that originate with the state and of those which were started by voluntary action. Inasmuch as this is so, there is a double contingency which explains why, paper to paper, certainly not flint to flint, the invited advisers tend to come up with administrative reforms only if reforms at all. The co-operatives are in themselves administrative agencies towards the solution of problems that far transcend the administrative realm. As such they offer, so to say, ready-made receptacles for the attentions of liberal studies and officially commissioned social science research.

Eastern Africa

In co-operative policies as well as in other respects the trend is strongly established at the present time, for Tanzania and Zambia to march side by side. Co-operative principles are interpreted in those two countries as being central not only to the agricultural sector of the economy. (In Zambia recently there has been some discussion of possible partial co-operativization even of mining.[2] Tanzania indeed stands out perhaps from all Africa in the emphasis the government put there on structural change as a necessity for economic development based, though this sometimes is, on rather a fanciful ideology about what "traditional" African society is supposed to be or to have been. In Uganda, the private sector in agriculture as in industry has showed much viability of its own and on the whole, but with major exceptions, government policy has not heavily discouraged this. Much, however, is anomalous and in transition in Uganda at the present time[3] and it would be difficult to find any other very convincing single formula.

The political culture of Kenya is different again. To the extent that "organizational rationality" is one of its watchwords and relatively more emphasis is put on this than on structural change, the case material to which I will turn next may be very opposite in that country.

A Kenya Case: a Fall in Pyrethrum Production in the Million Acres Scheme

The case material chosen for discussion here concerns the Kenya Highlands and especially the Million Acres Scheme of land re-settlement.[4] Of all the rural development projects in the entire continent today, this Scheme as a whole has unusually vast fiscal, administrative, economic, infrastructural, political and social dimensions, all these being in addition to its primary agricultural and technical objectives. Almost as soon as it started in the early 1960's, it was officially and popularly widely affirmed by almost all classes of commentators other than, significantly, the plot-holders themselves, that the economic performance of the Scheme, as well as certain other of its aspects, would depend very largely on the single factor of the role that primary co-operative societies, that were to be responsible for much of the day to day business, would play. It has become common in many countries in Africa today for policy recommenders to expect the performance of primary societies to be crucial for success as well as failure, however precisely these states are defined.

Soon after the introduction of these marketing co-operatives in the highlands external evaluation was called for. It seemed in several respects that they were not achieving the performances that their planners had come to hope of them. Unfortunately, it is rare for evaluations to be sought at less pessimistic moments. This goes some way to explain why so many development studies focus on supposed failures. Furthermore, as in this case, most African studies of co-operatives are no exception to the general rule, it is so often only economic problems that are singled out even for social analysis in development studies. It tends to be specifically problems of economic performance, in decline, which come up "for evaluation" even when someone has defined in advance the nature of solution to them as something to be sought in, say, some form of social rather than economic planning.[5] This in itself leads to curiosities of analysis in development studies that, in the context of one or another single social science discipline, not consciously given to "interdisciplinary" aims (yet concerned with development and planning all the same) would give rise to doubts and frowns if not sheer gaping disbelief.

One of the concerns about the highlands co-ops was a fall in the output of pyrethrum in the Scheme. This was blamed on to the co-operatives and it is this that is my subject here in a somewhat dramatized form for expository purposes but factual in its essentials, although the statistical dimensions of these have not been established and the material is incomplete in other ways. Following *uhuru* a decolonization of the Kenya highlands which had been reserved for White settlement for nearly two generations was set in process. Since Kenya is among the world's largest producers of pyrethrum central economic planners were quick to find that decline in its output posed a serious problem. We note here that as in many other cases this problem, albeit an economic one, was identified as such because of its implications for that abstraction, "the national economy" (also the world economy here given the Kenya share in the world pyrethrum output). There was much less thought or knowledge of the plight of the immediate causualties, namely the people who actually derived their livelihood from the production of the crop in question in the fields.

To account for this fall in production several modes of explanation were fashionable in Kenya in the mid 1960's— among central planners, that is, not the new settlers themselves. These "general theories" were not scientifically derived from an analytical study of the particular circumstances and situations involved. Rather, they were aspects of the belief-systems of planners at the time. As such, certainly they must be included within the scope of any analysis which aims to take "the human factor" into account. There is no reason to confine this latter—inaptly characterised though it may be—only to the receiving end of central planning.[6] Any evaluation of a development project must concern itself *both* with the circumstances themselves locally judged to be problematic *and* with the locally prevailing assumptions and theories which give them this complexion.

First of all, in Kenya in the middle 1960's, one heard this

shortfall in pyrethrum production being attributed to what was called "the political situation". Formerly under the regime of European settlerdom, there had recently been a transfer of power in Kenya following independence. It was widely believed at and shortly after that time, among both African and European central planners,[7] (and no doubt with an understandable measure of realism given the circumstances especially of Mau Mau which was then understood more in political than agrarian terms) that a wide range of disasters was bound to be part of the price paid for Independence. Of these perils, the fall in the output of pyrethrum was said to be merely one instance. According to one account, indeed, the entire Million Acres Scheme was devised in order to minimise the risk of grave security problems given the political sensitivity about the highlands and their white settlement. Above all in the highlands the colonial regime had been a European settlerdom characterised by large scale land holdings and extensive farming operations. Independence had led to the replacement of this pattern with one based on intensive land utilisation by African small-holdings (but in actuality each of the regimes was characterised by a combination of extensive and intensive features). The scatter of primary marketing societies was instituted mainly for the benefit of these small farms.

It was widely believed, if for the wrong reasons, that inevitably the problems of Kenyan agriculture would be particularly acute in this time of political transition. Given the importance of the highland region in the overall agricultural and political scene, it was thought that this would be the part of the country most affected. This kind of approach that lays the blame, actually or potentially, so squarely at the door of "the political factor", is something commonly resorted to by the practitioners us well as theorists of development administration theory. The credit for success it lays at its own door, praising the technical and functional qualities of the managers and officials responsible. The blame for failure is put into the political sector and politics from which administration distinguishes itself. For administrators it is politicians who are the scapegoats. The politicians, on the other hand, lament the inertia of the administration.

Second, it was also *à la mode* at the time for central planning to take it for granted that, in any event, the country's development problems would be solved not in the rural sector at all but in the industrial and urban sectors. This particular belief had disappeared in Eastern Africa almost altogether in 1967 no less suddenly than it had appeared and had become fashionable three or four years earlier, but it dominated many points of view in planning in 1965 particularly. No doubt it will become fashionable again some day. It was a general assumption about African economic development that was applied to labour and labour considerations as follows. For agricultural productivity it is held that much hard work, skill and selfdiscipline is required, qualities that planners tend to believe are not readily found among peasants. In the setting of industrial enterprise it was planned that "discipline" should and could be effectively enforced corporately from above, and that unskilled and part-time labour would do. Thus it was believed that the social obstacles that allegedly "economic development" would encounter in "tradition" could be controlled adequately again according to the extremist interpretation of the theory of the centrally planned economy fashionable at that time.

Rural irrigation schemes from this point of view are considered to form a class of development projects apart from others insofar as both the social and technical problems they pose seem to be amenable to direction and control from above.[8] The reason why co-operatives (of any kind) are *not* integral to irrigation schemes as planned in Kenya is a subject for discussion in itself.

It was added as a kind of modification of the general labour theory sketched above that, while perhaps there was some evidence to the effect that (according to the stereotype, especially Kikuyu) African women in the fields might work harder than African men, this was true only for subsistence or domestic purposes and not in the context of the money economy, except where tedious and repetitive work such as coffee and tea picking is concerned. This particular line of argument, however, was also peculiarly inapposite when applied to the pyrethrum problem as will also be pointed out in a moment.

Here we have an instance of the "social values philosophy of development".[9] It puts the blame when things go wrong on socially—and culturally-based, obstructive, destructive of indifferent motivations or attitudes, said to be "typical"—of "peasant society". A spate of government enquiries into co-operatives as well as other organizations has recently, now as in the colonial period, invoked this theory, to argue that the overall record of co-operation thus far has not been very successful. This is of course to state another complicated development theory only in crude terms reduced to bare essentials. Nonetheless, here we have another very pervasive theme. With the proviso that this and the development administration philosophy above manifests itself in subtle as well as simple formulations, there is an inkling here of a rudimentary framework within which one aspect of the following case material can be explored, since this is socially current and acted upon in the country concerned.

Third, there was a more subtle and technocratic explanation.[10] It was reckoned that social as well as economic and all other kinds of progress necessarily "went with" progressive economies of scale. Large scale organization was supposed to be somehow inherently more efficient than smaller-scale organization, especially for production but also for marketing. The Kenya highlands had seen a reversal of this trend. It was said that events had gone against the "logical" grain of economic progress. It was only "inevitable", therefore, so the explanation went, that output would fall. Not only were the land resettlement schemes and co-operatives merely a political expedient and running headlong into socio-cultural obstacles, but "evolution" was against them too.

Discussion of this would need to make careful distinction between the "efficiency" of production—though "efficiency" is one of the most elusive concepts in development studies—on the one hand, which involves cost analysis, and levels of output on the other, which could be discussed in broad aggregate terms. If it were necessary to attach a name to a general class of development theories of which this could be said to represent one instance, we could speak here of "intellectualist" approaches. There are of course no fewer kinds of these as there are of both "social values" and "administration" theories, not to mention practices. A future exercise would have to explore some of the detailed problems to be solved before our classification could be taken very seriously.

This third approach relies very heavily on a kind of mental formalism that finds it difficult to disentangle the short run in human affairs from the longer span, the very long span, to which evolutionary ideas pertain. It is by no means a cast of mind confined to centres of learning. It is rampant in governments too. "Intellectual" refers to a kind of activity that anyone can and often does engage in; it refers to a mode of action not an individual actor.

On investigation of why the pyrethrum output fell at the beginning of the Scheme, the matter appeared very differently indeed. In fact none of the accounts given above could be found to explain very much. What proved to have happened was, essentially, that an organizational change in the form of the introduction of a co-operative, had severely and adversely affected the marketing and pricing of the crop for its working growers. In particular, the introduction of this new structure had alienated the labour input in pyrethrum production from the return previously accepted as commensurate. Before this change the growers, who were predominantly women, had taken the dried flowers direct to the Board. They had been paid a "picking wage" immediately accordingly and directly without deductions or delays. The new system of marketing through the co-operative was very different. It meant that payouts were made only to the members of the co-operative society —the plotholders—who were mostly men. Only the plotholder-members (the men) were entitled to hold an account with the society. In any event the payout was finally made only after a period of delay and with deductions for the running of the co-operative and other expenses. The cultivation in the fields, and the drying of the pyrethrum flowers, continued as before to be very largely carried out by women, the wives. But now it was their husbands and not themselves who received the returns on their labour albeit with delays and deductions. The women said they received too little to make it materially sufficiently worth their while to continue to labour for long hours. So, rationally and realistically in the circumstances, they worked less.[11]

This is not to say that the role problem of the differing interests of the sexes though highly important and much neglected in this as well as in many rural development projects was the only factor responsible for the fall in pyrethrum output. It was not. All kinds of other considerations must be taken into account in this as in any other case. The European settlers had grown pyrethrum in large blocks which took time to split up and replant in smaller ones. Between the end of one settler regime and the beginning of another there was a period of neglect that took time and efforts to recover from. Also, not only do new plants take time to come into production, but many of the settlers and their wives gave priority to house building and subsistence crops,[12] with cash crops coming only second. Moreover, eventually the new settlers came to produce a great deal of pyrethrum and certainly it would be difficult to say from a general point of view that the Scheme as a whole, not even to limit ourselves to its pyrethrum aspect has been "a failure". On balance, the evidence is significantly to the contrary,[13] even given that "a success" is equally elusive of definition.

To some extent, indeed, it would be true to say that in Nairobi at the time few thought of there being a pyrethrum problem as such. To an extent this essay has created it as a separate phenomenon to serve as a rallying point for some thoughts on the evaluation of evaluation studies. But, make no mistake about it, it is true certainly to part of life in the pyrethrum fields. I will turn now to some implications of this case that have a more general relevance at the same time as they are part of Kenya's social history.

Some Wider Implications

First, the problematic change in productive performance was not due to any qualitative change in the labour force and its social values. Indeed, no change occurred on the labour front at all in the sense that for the most part the same people worked in the fields as before (but there are no reliable statistics on the population changes brought about by the settlement programme). Too many theories about productivity and co-operatives as well as other rural development projects focus exclusively on labour and its qualities virtually to the exclusion of other factors and always in the broadest of terms. Too few take account in any systematic way of either the special circumstances of the product, or those of its market and marketing analysing the various differences and any similarities there may be between the points of view of (a) the peasants and (b) the planistrators. Few, if any, allow for anything like the full plurality of causes—and functions. The older social studies on Africa that sought to relate labour productivity to single-factor causes such as its residential stability exemplify the very narrow approach that used to be so characteristic.

Certainly it would have no practical meaning to plan even for the very limited objective of labour productivity, without having reference to particular forms and bases of leadership, given and possible communications methods and organizational skills, and stated marketing conditions. Similarly, it is completely unrealistic to appeal to "co-operation" as a kind of social magic that regardless of everything else could bring about economic or social change.

Detailed marketing considerations and the need for local facilities such as transportation to and from collecting points are overlooked so regularly in development projects laid down in a highly centrally planned economy that this cannot be just written off just as an error in planning, due to chance. Partly, no doubt, this systematic omission relates to the innocence of most planistrators in Africa of commercial marketing experience of their own—other than with reference to their own wage-careers in another sector altogether. More important, however, may be the posing of a policy dilemma at the outset as necessarily involving a crucial choice between *either* the market economy *or* the planned economy. In going completely for the latter, according to socialist principles in various interpretations of these, the importance of local aspects of the former seems to get left out of the picture altogether. Specifically with regard even to marketing co-operatives there

are instances (though they are not discussed in this brief analysis) which I think cannot bear any other interpretation but
the view that the co-operative principle appealed to becomes
(a) virtually a substitute for adequate thought about local
marketing facilities, and (b) a version of that management or
human relations theory of production in which altogether the
effects of the market and marketing are given little, if any,
place. In so many instances the introduction of marketing co-
operatives in effect leaves the actual provision of local marketing facilities on the ground to the same non-resource that was
to produce the instant harmony and consensus of interests
and leadership in the organization of the co-operative itself.

Second, the assumption recurs, in development planning
for rural areas especially, that there is, necessarily, some peculiar and inherent relationship between land, and thence
land reform, and agricultural and rural change. Certainly
land questions *may* and in some situations do figure very
prominently in problems of rural society and its re-organiza-
tion. But this has led to generalizations about land as a factor
in efficiency being not less vague than those about labour
which were referred to above, ignoring situational exigencies
such as local scarcities or specialised use. The strong tendency,
especially in social anthropological African studies in the
1950's to regard land in "traditional" or "tribal" society as
subject to control simply by the political body corporate[14] is
still prominent. The social facts that, depending on circumstances and intentions, land may be treated diplomatically,
religiously, economically or domestically as well as politically,
regardless of however traditional or traditionalist the obtaining
social system may be by one standard or another, are seldom
given enough weight. The social structures and organizations
of authority involved in these different contexts simply cannot
all be reduced one to another as if they were all the same or
always dominated by a single one.

It would, of course, be absurd to deny the relevance of
certain soil and ecological circumstances for the cultivation of
tender plants with special requirements. But, it is neither
logically nor empirically the case—excluding gravitational pull
—that because a farm or a co-operative is on the land then

necessary it depends on it in a peculiarly significant way contrasted with all other kinds of human organization. Organizational and marketing factors might far outweigh any questions pertaining to land use, land ownership, or land exchange in certain regards. This is so in the material under discussion here. Most enterprises on the ground, and even an aeroplane in flight, require some sort of ground contact. Clearly a farm or any other social organization in a rural area, is no exception to this. But it is not necessarily a special case either. African land reform is much in need of re-thinking.

Third, a problem for that abstraction a "national economy" is also a problem for a number of individuals and groups. As such its solution is not to be found in isolation from the groups and individuals who are immediately affected. The pyrethrum case illustrates price reward return responsiveness on the part of, here, especially women cultivators. Such price responsiveness on the part of the intended beneficaries of plans often tends to be systematically under-estimated by the central planners, who like to think that the most significant factors in social behaviour in what they term "peasantries" are socio-cultural factors rather than economic responses. In Eastern Africa the outstanding example of such a line of reasoning is embodied in "the cattle complex", a complex about cattle that belongs as much if not more to the pre-conceptions of planners about cattle-owners than to the norms of the owners themselves. As many of the co-operatives in Kenya and elsewhere are dairying concerns, it may be of interest to digress here for a moment.

The cattle complex was a phenomenon in the colonial period as familiar to social science as it was to administration and planning. It amounted to a theory that people would not sell their cattle because they loved them too dearly, because their religious, symbolic or aesthetic value was greater by far than any price that could be put on them. Categorically, economic underdevelopment in the region concerned was put down to "the cattle complex" which was explained as some kind of alternative to, or substitute for, "market behaviour". Seldom was the economic importance of husbandry given its due in the plethora of cultural affirmations made about it.

Usually, the economic underdevelopment that it was supposed to account for was not described in any detail. If it had been it would have become perfectly clear that in many contexts and for many people, cattle spelled wealth rather than poverty. Due to the system of intersecting rights of ownership, few cattle were owned (or used or disposable) by individuals and individuals alone. (This does not mean though that all individuals had many cattle.) Often many people enjoyed rights of various kinds in the same animal.

Now it was and continues to be, perfectly true in societies in eastern African countries where animal husbandry affords the principal mode of livelihood, that cattle represent social as well as many other kinds of value. So does land in societies based on cultivation and sedentary residence. Why was husbandry and the nomadic or migratory way of life that went with it vested with so much cultural peculiarity as seen by planners, administrators and others? I think the answer must be that the Masai, the Gogo, the Turkana, the Suk, and many others followed a way of life so apparently alien to the experience of those who, from a distance, observed it superficially, that they believed they had no alternative except to wrap it in mystery and exoticism. The parallel with land in land-based societies that it would have been more apposite to make with cattle and cattle-based societies was, simply, overlooked.[15] It was too familiar.

Long before the cash economy land entered into various kinds of transactions in Eastern Africa, and cattle did too. The factors which influence the buying and selling in the market for cash of both land and cattle in their respective contexts as described above, depend on a number of circumstances. One of these in the case of cattle especially is simply how near or far in terms of local communications the market is physically. What has been well documented for cattle sales is that, when the price is right, cattle sales have increased steadily as the market facilities for selling them have increased, with buying points being extended deeper and deeper into, for example, Masai country.[16] Of course,, where there is evidence of the existence of a "cattle complex" of beliefs, certainly this may have some implications for "market" behaviour. But primarily it relates more to other aspects (e.g. religious) of social structure which are not necessarily concerned with the same matters.

All this is not to say either that behaviour *like* optimising behaviour is necessarily the same *as* optimising behaviour.[17] Neither is it to say that peasants either do or should "respond to the market" anymore than anyone else does or should. Also, and the importance of this cannot be over-estimated, "the market" is anything but a given. Its prices vary enormously especially for agricultural products, given especially that the economic value of land and of cattle outside the market is consistently high when a mode of life that is also more outside the market (and more inside subsistence, in the conventionally misleading terminology) heavily depends on them. Moreover, and it is another vital point, here again it is not production that is underdeveloped (although of course there is room always for new breeds, as for new seeds) so much as the distribution, marketing and advertising facilities to promote this. It tends to be a consequence of the administrative approach to economic development in the rural sector in much of Africa that the benefits of specialisation and advertising especially from which industrial development gains so much are seldom extended to agriculture to anything nearly like the same extent.

Fourth, our case shows that it is an interrelation between on the one hand "traditional" social and cultural factors, these being here husband–wife relationships, and on the other an "organizational" policy decision, here the introduction of a marketing co-operative, that accounts for the fall in output.[18] But while both are to be taken into account overall, more crucial was the policy decision from above that (*a*) introduced co-operatives and (*b*) limited membership in them to the plot-holders who, in most cases, are men. The sex-based division of work and control over its proceeds is crucial here. A different organizational policy decision need not necessarily have broken the link between labour and its reward that thus far had worked in the interests of output and not against them.

Again it is to be stressed that only a much more comprehensive analysis than is possible here could put all of the blame on to the introduction of co-operatives. And, clearly, it would be absurd to judge the whole idea and organization of a co-operative by only one detail, the limitation of membership in it to the plotholders, widely reported though this, and the delay in payments and deductions that was also mentioned above, has been in co-operatives studies from all parts of Africa. On the other hand, since one of the much stated general aims of "the co-operative movement" to promote socia-lism and to inhibit social class formation, especially social class with a basis in landed property, it is to be specially re-cognised here that a co-operative organization can have pre-cisely the contrary effects. When a co-operative is intended to be communal in orientation and to be based on maximum social participation, but when membership in it is denied to all hired labour and other people in the area whose occupa-tions are not mainly agricultural, then, as in this Kenyan case, what happens is that a majority of the people in the area concerned is excluded. A new exclusive social authority is created. This is conferred on a small minority who, insofar as the committee members are concerned, may and probably do have outside interests in any case, and thus are in less economic need of the co-operative than are others. Without such assets, whether even in a limited economic sense the small or the smallest farmer does or does not gain from having to sell his crops to the co-operative compared with the prices the private buyer can or could offer, is very much a matter open to doubt on the basis of the available evidence. But it is not possible to enter this debate here (which is in any event not susceptible to an answer in general terms). Much will depend on the nature of the crop, e.g. whether it is easily stored or not, or for home or overseas domestic consumption in its raw state or only after manufacture or processing, etc., etc. One must return and then return again to such particulars.

In discussing one aspect of a single case to bring into relief some aspects of the problem "of evaluating" even the micro-economic performance of co-operatives limited to questions of output, I have attempted to touch on several issues. Each of these would deserve further examination in itself. And there are several case studies we could draw upon in addition. Those engaged in development studies and development planning are very familiar with the experience that the results even of liberal studies officially commissioned may not be acted upon by the authorities concerned. Sometimes this is because the researchers themselves are at fault, or have badly (e.g. too narrowly) interpreted their terms of reference. Sometimes it is because the obstacles that policy aims to overcome lie more in the circumstances surrounding the formulation of that policy itself than in "the human factor" in the rural area concerned.

We have urged that "another human factor" is to be taken into account—in the staffing of the central planning office, and in the currents of popular or public opinion, that are very changeable, about what and where precisely *is* the problem to be worried about. In attempting for expository purposes to go as far beyond the details of one aspect of one particular case that formed our starting point as possible, I have nevertheless confined myself to the very narrow,—if, for some people, basic—criterion of one of its economic features. Like many similar organizations for rural development a co-operative may or may not act as well as an economic organization as: an agent of local government, as a source and a disseminator of social services, as a means—however limited—of social and perhaps limited political expression, or as a far-flung presence of the centre at the periphery of a country—as a link, that is to say, between the local and national levels where it is possible to separate these.[19] These are only a few, if perhaps the most prevalent, of the possibilities along one dimension of our subject.

Moreover, a comprehensive socio-economic analysis would, eventually, ascend to the level of sectoral considerations, for example, asking among other things whether the primary societies if it is these that are under review (secondary societies and higher unions of course present different problems again) are merely atoms within but one sector of national affairs which may be confined to agriculture (or some agriculture) alone. Is the expansion of "co-operative principles" to other sectors anticipated and if not, then why not? Then again, many aspects of the structure and organization of co-operatives as such must be taken into account in any relatively more complete evaluation. The question of membership alone is only one of these. And co-operatives in new schemes rather than in long settled communities have some special problems.

Then again, careful reference will have to be made even in a brief account to the aims of "the co-operative movement" within or for which "co-operatives" are started, as these are understood in government and in social and economic development policy. Co-operatives are the outward expression of an economic religion in Eastern Africa, It is in this guise that socialism there is conceptualized if somewhat differently in the four countries. As such co-operatives acquire a kind of ideological, or theological untouchability. The allusion to "the catholic church" at the beginning of this study was not fortuitous. Co-operatives stand for a means that also is taken to be an end in itself, however differently either their propagators or participants (and we have seen they are not always the same people) interpret this. When they are thus conceived of as being greater than their parts, co-operatives defy being dismantled into them for purposes of analysis. A less ideologically charged organization may be more essily broken down for study. For the faithful the worst that can happen is a few heresies. For the faithless, co-operatives were non-starters in any event.

We would do badly to underrate just how deeply rooted commitment to co-operation may be in present government policies in Eastern Africa. This is, however, probably as in many countries where government priorities are heavily committed to central economic planning of the directive kind, not a dogma that may be shared to the same extent by the peasants as well as by the planistrators. Again, we have touched on this here, and many other studies could be referred to for the sake of comparison. At the local level there may be little knowledge of, or identification with government objectives as stated in the officially promulgated principles of co-operative organizations (although, on the Million Acres settlement schemes and subject to various qualifications the level of identification with the co-operatives objectives appeared relatively high in 1966).

A problem for evaluation studies of co-operatives that we have not touched on in this discussion concerns the interconnection between co-operatives and marketing boards—which varies from crop to crop as much as from country to country—especially insofar as price fixing is concerned. It cannot be taken for granted that price fixing by the State is done mainly in the interests of the co-operative sector. A national economy is made up by several sectors. It must be discovered how and in whose favour conflicting interests as between these sectors have, for this crop or that, been resolved.

In Eastern Africa pricing policy has a special historical relevance to co-operatives. Both ideologically and in practice the co-operative movement there has been waged against private trade which often is not in the hands of nationals—or if it is, then sub-nationals only. The continued existence of these private traders in the country is seen as a remnant of the colonial period whether they are expatriate or not. Highly paid civil servants in virtually free housing are similarly redolent of the colonial period objectively speaking, but this tends to be looked at in a different light. The usual argument about private trade is that this works to the benefit of that historically privileged mercantile class because it is to the detriment of the small individual grower looking for good prices for his crops. In Eastern Africa "the co-operative movement" is directed less against class and capital than caste and commerce—to summarise some of the findings of this study in a few words. We have commented on the role of co-operatives in class formation. It is to be added that members of the primary societies not uncommonly put their revenue to capitalist use without this seeming to them to contradict any co-operative principle. A key question for analysis in those circumstances turns on the extent to which continued private selling to private buyers where co-operatives are legally instituted with monopoly powers represents rational or irrational subversion with positive or negative consequences for the individuals and the wider groups concerned.

With co-operatives there are so many facets to take into

account. If one thing is certain at the present stage of co-operative studies, it is that *an evaluation* of a policy *is itself and should be* a policy if only for the evaluation of evaluation studies. The implied criticism of "the social values philosophy of development" that this and my Makerere work on planned change has made is not a rejection of social values themselves either as a spring for action or as an explanatory device for certain purposes. No. It is, rather, to take a stand against that policy bias in social science which looks always for social values—especially at "the receiving" end of a plan—as if other variables were always systematically secondary. They are not. It is a continuing colonialism in social science to suppose otherwise.

Carl Gösta Widstrand

Efficiency and Co-operatives

Several of the contributors to the seminar have discussed the question of efficiency in co-operatives. From their discussion it would seem that efficiency has several aspects but that the major aspects are *what makes co-operatives successful*—which usually leads into a discussion of economic considerations, technical problems of checks and controls, education of membership and management, and analyses of economic performance—and *how can co-operatives contribute to social development*? The last aspect concerns the basic problem of what kind of rural society we want to have and what social structures will underpin a socially and economically successful co-operative. This is a much more complex efficiency problem, related to the problems of the prerequisities—if any—for co-operative development, which in turn leads to a discussion on "traditional" values and efficiency. It is related to substantive democratic issues, such as the development roles of various types of co-operative, the efficiency of control and problems of government and/or membership control of co-operatives, and to the question whether it would make any sense at all to modify the co-operative structures—which are basically European—to form something else. Finally any discussion of efficiency in any of the above categories inevitably leads to the problem of *evaluation*.

Let me take up some of these points, as they were discussed in the seminar.

Lionel Cliffe, Göran Hydén and Shem Migot-Adholla have looked critically at the inheritance of *traditional structures* to see whether there is anything left after the various traumatic changes of the colonial period and what relevance this may have for a range of different purposes.

One relevant question concerns how far these various societies have been transformed or changed by modernisation or
rather by the spread of capitalist relationships within East
Africa and what the results have been of this historical development, class formation, class consciousness, etc.

John Saul has shown that socio-economic differences can be
related directly to the development of capitalism in East
Africa.[1] There has been a process of socio-economic differentiation at the local level and in many cases this has led to a
situation in which the better-off farmers—those more actively
or successfully engaged in the modern economy—have been
taking advantage of the co-operatives for their own benefit.
The relevance of this observation to the above question about
the contribution of co-operatives to development is obvious;
the ability of the co-operatives to spread development instead
of concentrating it in the hands of the more progressive
farmers has been reduced by this process.

This relates to another kind of judgement about the long-
term potentials of the capitalist and co-operative agricultural
systems in East Africa. One could argue that in some ways
effective co-operation is dependent upon effective socialism.
As the capitalist relationships affect the way marketing co-
operatives are operating, it obviously affects the implementation of the strategy of the *ujamaa* villages as well, if, as in
Tanzania, that happens to be the goal.

This differential development in Tanzania has produced
many of the problems of the co-operatives. The gap is not
between the urban elites and the rural population but between the activists, the entrepreneurs and the parochials on
the local level. This gap is not being significantly narrowed
by the forces of capitalism drawing the vast masses of the
rural peasantry into an activist arena, nor is it leading at
a very rapid pace to a polarisation in preparation for a revolutionary transformation. These are obviously both romantic
notions.

But the government has the power to control this at every
level and one possible argument is that the most effective way
to mobilize the masses is to involve them in a new way.
Participation is participation in something and this something

could be the changing of the mode of agricultural production within which they operate.

This is in effect to expand the range of ways in which the co-operative impinges on the peasantry, bringing it new duties and moving it in the direction of co-operation in production. When a different mode of production becomes the base for the marketing co-operatives, then we shall have a situation in which more members of the co-operative are likely to control it in their own interest rather than having it manipulated against their interest in some way and falling into apathy. That is, if they avoid turning the administration of co-operatives into a bureaucracy.

But, in order to make rural institutions work, it may be necessary to transform the mode of production in the direction of a socialist mode of production. Hence the often-quoted statement by John Saul that socialism is a prerequisite for efficient co-operative development in Tanzania:

"Rather than co-operation being necessary for socialism, socialism may be necessary for co-operation."[2]

Generally it would seem that *social prerequisites* are often the desired consequences of action. They do not exist automatically on the basis of African tradition; they have to be created. This is a political challenge how to find the most effective blend of class consciousness, moral appeal and economic benefits to put co-operatives across.

More specifically, discussion about prerequisites seems to circle around the importance of "traditional" values. It has been pointed out that settlements where former labourers from plantations have been resettled, such as the ex-sisal workers' *ujamaa* village at Mbambara in Tanzania, have been successful. The reasons given have been that through their work on the European plantations they see the economic aspects, in addition to the social ones, more clearly, that they have an experience of working together not because of any social obligations but because of the economic necessity in the situation created, and that they are able to exercise better control because of their joint experience of exploitation. On the other hand, there is, for example, the Meru ability to organize their clans on a large scale, transcending kinship groups and age-grade organization. This ability to organize on a large scale has affected the development of co-operatives, but in the creation of these co-operatives both the experience to organise on a large scale and the traditional definitions of who has the rights and duties to expect co-operation are important.

What this means is that many of the questions posed in terms of *values* turn out to be problems of actual *social structure,* and it is not possible nor beneficial for the questions of values and structure to be separated.

Turning to the problem of organizing any kind of co-operative or collective method of animal husbandry among pastoral peoples we find one of the longest-standing myths of Africa is the idea of the cattle complex. (I am, however, sometimes at loss whether the term is used to mean "obsession with cattle" or "complex whole" of various usages peculiar to pastoral cultures). It comes up in situations involving attempts to limit the size of herds or to prevent overgrazing. As Raymond Apthorpe has said in his paper, the common argument is that these people have an attachment to cattle and that they will not get rid of cattle. The problem is rather that cattle or rights in cattle are individual, but at the same time access to grazing is completely free. No individual has any incentive to reduce his own herd, as he is only going to suffer relative to the rest. An additional difficulty is that livestock programmes finish up in the hands of the large cattle-owners with distorting effects.

It would seem that in segmentary societies, like that of the Nyaturu, even literacy groups and co-operatives become segmented, because whereas there is a tradition of co-operation within the family, there are also traditions of conflict and rivalry between extended family units which almost preclude any co-operation on a larger scale than the family. The very marked differences in success between neighbouring primary societies in Arusha would again seem to be due to the kind of social structure which exists.

In one of the two most successful primary societies in the area one clan is dominant and in the other there seems to be a lot of different clans and none of them occupies an influential position. In the case of the least successful primary societies the population is drawn from two traditionally rival clans.[3] Then what becomes important in a co-operative activity is not what we normally speak of as "traditional" values but the kinds of structural relationships existing between units (family, kinship groups, clans). In circumstances in which there may be various kinds of identification with some "traditional" factor—usually kinship—in the local area, the politics of co-operatives may be broken down into these kinds of loyalties. Traditional relationships and traditional cleavages which define the rights and duties of co-operation tend to perpetuate themselves in the new organisations.

These structural phenomena have special implications for the *development role of co-operatives,* the problems of democracy in co-operatives and the problem of power and conflict within co-operatives. In this situation a problem may arise due to the fact that the chairman and the committee members are making a lot out of their position, getting the first use of the tract or, sharing the all-too-few available bags between them, and covering up for each other at inspections etc.

This is not regarded as a problem of class differences but as a problem of a rather parochial nature. These people are manipulating the primary society because the society is in the hands of that clan or that village, and they must mobilize efforts to get their men in at the next election, which means that the situation is not changed at the election but that it "is somebody else's turn to eat". Thus, the more potential there is for this kind of parochial cleavages, the more a situation is created in which a co-operative can be exploited by its leadership.

This type of problem is not easily overcome. It is not possible anywhere to educate people out of the habit of considering power as a way of improving their position. When conflicts arise along the cleavages mentioned above, they are usually, as Göran Hydén points out, not about substantive issues but are on the basis of personal relations. It is not a substantive conflict but an affective conflict and usually affective conflicts are much more difficult to solve, particularly within organisations.[4] Here, however, there seems to be a case for an educational effort, as so much co-operative conflict is in fact substantive or, in plain language, about money.

Finally, in a discussion on "traditional" values and structures the philosophy of *ujamaa* and its relationship to co-operatives has an obvious place. Lionel Cliffe has devoted his paper to a thorough discussion of most of the implications of the *ujamaa*. Göran Hydén has also discussed them.

The ujamaa ideology has been outlined by President Nyerere in his *Socialism and Rural Development* from 1967, and of course in the Arusha Declaration, and aims at the creation of villages with production—and later other things as services—collectively or communally organized. The extended family—the *ujamaa*—has according to Nyerere three basic qualities: there was a basic solidarity that provided security for the individual and guaranteed a certain amount of equality. "All the basic goods were held in common and shared among the members of the unit",[5] and everyone had an obligation to work: "in traditional African society everybody was a worker".[6]

What is the impact of this ideology of traditionalism? It can be argued that the whole ideology of African Socialism, to which *ujamaa* is related, has served in East Africa as a kind of mystifying ideology and is manipulated by those in power as a means of papering over potential contradictions in their societies.

If you can convince people that they are still operating in this traditional kind of situation, that everybody is everybody else's brother, and that these various traditional forms of social relationship are still the most important ones then perhaps fewer embarassing questions about economic distinctions will be raised. In that sense there is a danger that ujamaa may become a mystifying ideology.

The second possibility is that it may become a constructive myth. It may either be a myth used to try to recreate and mobilise whatever residual aspects of communal feeling there still are for nation-building purposes or it may be used merely to legitimate attempts to build socialism at the present time, by drawing on historical precedents and by saying: "These are the values we have had in the past, what we want to do now is to live up to these values and find new ways of making them work".

The final possibility is that, even when this idea is used sincerely, it may become a rather dangerous instrument. If people believe that capitalist individualism is still prevalent in East Africa society and in Tanzania particularly and you wish to counter this belief, you may feel that, by falling back on this myth of *ujamaa,* you are giving away too much. It is necessary to face up to the fact of differentiation, to try to rally the poor people against the richer people, even in the rural areas, and maybe even to draw upon a theory of class struggle, as a means of bringing change into rural areas and perhaps making effective co-operatives possible.

Clearly this kind of choice is necessary, as is this kind of assessment of where *ujamaa* fits as an ideology, how useful it is, and what its costs and benefits are likely to be. It refers to the people's interpretation of the realities of the different societies and to how far they have moved away from *ujamaa* —insofar as *ujamaa* ever existed. It refers to the goals of the society and how genuinely socialism is desired. It would seem that traditional *ujamaa* in a general sense has pretty well disappeared in most areas of Tanzania. It may be that some aspects of it are still relevant to new kinds of collective modes of agricultural production, but it does not show how to make marketing co-operatives work, and it is not advisable for producer co-operatives to rely very heavily on the pre-existent socialism of the "traditional" society.

On the other hand, the alternative of raising *class consciousness* is in itself a rather difficult weapon to use. It may be useful in some ways to rally the masses of the rural population against the potential exploitation of the urban classes, the elites, the bureaucracy, and so on. But how effective it is in the rural areas in really creating socialist modes of production is not clear.

Africa is very different from other developing regions. Feudal relationships exist that touch people right at the local level and make them potentially receptive of an increasingly radical critique of their society. The form of capitalism that has come about in Tanzania, for example, is not so well developed.

236

There are some rich peasants, and they play a dominant role in the activities of the co-operatives. There are some very poor and even landless peasants in Tanzania. But there is also a large mass of *middle peasants,* not wholly committed to the market economy, and still engaged in subsistence production. There is a challenge here for the person who thinks that the raising of class consciousness is going to be an easy way of involving people in new sorts of co-operative enterprises.

In this connection it may be of interest to mention the ongoing discussion about how *ujamaa* could become or be made relevant also for the more developed areas of Tanzania, where there is already an individualistic agriculture. Most of the *ujamaa* villages so far have been newly created. In this situation, in which existing economic systems in particular areas are gradually to be transformed into communally or collectively oriented systems, the co-operative movement is one of the obvious points of interest. Instead of establishing new villages, the existing local co-operative might become the focal point by taking on new projects and expanding to become a communal growth point. As Lionel Cliffe has pointed out in his paper in a similar context, one raison d'être for co-operatives is to expand the scale of effective co-operative organisation. This development is, of course, in its initial stages, but it would seem to command considerable interest in Tanzania. The recent statements by the party that they are responsible for the *ujamaa* policy, together with the appropriate ministries, is also interesting and may give the party an increased presence at the local level.

Let us now turn to the basic problems of democracy, the *involvement of the government* and the effective involvement of members. In some cases the co-operatives are in fact manipulated by the wealthier peasants, and with "traditional" cleavages. There is also the case in which the government has pressed or forced a co-operative upon a peasant community which has not asked for one. In both cases the alienated membership may react with indifference and apathy, and with a feeling that they cannot influence the decisions about their own co-operative and about their own future. In the long run the efficiency of co-operatives can only be guaranteed when the members are prepared to take an intelligent and continuing interest in the efficiency of their own co-operatives.

Göran Hydén has dealt at length with the problems of government involvement in co-operatives and *participation from below*. One major problem is how to strike a balance between membership participation from below and government control of what are often the legitimate interests of national priorities.[7]

Bismarck Mwansasu has pointed out that co-operatives often have surpluses that are an important asset in rural development. These surpluses are at least theoretically available for development purposes. There have been instances in which the government and the co-operative union have had different views on the best uses to which these surpluses should be put. The union felt that the balance should be used mostly for things like office buildings, processing equipment and similar investments, whereas the government considered that tractor programmes and fertilizer programmes were more important. This is an instance in which the government could intervene, because it was difficult to get the co-operative to play their development role efficiently in terms of national objectives.

However, when government controls are discussed, we usually mean the more traditional type of efficiency control. Where the government has forced people into co-operatives, it uses government control as a mechanism to make them efficient, that is, to operate efficiently and honestly within that framework. But the 1966 Co-operatives Act in Kenya—which gave the Commissioner wide powers—has been experienced by the societies only as additional routine work, filling in forms for the Commissioner, getting cheques countersigned by co-operative officers, etc.

Ideally, in the long run it is not until the members themselves feel a sense of involvement and that they have some control over the co-operative (through education, involvement in productive activities, etc.) that efficiency can be guaranteed by pressure from below, by active participation by the membership, both in marketing and producer co-operatives.

It can, however, be argued that it only requires pressure from below to keep management efficient: since the more the government gets involved in processing monopolies for coffee and cotton, for example it is going to raise the question of to what extent the ordinary farmer is to be consulted *at all* in the operation of co-operative unions. It is going to be increasingly difficult to put forward justifications for policies which permit the farmer fuller control. The question is what can the individual farmer-member contribute to his union in this kind of situation? He may contribute his participation, but participation must be about something and cannot be a function of something else.

This situation is related to the *problem of scale*. Both Lionel Cliffe and Göran Hydén have argued that it is necessary to think about kinds of co-operative organisation and whether they are appropriate when discussed both in terms of 38 members or 10,000 members.

There are two aspects of this problem of *scale and efficiency:* one is economic and the other is about scale and efficient democracy. If we look at the economics of marketing, this is in practice a multi-purpose function. It includes storage, transportation, collection, very often processing and the actual arrangement of sales. In trying to suggest an appropriate economic scale for this undertaking it is necessary to break down the separate parts of the marketing functions and consider their relative importances in terms of a particular crop. Some crops like tea are fairly costly to process. A tea factory cannot operate properly below a certain size. In order to concentrate on getting the maximum benefits from the processing, the body handling tea is going to be a fairly large body. The economies of scale in connection with vegetables or other perishable foodstuffs are those to be gained from rapid handling. You will have a fairly small body handling this type of crop. To aim at economies of scale is an important aspect of efficiency.

But democracy as a means of control that will, it is hoped, produce economic efficiency is also a problem of scale. Effective organisation and effective participation are governed by the rule of optimal size, as well as the processing of tea or coffee. Effective participation decreases sharply with increasing membership. The problem here, of course, is that in

239

many cases the economies of processing and marketing need an expanding scale, while effective participation needs a drastically increasing scale.

Most of the primary societies in East Africa are by any standards, even in terms of economic criteria, very large organisations and probably all of them are too large for effective membership participation, let alone effective producer organisation.

Another way of looking at efficiency and controls from above and below is to look at the relationships between groups, such as the government, the co-operative leaders, the co-operative employees and the members. These are four social groups with different interests. The government can be considered as a group representing certain interests. For example, government manipulation of the prices of various crops in Uganda in the early 1960's was concerned with very wide issues of Ugandan politics. The manipulation of cotton prices in favour of cotton producers as against the coffee producers, was essentially a way of locating resources away from Buganda.

There is another aspect of the difference between these groups that Bismarck Mwansasu pointed out. It is important to draw a distinction between the group of committeemen, with powers to appoint and dismiss employees, and the group of managers and other employees. The interest of employees is partly in preserving the size of their hierarchy and, if need be, in expanding it and, of course, in getting better conditions and pay for themselves. This is quite contrary to the interests of the farmer.

After the government intervention in the VFCU, the manpower was reduced almost by half, with incredible savings to the organisation. This created another problem and exposed the conflict of interests. The people who got sacked were very directly affected by the government intervention. This group, which had very marked grievances, has been able to generate a lot of disgust over the new situation, especially as the tremendous savings from the cutting down on staff were not passed on to the farmers. This particular case brings up another point: you are likely to get control from below in order to get increased efficiency if the pricing system makes it possible for the improvement in efficiency to be passed back to the growers themselves. One of the very simple measures that could be taken to promote control from below would therefore be to introduce a system of pricing which allowed for the possibility of variation at the society level, in order that the efficient society and its members could really benefit from efficiency and control at the local level.

The government has been thought of as intervening in two ways: (1) through its rule-making functions and (2) through its controlling and supervisory functions. These two types of involvement imply a kind of movement from the top through the middle to the bottom in a succession of steps, as in any hierarchical type of downward flow. Ulf Himmelstrand suggested that it might be possible to have direct contact between top and bottom in order to control the middle. Instead of having an ordinary administrative model, one would have a model in which the masses were mobilized to control the efficiency of the middle group.

The government has to make the general environment receptive to the basic values of the policy and it has to have the confidence of those who stand to gain from co-operative institutions, as the recent Tunisian experience shows. There, a major move to introduce a very ambitious co-operative reform to put all arable land into producer co-operatives within a year failed, precisely because those who were promoting the reform did not have the confidence of those who stood to gain from the reform.

The important argument in discussing the *evaluation* of the efficiency of co-operatives is that it is necessary not only to apply economic criteria, but also to look at other criteria by which one can measure the success of co-operatives. In the development role, one such criterion would obviously be the general acceptance of the co-operatives among the population.

Rayomond Apthorpe has devoted his paper to these very difficult questions of evaluating social performance. One reason for the difficulties is that not very much effort has been put into finding suitable social indicators. Even if one finds or establishes such indicators, there are additional problems. It is very difficult to find ways of judging increased social participation in the fields of nutrition, health, and education, for example.

Even if one could find some way, there is then the problem that the unit that may be crucial for nutritional improvement may have nothing to do with the scale of the social unit which could be engaged in educational or health policies. Furthermore evaluators are usually called for when things go wrong—hence the gloomy writings of evaluators. To try to evaluate a complex set like co-operation, as Raymond Apthorpe said, is like trying to evaluate the Church.[8]

Dan Nyanjom

Some Observations on the Seminar on Co-operatives and Rural Development in East Africa

Thanks are due to the Scandinavian Institute of African Studies and any other sponsoring agencies for organizing a Seminar at which a serious attempt has been made, presumably for the first time, to critically and objectively analyse and highlight problems of co-operative development in East Africa. This appreciation will no doubt be shared by other leaders, both at the Seminar and back home.

From the papers submitted, it has been amazing to see the amount of research interest taken in the co-operative movements of East Africa by people not directly concerned with co-operative development, and even more, the extent to which research work has been carried out in a manner that has provoked lively discussion on some very urgent and vital aspects of the work such as: "Co-operative Democracy versus Efficiency."

The need has been felt, right through the Seminar, for closer collaboration between the research workers and those practically engaged in co-operative development in the field. This would facilitate a constant exchange of ideas and help to eliminate obvious inaccuracies and discrepancies.

Another need that has been apparent during the Seminar is the listing of priorities when deciding on the areas in which research is to be carried out. Whilst appreciating the need for freedom of choice of subject by individual research workers initial consultations prior to commencement of research could lead to projects being undertaken that would be more relevant to and directly applicable to current problems. Here the ICA

Regional office could probably play a useful co-ordinating role.

Finally, the question of follow-up. It is suggested that the task be now undertaken to carry out a comparative analysis of the facts and figures already available form research carried out so far in all the three East African countries. This exercise would help highlight problems of mutual interest such as: "Efficiency in the Performance of Co-operatives", and provide background material for a follow-up Seminar which should take place in East Africa under the auspices of the Institute and other interested organizations. The second Seminar would draw in, not only the researchers and Government officials, but also a cross-section of the leadership within the Co-operative Movements of East Africa, whose contribution would be invaluable to the discussions.

The conclusions of the two Seminars should then be published in an authoritative document which can be used by those responsible for co-operative development in tackling and finding solutions to the various problems within their respective countries. Unless this vital follow-up is carried out, the usefulness of this worthy effort is likely to be restricted to a mere get-together and exchange of ideas with literature to carry back home—while the actual problems still live on.

Contributors

Raymond Apthorpe is at present Senior Consultant on African Social Planning and Rural Institutions at the UNRISD, Geneva, and was engaged in social-science research in Kenya, Tanzania, Uganda and Zambia in 1957–68. He was also Professor of Sociology and Dean of the Faculty of Social Studies, Makerere University College, Kampala.

Göran Hydén is a member of the Department of Government, University of Nairobi, Nairobi, and has published many works on East African problems, both in English and Swedish. He took his Ph.D. at Lund University in Sweden and his thesis *Tanu Yajenga Nchi* was recently published in East Africa.

Nelson Kasfir is a member of the Department of Government, Dartmouth College, New Hampshire, U.S.A., and was visiting lecturer in the Department of Political Science and Public Administration, Makerere University College, from 1966 to 1970. He is currently working on a larger study of organizational dynamics in Ugandan co-operative unions.

Patrick McAuslan went to Tanzania as one of the founder-members of the Faculty of Law of the new University College, Dar-es-Salaam, which he left to go to the London School of Economics in 1966. He was Visiting Professor of African Law in the University of Wisconsin School of Law in 1969 and is at present a member of the School of Law of the University of Warwick. He has written on several aspects of the law in East Africa and has published *Public Law and Political Change in Kenya* (with Y.P. Ghai) and an essay on the law of agricultural development in Kenya and Tanzania in East African Law and Social Change.

S. E. Migot-Adholla was educated in Kenya and participated in a number of social-research projects before attending University College, Dar-es-Salaam, from which he graduated in

1969. He is now studying for a Ph.D. in sociology at the University of California, Los Angeles. Together with John S. Saul, he edited *Marketing Co-operatives in Tanzania*.

Dan Nyanjom has been Commissioner for Co-operatives in Kenya and has recently been appointed Regional Director of the Office for East and Central Africa of the International Co-operative Alliance.

Okoro Okereke took hos B.A. at Fourah Bay College, Freetown, Sierra Leone, and was the principal of a Methodist teacher-training college in eastern Nigeria. Since he received his M.A. from Makerere University College, he has been employed as a Research Fellow at the Makerere Institute of Social Research. His study entitled *The Role of the Co-operative Movement in the Economic Development of Uganda* is forthcoming.

Poul W. Westergaard graduated from the University of Copenhagen in 1967 and was appointed Research Fellow of the Economic Research Bureau, University College, Dar-es-Salaam, the same year. Since August 1969 he has been working on the Joint Research Project on Co-operatives sponsored by the E.R.B., University of Dar es Salaam, Dar-es-Salaam, and the Co-operative College and the Co-operative Education Centre, Moshi.

Carl Widstrand has been the Director of the Scandinavian Institute of African Studies since 1962 and is a member of the Department of Social Anthropology, University of Uppsala. He was the first Professor of Sociology at the University College, Dar-es-Salaam, and has also visited the University of Manitoba, Winnipeg, as Professor of Sociology. He has written on African and Arctic sociological problems and contributed to and edited several series of volumes published by the Institute.

List of participants in the seminar

Prof. Raymond Apthorpe
c/o UN Research Institute for
Social Development
Palais des Nation
CH-211 Geneve 10

Dir. Mauritz Bonow
KF
Fack
104 65 Stockholm 15

Mr. Jannik Boesen
Institute for Development
Research
Sct. Annae Plads 5
1250 Copenhagen

Dir. Alf Carlsson
Swedish Co-operative Centre
Fack
104 65 Stockholm 15

Mr. Lionel Cliffe
Director of Development Studies
University College
P.O. Box 35042
Dar Es Salaam

Dir. Rune Forsberg
Swedish Co-operative Centre
Fack
104 65 Stockholm 15

Dir. Sven Hamrell
Dag Hammarskjöld Foundation
Övre Slottsgatan 2
752 20 Uppsala

Mr. Tage Hjort
Ass. Project Administrator
Ministry of Foreign Affairs
Amaliegade 7
Copenhagen

Dr. Göran Hydén
Department of Government
University College
P.O. Box 30197
Nairobi

Dir. Gabriel Kagaruki
Co-operative Education Centre
P.O. Box 3091
Moshi

Mr. Edward Karanja
Institute of Development
Studies
University College
P.O. Box 30197
Nairobi

Dr. Nelson Kasfir
Department of Political Science
and Public Administration
P.O. Box 7062
Kampala

Konsulent Olav Lindstad
Senior Planning Officer
Norwegian Agency for Inter-
national Development
Dr. Maudsg 11
Oslo DEP

Mr. Kristian Lund-Jensen
Central Co-operative Committee
HC Andersens Boulevard 42
DK-1553 Copenhagen

Mr. J. P. W. B. McAuslan
School of Law
The University of Warwick
Coventry
Warwickshire

Mr. S. E. Migot-Adholla
919 Levering Avenue 10
Los Angeles Calif 90024

Mr. M. K. M. Mulinde
Senior Co-operative Officer
Department of Co-operative
Development
Ministry of Marketing and
Co-operatives
P.O. Box 3585
Kampala

Mr. Bismarck U. Mwansasu
Department of Political Science
University College
P.O. Box 35042
Dar es Salaam

Mr. Dan Nyanjom
Commissioner for Co-operatives
Ministry of Co-operatives &
Social Services
P.O. Box 811
Nairobi

University Lecturer
Astrid Nypan
Institute of Sociology
University of Oslo
Box 1096
Blindern Oslo 3

Drs. S. O. Odede
Institute of Development
Studies
University College
P.O. Box 30197
Nairobi

Dr. O. Okereke
Social Research Institute
Makerere University College
P.O. Box 16022
Kampala

Pol. mag.
Marjatta Oksanen
The Finnish Institute of
International Affairs
Africa-Group
Museokatu 18 A 9
Helsinki 10

Mr. Thorvald Persson
Swedish Co-operative Centre
Fack
104 65 Stockholm 15

Docent Lars Rudebeck
Department of Political Science
University of Uppsala
Uppsala

Mr. John S. Saul
Department of Political Science
University College
P.O. Box 35042
Dar es Salaam

Prof. K. F. Svärdström
Agricultural College of Sweden
750 07 Uppsala
University Lecturer Mariken
Vaa
Institute of Sociology

248

University of Oslo
Box 1096
Blindern Oslo 3

Mr. Poul W. Westergaard
Economic Research Bureau
University College
Dar es Salaam

Agronom Lars Wicknertz
Association of Swedish Livestock
Breeding and Production

(Svensk Husdjursskötsel-SHS)
Hållsta-Eskilstuna

Mr. Jörgen Wide
Swedish Co-operative Centre
Fack
104 65 Stockholm 15

Fil. mag. Lars Zanderin
Department of Political Science
University of Lund
Fack
220 05 Lund 5

Notes

Introduction, pp. 11–16

1. Admittedly there are differences of definition. See also C. K. Wilber, *The Soviet Model and Under-developed Countries* (Chapel Hill, 1969).

2. Anonymus, "Back to grass roots", *The Times Literary Supplement*, (December 19, 1968) a review article dealing with Alexander Chayanov's *The Theory of Peasant Economy* and with a lucid and critical discussion of fashions in rural development studies.

3. John S. Saul, "Marketing Co-operatives in Tanzania", Paper given at the University of Sussex Conference on Social Prerequisites of Agricultural Co-operation, March, 1969. Also in Swedish translation in a publication by the Scandinavian Institute of African Studies: *Kooperation i Östafrika* (Uppsala, 1970). Several of the arguments in the following have been borrowed from this paper.

4. Cf. M. Paulus, *Das Genossenschaftswesen in Tanganyika and Uganda*, Afrika-Studien 15 (München: IFO-Institut, 167), p. 4.

5. Cf. also Xavier A. Flores, "Institutional Problems in the Modernization of African Agriculture, *"A Review of Rural Co-operation in Developing Areas*, I (Geneva: UNRISD, 1969), pp. 201 ff. This is a good survey especially of the francophone African experience. Also Harald Voss, *Kooperation in Afrika, Das Beispiel Equatorialafrikas* (Hamburg: Weltarchiv, 1965).

6. Guy Hunter, *Modernizing Peasant Societies* (London: Oxford University Press, 1969), p. 154 f.; John Saul, op. cit.

7. Hunter, op. cit., p. 157.

8. John Saul, op. cit., and also "Towards a critique of Modernization Theory", G. Arrighi and John S. Saul, *Ideology and Development, Essays on the Political History of Africa* (Nairobi: East African Publishing House, forthcoming).

9. It is interesting to see how little impact the deliberate introduction of such forms of ideologies of traditionalism have had on co-operatives in other places. Nevertheless it is still used, especially when government agencies are promoting the setting up of co-operatives, for example in the Canadian Arctic. Traditional Communal methods in hunting (polar bear drives, seal hunting)

are invoked to promote the setting up of carvers' co-operatives. Cf. *Qaujivaallirutissat* (Ottawa: The Queen's Printer, 1964), p. 286; S. E. Arbess, *Social Change and the Eskimo Co-operative at George River, Quebec* (Ottawa: Department of Northern Affairs and Natural Resources, 1966); A. Balikci, "Two attempts at Community Organization among the Eastern Hudson Bay Eskimos", *Anthropologica* 1 (1959); Frank Vallee, *Povungnetuk and its Co-operative. A case study in Community Change* (Ottawa: Department of Indian Affairs and Northern Development, 1967).

S. E. Migot-Adholla, pp. 17–37

1. See Frank W. Holmquist: "Community History and Reactions to the Launching of a Co-operative Farming Scheme", University of East Africa, Social Science Conference, Makerere University College, Kampala, Uganda (1968).

2. For a discussion of this concept see George M. Forster: *Traditional Cultures and the Impact of Technological Change* (New York: Harper and Row, 1962).

3. Concepts of the family in Africa are rather illusive. Very few vernaculars have a single word for the family as such, a fact which led to a number of administrative difficulties during colonial rule. See, for example, William L. Sytek: "A History of Land Consolidation in Central Nyanza, 1956–1962", East African Institute of Social Research Conference, Makerere, Kampala (1966).

4. See Beverly Brock: "Customary Land Tenure, 'Individualisation' and Agricultural Development", *Seminar Paper 65*, Rural Development Research, Department of Agriculture, Makerere University College, Kampala (July, 1968).

5. *Ibid.*

6. I am greatly indebted to this analysis of problems of order among cultivators which was developed by an Albanian scholar, Mehmet Beqiraj, *Peasantry in Revolution*, Center for International Studies, Cornell University (1966).

7. See W. A. Anderson, "Community Society Continua", *The International Encyclopaedia of the Social Sciences*, Vol. 3 (1968), pp. 174–81.

8. See, for example, the description of the *basumba batale* in D. W. Malcom, *Sukumaland: An African People and Their Land* (London: Oxford University Press, 1953).

9. See p. 73 of Karl Polanyi, *The Great Transformation: The Political and Economic Origins of Our Time* (Boston: Beacon Press, 1957).

10. One commission was set up, among other things, to make

recommendations on "the adaptations or modifications in traditional tribal systems of tenure necessary for the full development of the land". See *East African Royal Commission 1953-55.* Cmd. 4753, (1955), p. ix.

11. See J. S. Saul, and Roger Woods, "African Peasantries", University of East Africa, Social Science Conference, University College, Nairobi (December, 1969).

12. *Ibid.*

13. For a brief general description of co-operative development in East Africa, see Roy C. Cave, *Co-operative Development and Outlook in East and Central Africa.* Consumer Research Institute, San Francisco State College (1961).

14. See, for example, the report by a Special Committee of the Fabian Colonial Bureau, *Co-operation in the Colonies* (London: George Allen and Unwin, 1945) and Cave p. 2–3 containing a citation from the dispatch to colonial administrators in 1946 recommending the appointment of Registrars of Societies and enactment of Co-operative Ordinances.

15. For accounts particularily examing this aspect of growth organisations, see for example Andrew G. Maguire, *Toward "Uhuru" in Tanzania. The Politics of Participation* (Cambridge: Cambridge University Press, 1969), pp. 81–111. For a discussion of conflict earlier in the development of nationalism, see Lionel Cliffe, "Nationalism and the Reaction to Forced Agricultural Improvement in Tanganyika During the Colonial Period." East African Social Science Conference, Makerere University College, Kampala (December, 1964).

16. See, for example, policy papers on Socialism by the Kenya government *African Socialism and Its Application to Planning in Kenya* (Nairobi: Government Printer, 1965) and Julius K. Nyerere, *Socialism and Rural Development* (Dar es Salaam: Government Printer, 1967).

17. Compare, for example, the first *Co-operative Societies Ordinance of Tanganyika* 1932 and the recently enforced *Co-operative Societies Act,* 1968.

18. See the biographical sketches of the dominant figures in the Kilagabageni Union (now Sola Zone) of the co-operative movement in Sukumaland. S. E. Migot-Adholla, "The Politics of a Growers' Co-operative Society", unpublished undergraduate dissertation, Department of Political Science, University College, Dar es Salaam (1969).

19. *Ibid.*

20. Westerners are always quick to point at the particularistic

tendencies of tribal peoples in Africa, little realising the "tribalistic" characteristics in their own societies like Belgium, Canada, or Great Britain. Other "backward" practices that go along with particularism are equally evident, for example, President Kennedy's nepotism in appointing his brother as Attorney General or Nixon appointing his former lawyer-partner to the same post. Nor is corruption unknown in these societies; it is only called by a different name.

21. See Richard S. Odingo, "Agricultural Land Settlement and Rural Development in Kenya", paper delivered to a seminar at the Department of Geography, University of California at Los Angeles (8th January, 1970).

Lionel Cliffe, pp. 38–60

1. J. K. Nyerere, *Socialism and Rural Development* (Dar es Salaam, 1967).

2. This set of principles is a feature of his 1962 discussion of "Ujamaa—the Basis of African Socialism" as well as his 1967 policy statement *Socialism and Rural Development*.

3. Conflicting interpretations have been offered for the "Arusha ideology". Ahmed Mohiddin of Makerere has stressed the continuity in Nyerere's ideas from the 1950s, see, for instance, "Ujamaa na Kujitegemea", *Mawazo*, No. 2 (December, 1967). My colleague John Saul has seen a qualitative step forward from a mere ideal towards the definition of a *strategy* that is in turn based on a class *analysis*, see his "Class and Penetration" in *Political Penetration in East Africa*, a forth-coming volume edited by J. S. Coleman, L. Cliffe, & M. Doornbos. Both these essays and other material on Tanzania socialism are to be found in a reader on Tanzania politics edited by Cliffe and Saul, which will be published later this year.

4. J. Goody, "Economy & Feudalism in Africa", *Economic History Review*, 2nd Series, Vol. XXII, No. 3 (December, 1969).

5. P. Gulliver describes how competition for, and effective control over land were two of several lines of cleavage and stratification following the introduction of cash crops in Rungwe—see his *Land Tenure and Social Change among the Nyakyusa* (Kampala, 1960).

6. In Pare District, clans with a monopoly over land rights represent one obstacle to co-operation in that they are hanging on to the only spare land in this crowded area; recent legislation appointing local Land Tribunals is aimed at preventing these elements retaining unused land. (This information I owe to University College students, Miss Mtamba and Mr. Mndeme).

7. For an indictment of the premises of which many past plans

have rested, see P. Rigby, "Pastoralism & Prejudice", *Nkanga* 4 (Kampala 1969).

8. These data on the formation of livestock co-operatives from R. ole Kuney, "Ranching Associations in Masailand" undergraduate dissertation, Dar es Salaam University College.

9. While, in highland-banana areas, the "natural" surplus made possible the emergence of political and social hierarchies, it has been suggested that only the emergence of more sophisticated forms of political organisation made possible the settlement of the often tsetse-occupied, fairly dry, bush-woodland areas in central and western parts of Tanzania and led to the establishment of the chiefdoms of the Kimbu, Sukuma, Nyamwezi and other areas; see the cases in A. Roberts (ed.), *Tanzania Before 1900* (Nairobi, 1968) and I. Kimambo & A. Temu (eds.), *A History of Tanzania* (Dar es Salaam, 1969) esp. Chs. 2–4.

10. Even in the more egalitarian, segmented societies, problems are forced in moving towards modern forms of co-operation, for instance, M. Jellicoe, "Community Development in Singida", unpublished M. A. Thesis, Makerere University College, has argued that the solidarity *within* the extended family, and the segmented nature of Turu Society as a whole, makes permanent co-operation *between* family groups very difficult to achieve.

11. The individualist elements, as supposed to the communal, are stressed in a detailed survey by H. Schneider, *Wahi Wanyaturu: A Traditional Economy,* (forthcoming), in which he argues that the typical Nyaturu is an excellent example of economic man, that intra-family obligations to supply labour cannot always be assumed, and that labour exchange is undertaken on a reciprocal basis motivated by mutual profit.

12. R. G. Abrahams, "Neighbourhood organisation: A major sub-system among the Northern Nyamwezi", *Africa,* Vol. XXXV, No. 2 (April, 1965).

13. Notable exceptions for Tanzania are the works of P. Gulliver on labour migration, cash cropping etc.

14. J. K. Nyerere, *Socialism and Rural Development,* p. 7.

15. President Nyerere's inaugural speech in December 1962, was the first occasion on which he talked about "villagisation"; this slogan was, rather inappropriately, given effect in the unsuccessful Village Settlement Programme in 1963–5.

16. In a survey of several villages in one district, a Dar es Salaam University student, Miss C. B. Mtamba: "Research on *ujamaa* villages in Pare" (unpublished), stresses that by for the most successful village she visited was the only one that had instituted specialist

teams for different activities. Some more general points in a similar vein are made in a paper L. Cliffe & C. L. Cunningham, "Ideology, Organisation and the Settlement Experience in Tanzania", shortly to appear in D. C. R. Belshaw & E. A. Brett (eds.), *Public Policy and Agricultural Development in East Africa* (London: Frank Cass 1970).

17. This survey was conducted by a team of university students who came from the district under the direction of my colleagues John G. Moore and William L. Luttrell and myself in January 1969.

18. The whole of the research which will be drawn on has been carried out by the team mentioned above, with the assistance of Poul Westergaard, Economic Research Bureau, Dar es Salaam.

19. For a full account of this history see the chapter on the Shambala by S. Feierman in A. W. Roberts, *Tanzania before 1900;* for an account of the political tradition see E. V. Winans, *Shambala: The Constitution of a Traditional Kingdom* (London, 1962).

20. Details of some of the colonial history are to be found in J. Iliffe, *Tanzania under German Rule* (Cambridge: C.U.P., 1969). I. Mnkondo, "The Political History of Lushoto", and J. Hoza, "The Hoza Rebellion", undergraduate dissertations, Political Science Dept. (University College, Dar es Salaam).

21. Over half of our sample had three or more plots of land.

22. M. Attems, "Permanent Cropping in the Usambara Mountains" in H. Ruthenberg (ed.), *Smallholder Farming & Smallholder Development in Tanzania* (München, 1969).

23. M. Attems, "Permanent Cropping in the Usambara ...".

24. W. L. Luttrell, "Proposals for Ujamaa Dairying in Highland, High-Density Areas" (unpublished) (Dar es Salaam 1969); P. Mmbaga, "The Economies of Dairy Cattle in Arusha" (unpublished) (Makerere, 1968).

25. The Lushoto study group, mentioned earlier is in fact at present conducting detailed research in a few pilot villages for these purposes, in support of a programme of intergrated rural development which has just been started in the district, under the sponsorship of the Community Development Trust Fund of Tanzania and the Kübel Foundation of West Germany.

26. A more detailed analysis of the ujamaa potential and the problems of implementation can be found in L. Cliffe, W. L. Luttrell & J. E. Moore, "Socialist Transformation in Rural Tanzania —A Strategy for the Western Usambaras" (University of East Africa, Social Science Conference; 1969).

Gösta Hydén, pp. 61–80

1. *Sessional Paper No. 10. 1965* (Government Printer, Nairobi), p. 11.

2. *Government Paper No. 4, 1967* (Government Printer, Dar-es-Salaam), p. 15.

3. *The Common Man's Charter* (Consolidated Printers, Kampala 1969), p. 18.

4. *Development Plan 1966–70* (Government Printer, Nairobi), p. 200.

5. In the Second Plan it is expressed in the following terms: "... given the many problems experienced by co-operatives, emphasis, at least during the early part of the Plan period, will be given to measures designed to improve the efficiency of existing co-operatives rather than to expanding rapidly the number of societies" (p. 277).

6. Cf. Nelson Kasfir's paper on "Organization Theory and Ugandan Co-operative Unions" in this volume.

7. A free peasantry is likely to be a condition for the growth of strong voluntary associations in the rural areas. In this respect, African peasants, seem to have an advantage over their counterparts in Latin America and many parts of Asia.

8. See, e.g., John Saul, "Marketing Co-operatives in a Developing Country: The Tanzanian Case", University of East Africa, Social Science Conference Paper (Nairobi, December 8–12, 1969), reprinted in Göran Hydén and John Saul, *Kooperation i Östafrika* (Uppsala 1970); also G. Hydén, *Political Development in Rural Tanzania* (Nairobi: East African Publishing House, 1969).

9 *Annual Report of the Registrar of Co-operatives* (Nairobi, 1946), p. 4.

10. Cf. Audun Sandberg, "Generational Conflict and Entrepreneurship in Meru", *Staff Paper No. 52* (Institute of Development Studies, University of Nairobi, 1969).

11. Karl Marx and Friedrich Engels, *Basic Writings on Politics and Philosophy*, "Eighteenth Brumaire of Louis Bonaparte", (New York: Anchor Books, 1959), p. 338.

12. Karl Marx, *Pre-Capitalist Economic Formations*, "Marx to Zasulich, March 8, 1881" (New York: International Publishers, 1966), p. 143.

13. Saul, op. cit., p. 13.

14. Cf. Kasfir's account of the Uganda Growers' Co-operative Union in this volume.

15. In some cases action has been taken against only one union

256

at a time. In Tanzania, the Victoria Federation of Co-operative Unions has been subject to separate government intervention. The same applies in Kenya to the Mount-Elgon Co-operative Union in Bungoma District, Western Province.

16. Poul Westergaard in his paper in this volume discusses some experiments made in this direction in Tanzania.

J. P. W. B. McAuslan, pp. 81–120

1. P. J. Nkambo Mugerwa, "Land Tenure in East Africa—Some Contracts", *East African Law Today* (London: British Institute of International and Comparative Law, 1966), pp. 101–114.

2. I. Potekhin, "Land Relations in African Countries", *Journal of Modern African Studies*, 1, 1 (1963), pp. 39–62.

3. J. P. W. B. McAuslan, "Control of Land and Agricultural Development in Kenya and Tanzania", G. F. A. Sawyerr (ed.), *East African Law and Social Change* (Nairobi: East African Publishing House, 1967), 172–258 at pp. 196–9 for a brief description of this process.

4. Constitution: s. 115 (2).

5. R. L. A. Cap. 300, s. 102 (1) (b).

6. R. L. A., s. 103 (1).

7. *Report of the Mission on Land Consolidation and Registration in Kenya* (Nairobi: Government Printer, 1967), Chap. 8.

8. Op. cit. para. 96.

9. Op. cit. para. 107.

10. Nos. 36 and 35 of 1968.

11. Land (Group Representatives) Act, s. 8.

12. O. Schiller, *Co-operation and Integration in Agricultural Production* (Asia, 1969), p. 36.

13. J. W. Maina, "Land Settlement in Kenya" (Rome: World Land Reform Conference, F.A.O., 1966).

14. The next two paragraphs are based on McAuslan, op. cit. 218–8.

15. Reported in D. Warrinder, *Land Reform in Principle and Practice* (London: O.U.P., 1969), p. 70.

16. Other possible tenure problems are discussed in L. Cliffe, supra.

17. This and the next paragraph are taken from McAuslan, op. cit., 187–9.

18. H. F. Morris and J. S. Read, *Uganda, the Development of its Laws and Constitutions* (London: Stevens, 1966). Chap. 15 for an excellent survey of Uganda's land laws.

19. S. Charsley, "The Group Farm Scheme in Uganda in Land

Settlement and Rural Development in East Africa", R. Apthorpe (ed.), *Nkanga 3* (Kampala: Transition Books, 1968), pp. 56–64.

20. Op. cit., 58.

21. Op. cit., 63.

22. D. Warrinder, op. cit., 70.

23. A successful example of a combination of large scale production and individual peasant holdings is the Kenya Tea Development Authority discussed in G. Hydén's paper and in Y. P. Ghai and J. P. W. B. McAuslan, *Public Law and Political Change in Kenya* (London: O.U.P., 1970), pp. 297–300.

24. Cap. 490, s. 5. Though phrased differently, the Tanzanian Co-operative Societies Act (No. 27 of 1968) confers similar powers on the Registrar of Co-operative Societies. He shall register a co-operative society unless he is of the opinion that, inter alia, it would not be desirable to do so.

25. The 1964 Ugandan Co-operative Societies Act did not have any provisions for compulsory marketing. I have not dealt with the Ugandan situation in this part of the paper as a new Co-operative Societies Bill was scheduled for publication and debate during the writing and revision of the paper. The Bill will presumably be based in part on the Arain report, discussed in O. Okereke and N. Kasfir infra.

26. *Dairy Commission of Inquiry Report* (Nairobi: Ministry of Agriculture, 1965), 19 para. 126.

27. S. M. Aktar, "The Possibilities of Co-operative Farming,", K. H. Parsons, R. I. Penn and P. M. Raup (eds.), *Land Tenure* (University of Wisconsin, 1956), pp. 590–7 for a good statement of the classical position.

28. Government Printer (Dar es Salaam, 1966).

28 a. This was implemented by the Unified Co-operative Service Act, No. 44 of 1968. The Act applies to national and secondary societies and such others as the Minister shall specify. The Commission consists of a chairman and from four to six members of whom one represents the Ministry of Co-operative Development and one is nominated by C.U.T. The Commission has authority over terms and conditions of service discipline and joint negotiating machinery. It may advise co-operatives on training schemes and promotion exams. Its decisions are binding on all officers and societies.

29. *Proposals of the Tanzania Government on the Recommendation of the Special Presidential Committee of Enquiry into the Co-operative Movement and Marketing Boards,* Government Paper No. 3 of 1966.

30. I was informed at the Conference in an informal session, that

Uganda does operate an insurance scheme for defaulters, but I have not been able to find out any details of the scheme.

31. M. P. Collinson, *Agricultural Credit in Tanzania in Agricultural Planning in East Africa,* ed. G. K. Helleiner (Nairobi: East African Publishing House, 1968), 139–156, at pp. 140–2. See too, McAuslan, op. cit., 228–34.

32. Laws of Tanganyika, Cap. 210.

33. M. P. Collinson, op. cit., 142.

34. C. Geertz, "The Rotating Credit Association: A Middle Rung", *Development,* 10(3) Economic Development and Cultural Change, 241–63 (reprinted in *Social Change, the Colonial Situation,* ed. I. Wallerstein) (N.Y.: Wiley, 1966), pp. 420–446.

35. Y. P. Ghai and J. P. W. B. McAuslan, op.cit., 86–88.

36. According to information given at the Conference 29 million shs has been lent by farmers in Uganda without security, much of it via revolving credit associations. 89 per cent of the money has been repaid. The proposal in the test is to tie in these successful associations with primary societies.

37. C. Geertz, op.cit., 439.

Poul W. Westergaard, pp. 121–152

1. *Acknowledgements:* I wish to express my sincere gratitude to Mr. A. Holmberg, Director, Office for East and Central Africa of the International Co-operative Alliance (ICA), and Mr. B. Zlataric, Agricultural Secretary of the ICA, as well as the Registrar of Co-operative Societies in Tanzania for pointing out errors in earlier versions which have been taken into account in this version. The views expressed in this paper are, however, my responsibility alone, as are any errors and omissions made.

2. Statement by the International Co-operative Alliance in connection with the 46th session, in 1969, of the ECOSOC of the UN.

3. *Wages, Incomes, Rural Development, Investment and Price Policy,* Government Paper No. 4, 1967.

4. The paper refers to mainland Tanzania only.

5. *Tanzania Second Five-Year Pland for Economic and Social Development, 1st July, 1969, to 30th June, 1974.*

6. International Co-operative Alliance, *23rd Congress Report,* 1966. Quoted from the inaugural address of the President of the International Co-operative Alliance at the 23rd congress of the ICA.

7. Co-operative Societies Ordinance 1933, as amended in 1964.

8. R. J. M. Swynnerton *et al., All about "KNCU" coffee* (Moshi, 1948).

9. *Ibid.*

10. The following information is taken from M. Paulus, *Das Genossenschaftswesen in Tanganyika und Uganda,* Afrika-Studien 15 (München: IFO Institut, 1967).

11. R. J. M. Swynnerton, op.cit.

12. *Chagga Coffee.* Pamphlet issued by the KNCU on Independence Day 1961.

13. *The Co-operative Movement in Tanganyika* (1961).

14. *Report of the Presidential Special Committee of Enquiry into Co-operative Movement and Marketing Boards* (Dar-es-Salaam, 1966).

15. *Proposals of the Tanzania Government on the Recommendations of the Special Presidential Committee of Enquiry ... Government* Paper No. 3 (1966).

16. The Committee was, however, against a three-tier system, such as that in the VFCU (which was a federation of secondary societies). The VFCU was wound up in 1967 and replaced by the Nyanza Co-operative Union.

17. The manpower situation of the co-operatives had been aggravated by the fact that there was, in the years after Independence, a "great drain of trained manpower from the movement itself into more lucrative positions in government at both the political and the civil service levels, into the marketing boards and into private industry" (quotation from the report).

18. The Special Committee also recommended that the Registrar should be given powers to suspend or remove the committee of a society and to designate a new secretary. The Registrar already had such powers under the Co-operative Societies Ordinance of 1963, which had repealed the Ordinance of 1933, with later amendments. Under the Ordinance of 1963, the Registrar had, however, to act through the Minister in such cases.

19. C. K. Laurent, "Cotton Marketing in Tanzania", (Dar-es-Salaam, 1969) (mimeographed).

20. A complete description of the pricing system can be found in P. W. Westergaard and H. Kayumbo, "The Cashew-nut Industry in Tanzania", (forthcoming).

21. The reader is referred to P. W. Westergaard, "The Cashew-nut Industry in Tanzania: Marketing Costs", ERB (R), Paper 69.3 (mimeographed).

22. Cf. the following remark by the Presidential Special Committee of Enquiry: "... world prices for cotton lint have been falling for some years, cushioned by the LSMB price-assistance fund,

and we found very little appreciation by the cotton farmers that they have been receiving more than their crop was worth."

23. Nor am I competent to judge whether the present marketing boards are efficient or not.

24. Cf. C. K. Laurent, op.cit. and also J. K. Nyerere, *Socialism and Rural Development*; C. K. Laurent, "A background appraisal of marketing of selected agricultural products in the Mtwara Region of Tanzania" (Dar-es-Salaam, 1969) (mimeographed); B. K. Zegge, "Marketing tobacco in Tanzania" (Dar-es-Salaam, 1969) (mimeographed); B. K. Zegge, "Co-operative marketing in the Coast Region" (Dar-es-Salaam, 1969) (mimeographed); P. W. Westergaard, "Primary societies' marketing costs, a case study and some general remarks, mostly on efficiency", ERB Paper 69.6 (mimeographed); P. W. Westergaard and H. Pedersen, "The economic performance in 1966–67 of K.N.C.U. societies" (Moshi, 1970) (mimeographed).

25. The educational activities of the College and the Centre are not focussed only on the economic efficiency of management. Co-operative education is directed towards the "co-operative triangle" —members, committee and management.

26. Cf. ref. 6 above.

27. One possible way of presenting accounts informatively and understandably is shown in P. W. Westergaard and H. Pedersen, op.cit. (1970).

O. Okereke, pp, 153–177

1. See the policy speech to Parliament, by the Minister of Marketing and Co-operatives, Ministry of Marketing and Co-operatives, 1969, p. 3.

2. *Ibid.*

3. Livingstone and Ord, *Economics for East Africa* (1967), p. 149.

4. O. Okereke, "The Strengths and Weaknesses of the Co-operative Movement in Uganda", in E. B. Riordan (ed.), *Agricultural Marketing in East Africa*.

5. J. K. Gailbraith, *American Capitalism, The Concept Countervailing Power* (1952), p. 118.

6. R. L. Glodius and W. F. Mueller, "Market Structure Analysis as an Orientation for Research in Agricultural Economics", *Journal of Farm Economics*, 43 (1961), p. 516.

7. *Ibid.*

8. *Ibid.*, pp. 516–7.

9. Considering the composition of the 1962 Commission, it would seem that the Commission's recommendations supporting competition arose from the fact that alien business was gradually passing

into the hands of co-operatives which had begun to enjoy a sheltered position. The earlier Commissions had urged protection for the Buying Association and the Ginning Pools when immigrant businessmen were in control of the industry. There is, therefore, no wonder that the 1966 Cotton Committee, comprising mainly Ugandans, upheld protection for co-operatives as "a political necessity".

10. See *Report of the Committee of Inquiry into the Cotton Industry* (1966).

11. The pros and cons of monopoly cannot be dealt with in this paper. Arguments for, and against, this form of market situation can be obtained from an array of standard texts, like, P. W. Bell and M. P. Todaro, *Economic Theory*; I. Livingstone and H. W. Ord, *An Introduction to Economics for East Africa*; Joan Robinson, *The Economics of Imperfect Competition*, (1933); E. A. G. Robinson, *Monopoly*, etc.

12. Uganda Protectorate, *Report of the Commission of Inquiry into the Cotton Ginning Industry of Uganda* (1962), p. 37.

13. *Uganda Argus* (Sept. 20, 1963).

14. *Ibid.*

15. O. Okereke, "Co-operative Development in Uganda, 1900–1939", *East African Journal of Rural Development, I* (1968), pp. 60–71.

16. O. Okereke, *The Role of the Co-operative Movement in the Economic Development of Uganda* (M. A. Thesis, University of East Africa, 1968), p. 439.

17. 1962 Cotton Report, op.cit., p. 43.

18. Uganda Govt. *Report of the Committee of Inquiry into the Cotton Industry* (1966), pp. 32–33.

19. *Ibid.*, pp. 31–34.

20. Republic of Uganda, *The Report of the Committee of Inquiry into the Affairs of all Co-operative Unions in Uganda* (1966): Summary, para. 19–167. See also ch. XVIII of the report.

21. *Ibid.* This recommendation has been accepted by Government.

22. Associations of growers which persisted in the coffee industry until 1969, have been accused of abdicating their coffee processing rights to Asian businessmen who provided the capital for most of the coffee processing plants licensed in the name of associations of growers, under stringent terms inimical to the interests of these associations themselves. It was recommended that these associations of growers should either be abolished "in the interest of the coffee industry", or, become co-operatives or be treated like private companies. Co-op. Unions' Report, 1968, *op. cit.* Summary 19–181.

23. Republic of Uganda, *Govt. White Paper on the Report of the Committee of Inquiry into the Coffee Industry*, 1967, Sessional Paper, No. 3 of 1968.

24. Uganda Protectorate, *Commission of Inquiry into the Coffee Industry*, 1957. The "free side" of the coffee industry, in the past, consisted in the right of the coffee grower to make his own marketing arrangements for the sale of his processed coffee, including the right of export under his own mark. Such coffee, therefore, did not pass through the Coffee Marketing Board. Estate Coffee and pulped coffee producers, as well as the Bugisu Co-operative Union, were in this category. On the other hand, for the "controlled side" of the coffee industry, all marketing arrangements and the export of the processed coffee were vested in the Coffee Marketing Board. Yet, even during the period of differentiation, one vital aspect of the industry (as in cotton also) was apparent, in that the statutory marketing boards retained the overall control of both the coffee and the cotton industries. For example, in the coffee industry, even the so-called "free side" could not export coffee without the authority of the CMB. Hence all coffee (as it is now) was subject to central control, since all coffee must be graded and the quantity to be exported was dependent upon the Board for allocation of quota, in accordance with the International Coffee Agreement.

25. *Uganda Argus,* June 11, 1963.

26. *Ibid.*

27. Uganda Govt. White Paper on the Report of the Committee of Inquiry into the Coffee Industry, 1967, Sessional Paper, No. 3., March 1968. In the White Paper, the Government rejected the committee's recommendation that private coffee companies still have a useful role to play in the coffee industry, and asserted that "the Government's aim is that farmers should buy and process all their coffee through co-operative unions". The 1968 Co-op. Union report reaffirms the belief "that private traders have caused much harm to the coffee industry as a whole and to the co-operatives". (1968 Co-operative Union Report, *op. cit.*, parag. 10–17).

28. As the licensing of coffee and cotton buyers is the responsibility of the CMB and the LMB, respectively, so is the licensing of secondary crop buyers that of the Produce Marketing Board. The Board has a planned programme of taking over the export of secondary crops as it is now doing with tobacco, "as soon as legal adjustments are completed and necessary funds and storage facilities are provided". The BAT has handed over to cooperatives in West Nile and Acholi the sole right of tobacco buying. See the Uganda Argus, April 9, 1970, p. 1.

29. This risk element was removed in the case of the Busoga Growers' Co-operative Union in the 1962/63 season when Government subsidised the Union to offset the loss it sustained in its groundnut trade of that year.

30. See the recent policy speech of the Minister of Marketing and Cooperatives, *Uganda Argus*, Feb. 14, 1970, p. 1.

31. A. S. M. Hall, "Crop and Livestock Processing in Uganda", F.A.O./Makerere University College Rural Economy Dept. Conference Paper, No. 5 (1967).

32. Both unions appear to have recovered under their Supervising Managers, wiped out their deficits and made surpluses. See the policy speech of the Minister of Marketing and Co-operatives quoted above. More important, however, is the use into which the surplus is put—i.e. whether distributed to growers or used mainly for capital development.

33. Uganda Protectorate, *Report of the Commission of Inquiry into the Bugisu Coffee Industry* (1958), pp. 6.

34. Uganda Protectorate, *Government Memorandum on the Future Organisation of the Bugisu Coffee Industry*, Sessional Paper No. 19 (1958).

35. A Supervising Manager was appointed to manage the affairs of the union for a term of four years, but was later withdrawn after serving for a period of three years.

36. 1968 Co-operative Union's Report, op.cit. para. 10–18.

37. *Ibid.*, p. 154.

38. *Ibid.*

39. Republic of Uganda, *Govt. White Paper on the Report of the Committee of Inquiry into the Affairs of all Co-operative Unions in Uganda*, Sessional Paper No. 5 (1968), para. 19–174.

40. The Government has warned co-operative societies that they must pay growers promptly on delivery of their crop to them. See *The People* (May 19, 1970), p. 8.

41. 1968 Co-operative Union's Report, op.cit. 19–178.

42. Uganda Government. *The Report of the Committee of Inquiry into the Coffee Industry*, 1967, para. 3. 19.

43. *Ibid.*

44. *Ibid.*

45. The previous proposal allowed 50% of coffee processing to the private traders in Buganda, where most of coffee processing was in the hands of the indigenous coffee growers. Outside Buganda, co-operatives were to take over all coffee processing. But there was a proviso that Co-ops. would eventually take over all coffee processing. This was stated in a policy statement, in Parliament.

by the Minister of Marketing and Co-operatives. *Uganda Argus* (July 12, 1969), p. 6.

46. O. Okereke, *Agricultural Marketing in East Africa,* op.cit.

47. 1968 Co-operative Union's Report, op.cit. p. 50.

48. See, for example, A. Milton Obote, *The Common Man's Charter.*

49. See *Uganda Argus* (May 7, 1970), p. 10. Co-operatives are to acquire part of the 60% of shareholding in all bus services outside Buganda.

50. See G. K. Helleiner, "Agricultural Marketing in Tanzania: Policies and Problems", *Agricultural Marketing in East Africa,* op.cit.

51. P. T. Bauer and B. S. Yamey, *The Economics of Under-developed Countries* (London, 1957), p. 149.

Nelson Kasfir, pp. 178–208

1. *Report of the Committee of Inquiry into the Affairs of all Co-operative Unions in Uganda* (Arain Report) (Entebbe: Government Printer, 1967), p. 16.

2. *1967 Annual Report* of the Department of Co-operative Development, Uganda, p. 6.

3. *Arain Report,* pp. 15, 16 and 152.

4. *1967 Annual Report,* pp. 1 and 22.

5. *Ibid.,* p. 3.

6. *Socialism and Rural Development,* (Dar es Salaam: Government Printer, 1967), p. 9.

7. D. H. Laws, "The Problems of Management in the Uganda Co-operative Movement", in *The Role of the Co-operative Movement in Uganda* (Kampala: Milton Obote Foundation, 1966), p. 29.

8. A good summary of the scientific management school can be found in Nicos Mouzelis, *Organisation and Bureaucracy* (London: Routledge & Kegan Paul, 1967), pp. 79–96.

9. A case study of restriction of production is presented in George Homans, *The Human Group* (New York: Harcourt Brace, 1950).

10. For a discussion of the human relations approach, see Mouzelis, *Organisation and Bureaucracy,* pp. 97–119.

11. Herbert Simon, *Administrative Behavior,* 2nd. ed. (New York: Free Press, 1961), Ch. 2.

12. James March and Herbert Simon, *Organizations,* (New York: Wiley, 1958).

13. Chester Barnard, *The Functions of the Executive* (Cambridge: Harvard University Press, 1938).

14. Peter Clark and James Q. Wilson, "Incentive Systems: A

theory of Organizations", *Administrative Science Quarterly, 6* (September, 1961), pp. 129–66.

15. Michel Crozier, *The Bureaucratic Phenomenon* (Chicago: University of Chicago Press, 1964), p. 149.

16. Robert Presthus, "Authority in Organisations", *Public Administration Review,* 20: 2 (Spring 1960), pp. 86–91.

17. Dalton, *Men Who Manage* (New York: Wiley, 1959). Crozier, *The Bureaucratic Phenomenon.*

18. Mouzelis, *Organisation and Bureaucracy,* pp. 159–60. If Crozier had probed into the power relations within each of the occupational groups he studied, he might have found strategies of smaller groups (perhaps the most senior maintenance men) for controlling other members in their group (perhaps giving them the "dirtier" jobs). There is a problem of infinite regression here.

19. *The Bureaucratic Phenomenon,* p. 156. Dalton defines the term "power struggles" in precisely the same way. *Men Who Manage,* p. 19.

20. *Power in Co-operatives* (Oxford: Blackwell, 1965), pp. 102–40.

21. The most important study of the institutionalisation of a competitive political system within a voluntary association is Seymour Martin Lipset, Martin Trow and James Coleman, *Union Democracy* (Glencoe: Free Press, 1956).

22. Ostergaard and Halsey, *Power in Co-operatives,* pp. 222–28.

23. David Smock, *Conflict and Control in an African Trade Union* (Stanford: Hoover Institution Press, 1969).

24. *The Bureaucratic Phenomenon,* pp. 163 and 166.

25. "Comments on the Theory of Organizations", *American Political Science Review,* 46: 4 (December, 1952), pp. 1130–39. (Italics added).

26. "The Concept of Power", *Behavioural Science,* 2 (July, 1957), p. 201–15.

27. Abraham Kaplan, "Power in Perspective", in Robert Kahn and Elise Boulding, *Power and Conflict in Organizations* (London: Tavistock, 1964), pp. 12–17.

28. Talcott Parsons, "On the Concept of Power", *Proceedings of the American Philosophical Society,* 107 (June, 1963).

29. Mouzelis, *Organisation and Bureaucracy,* p. 156. Mouzelis makes the oft-repeated point that Parsons' view of the social systems places too much emphasis on harmony and not enough on conflict. For example, in the case of power Parsons concentrates on the productive aspects and not the consequences of the pattern of its distribution in the organisation. However, it is important to

keep in mind that this imbalance is not a necessary consequence of Parsons' definition of power, as I suggest in the previous paragraph.

30. For a general treatment of this position see Lewis A. Coser, *The Functions of Social Conflict* (Glencoe: Free Press, 1956).

31. March and Simon, *Organizations*, p. 115.

32. *Men Who Manage*, p. 68.

33. Donald Pelz, "Influence: A Key to Effective Leadership in the First-Line Supervisor", *Personnel*, 29(1952), pp. 3–11. The findings of this study and a similar one carried out later which demonstrated that the supervisor's "good efforts" were not sufficient, he had to be successful in exercising his influence in order to keep morale high are summarised in Robert Kahn, "Field Studies of Power in Organizations", in Kahn and Boulding, *Power and Conflict in Organizations*, pp. 52–57.

34. Kahn, "Field Studies of Power in Organizations", pp. 57–62. Kahn and Arnold Tannenbaum designed a "control graph" which seeks to simultaneously measure the amount of power and organisation has and how it is distributed. Thus, they encompass both levels of power discussed above.

35. *Ibid.*, pp. 62–64.

36. "Comments on the Theory of Organizations". The concept includes both Barnard's "executive" (who maintains the balance between flows of contributions and incentives) and his "leader" (who formulates the purposes towards which the organisation strives). See Clark and Wilson, "Incentive Systems".

37. See Dalton, *Men Who Manage*, pp. 248–52 for a discussion of business managers as politicians.

38. *TVA and the Grass Roots* (New York: Harper & Row, 1966), p. 10.

39. John Saul, "Marketing Co-operatives in a Developing Country: The Tanzanian Case", University Social Sciences Council Conference: Nairobi (December, 1969), pp. 3, 4 and 13. Saul puts forward a compelling argument that the conflict-free *Gemeinschaft* vision of traditional society has very little to do with behaviour in modern African co-operatives.

40. Under current regulations all co-operatives are required to pay cash to the farmers at the time of delivery, and for those crops in which co-operatives have a processing monopoly private traders have ceased to present an important a threat. It would be misleading to assume that these areas have necessarily been removed from the struggle for power by the new rules. While it is too early to tell, it seems that the farmers have gained an important ad-

vantage from the committee and union staff by restricting their ability to divert crop finance to other purposes. On the other hand, the monopolies should enormously strengthen the position of the staff, since the farmers will have no choice but to bring their coffee or cotton to the co-operative union.

41. *Arain Report,* p. 41.

42. Ostergaard and Halsey, p. 78.

43. *Arain Report,* pp. 22 and 24.

44. Similar practices have been reported in Tanzanian co-operatives. See Shem Migot-Adholla, "The Politics of a Growers' Co-operative Organisation", unpublished student dissertation: Department of Political Science, University College, Dar-es-Salaam, 1969, p. 26.

45. E. A. Brett and M. Crawford Young, "Survey of Uganda Farmers", unpublished, 1969.

46. With the processing monopoly each of the three new unions is growing larger at a rapid rate. East Mengo Union may well be larger already than Uganda Growers ever was.

47. See George Shepherd, *They Wait in Darkness* (New York: John Ray, 1955) and John Stonehouse, *Prohibited Immigrant* (London: Bodley Head, 1960) for accounts of FUAF and some of the strategies used to acquire resources within the organisation.

48. The authors of the recent commission of inquiry into co-operative unions argue that this might have been the crucial opportunity to phase out absolescent private ginneries and build new co-operative units. Unfortunately, at this time the government had not made a full commitment to co-operatives and the chance was missed. *Arain Report,* p. 102.

49. The following figures on the performance of UG have been taken from the union's balance sheets, which were prepared by professional auditors. These figures sometimes vary greatly from those reported in the co-operative department's annual reports.

50. Figures have been taken from the annual balance sheets of the union.

51. The advantage of this comparison is that size of the union and debt position do not affect the comparison. Slightly more accurate figures would be obtained, if surpluses or deficits generated solely by crop turnover were compared rather than net surpluses or deficits.

52. Lipset, Trow and Coleman point out that the opposition in the ITU also used general meetings to create opposition and embarrass the leadership as a campaign tactic. *Trade Union Democracy,* p. 65.

53. A frequent tactic of managers the world over is to clothe their power strategies in "technical" and "rational" arguments in order to prevent "interference" by others. See Lipset, Trow and Coleman, *Trade Union Democracy*, p. 11.

Raymond Apthorpe, pp. 209–229

1. Cf. Fredrik Barth "On the study of social change", *American Anthropologist* Vol. 69 (1967), pp. 661–669. Some criticisms of "social pre-requisites" in co-operative studies are included in my "The golden eggs of agricultural co-operation", a critique presented at the Institute of Development Studies, Sussex, in April 1969. The present paper derives from my work on agricultural co-operatives and planned social change in Africa nearing completion at UNRISD, Geneva.

2. I am indebted to David Phiri for this observation. For a change in policy in Zambia from production to service co-operative of various kinds see President Kaunda's speech January 12, 1970. I am indebted to Stephen Lombard for this reference.

3. The allusion here is specifically to the time at the turn of the year 1969–70 which saw the politics of *The Common Man's Charter*, by A. Milton Obote (published in October 1969), which is greatly critical of a class owing its privilege to wealth in the private sector.

4. What follows are reflections on the writer's own work in Eastern Africa 1964–8: He is indebted for many discussions on the problems of the Kenya Million Acres Scheme in particular to Brian van Arkadie, John MacArthur and William Omamo, with whom he carried out a joint enquiry into the problem in 1966 for the Governments of Kenya and the United Kingdom. I am indebted to Mr. MacArthur for comments on the content of the agreement that follows. No attempt will be made here to review the extensive bibliography on the Million Acres scheme. The most comprehensive source is Robert Chambers' *Settlement Schemes in Tropical Africa* (London: Routledge & Kegan Paul, 1969).

5. Cf. "Development studies and social planning" in *People, planning and development studies* by Raymond Apthorpe, Nicholas Bennett, *et al.* (London: Frank Cass, 1970).

6. Cf. the chapters on "Rural development planning and the human factor in Africa", *People, planning and development studies* (1970) (see footnote no. 5).

7. "Planners" here as elsewhere in this note refers to a professional category "of manpower" unqualified ethnically.

8. Eg. see E. G. Giglioli "Mechanical cultivation of rice on the

Murea irrigation settlement", *East African Agricultural and Forestry Journal* (January, 1965). I am indebted to R. J. Chambers for this reference.

9. Cf. the writer's "Two planning theories of economic development", E. A. Brett (ed.), *Public Policy and Agricultural Development in East Africa*. (London: Frank Cass and EAPH, Nairobi, 1970) a revised version of "Planned social change and land settlement", *Nkanga 3* (Kampala, 1968).

10. That finds expression for instance in part of the first of a two volume work on planning and development in Kenya, Uganda and Tanzania in a passage on the Kenya land decolonization schemes. A. Meister *L'Afrique peut-elle partir? Changement social et développement en Afrique orientale*. (Paris: Editions du Seuil, 1966).

11. Cf. J. C. de Wilde, *Experiences with agricultural development in tropical Africa*, Vol. 1 (Washington: Johns Hopkins, 1967), p. 55.

12. See the study cited in ref. no. 6 for an analysis of this.

13. See the Report cited in ref. no. 1.

14. Instances of this in the East African studies by the academic authorities in those years such as Max Gluckman and Thomas Fallers, oddly contrast strikingly with the work that in fact derives from approximately the same period by, e.g. the scholar-administrator, Charles White. Cf. the writer's "Land law and land policy in Eastern Africa", J. Obol-Ochola (ed.), *Land Law Reform in East Africa* (Kampala Press Trust, 1969).

15. A much less satisfactory analogy with cash crops rather than land is made in *Wilde,* 1967 op.cit., 67.

16. I owe a good deal of information on Masai cattle sales to an unpublished manuscript by Alan Jacobs shown to me by the then Chief Spokesman for the Masai in Tanzania in 1964.

17. Cf. Michael Lipton, "The theory of the optimizing peasant", *Journal of Development Studies* (April 1968).

18. The contrast expressed in terms of "traditional" versus "organizational" is conventionally misleading in that it relies on words which have many uses. It is *not* implied that the husband-wife relationship is *only* a traditional one in the sense that nothing has changed in it since time immemorial. And in central policy decisions in Africa it has indeed become traditional or customary for them to look to co-operatives for a solution sometimes of all their rural problems.

19. Cf. the writer's "Planned social change and land settlement", *Land settlement and rural development in Eastern Africa, Nkanga 3* (Kampala, 1968).

Carl Gösta Widstand, pp. 230–242

1. John S. Saul, "Marketing Co-operatives in Tanzania", Paper given at the University of Sussex Conference on Social Pre-requisites of Agricultural Co-operation (March, 1969).

2. John S. Saul, op.cit., p. 15.

3. Cf. however the experience of A. Weingrod (referred in Percy Cohen, "Traditional Societies and Modern Co-operatives", Paper presented at the VIth World Congress of Sociology, Evian, 1966) from Israeli *moshavim* recruited from North Africa, where the socially highly fragmented did not work well, whereas in the situation where there were two competing factions, the competition between the two groups produced better results. The main argument of the examples presented in that study is: where there is a single cohesive group there is relative success.

4. Ph. Gulliver's recent studies on action sets (non-permanent, non-political groups, set up by an individual to help him achieve something) and factions (persistent sets of individuals, clique of a corporate character for political action) in Ndendeuli in S. Tanzania is of theoretical importance for further studies of conflict in co-operatives.

5. *Socialism and Rural Development* (Dar es Salaam, 1967), p. 2.

6. *Ujamaa—the Basis of African Socialism* (Dar es Salaam: TANU, 1962), p. 5.

7. Cf. also E. Hasselman, "Staat und Genossenschaft in Entwicklungsländern", *Z.f.d. Gesamte Genossenschaftswesen, 12* (Göttingen, 1962), p. 89 ff.

8. The Church has in fact been undergoing a considerable process of evaluation in later years.